T0329092

Moisés Naím is a Distinguished Fellow at the Carnegie Endowment for International Peace in Washington, D.C., and one of the world's most influential opinion leaders. He publishes weekly in newspapers around the world on international affairs and is among today's most widely read Spanish language columnists.

Naím has authored over ten books, including bestsellers, which have been translated into many languages. In 2011, he received the first Ortega y Gasset Award for his illustrious journalistic career, which includes serving as the editor-in-chief of Foreign Policy magazine from 1996 to 2010. He is also a three-time recipient of the American Society of Magazine Editors' award for editorial excellence. In 2018, his weekly television show, *Efecto Naím*, won an Emmy Award.

Before his career in journalism, Moisés Naím was an academic, then Venezuela's Minister of Development, and later Executive Director of the World Bank. He holds a PhD from the Massachusetts Institute of Technology (MIT). His previous book, *The Revenge of Power* (St. Martin's Press, 2022), was selected by The New Yorker as one of the best books of the year.

What Is Happening to Us?

What Is Happening to Us?

121 ideas for analyzing the 21st century

MOISÉS NAÍM

GRUPOIII
IIIBOOKS

**GRUPOIII
IIIBOOKS**

An imprint of Penguin Random House Grupo Editorial

Copyright ©2024 by Moisés Naím
Copyright ©2024 by Penguin Random House Grupo Editorial, S. A. U.
Travessera de Gràcia, 47-49. 08021 Barcelona, Spain

English translation by Clàudia Fernández

Originally published in Spanish in 2024 by
Penguin Random House Grupo Editorial , S. A. U.
as "Lo que nos está pasando"

© 2020, Francisco Toro, for co-authoring
"Venezuela's Problem Is Not Socialism" (pp. 185-193).

ISBN: 979-88-909823-1-5

For Rubina Abravanel and Clemente Naím, my parents

Index

2017

2023

2016

Prologue

What Is Happening to Us?

As we take a collective breath after navigating one pandemic, we now find ourselves on the verge of another: a mental health pandemic. A staggering one-fourth of the global adult population wrestles with various disorders, with only one in three individuals receiving the treatment they need. Every forty seconds, a life is lost to suicide. Three hundred million people struggle with anxiety disorders, highlighting the pervasive nature of this globalized anxiety, a new, silent pandemic.

Fueling this crisis is the perception that earth-changing transformations are on the way. They will affect us all, and we do not know how, where or when we will experience the consequences of the new realities heading our way. What we do know is that they will be massive, and they will manifest themselves everywhere and in all social spheres. Some of them will be welcomed and others cursed.

We are already beginning to see the first signs of some of the most serious transformations: the climate crisis, the fierce polarization that manifests itself in increased social conflict, renewed superpower rivalry, the corruption that has penetrated many societies, and the digital revolution and, specifically, artificial intelligence and its broad menu of impacts on the way we have lived up to now.

The list of threats that will make it difficult to sustain our lives is varied and manifests itself in different ways in different geographies. But everywhere it translates into an anxiety boom that respects no borders and warps our behaviors, aspirations, work, education and communities — in short, it touches each and every one of us.

Where does all this anxiety come from? From not knowing what is happening to us.

In the 1930s, the respected Spanish thinker José Ortega y Gasset, worried about the conflicts shaking Europe to its core, wrote in one of his books: "We do not know what is happening to us, and that is precisely what is happening to us, the fact of not knowing what is happening to us.... That is always the vital sensation that assails man in periods of historic crisis."

Many of the elements Ortega y Gasset pinpointed in the last century are with us today, laden with threats. That's why it's urgent to understand what is happening to us, and what to do about it.

This book is not in any way a proposal for solutions to the great problems of our times. My goal is less ambitious: to identify the hidden elements that configure the threats we face, to name them and shed light on them. It is only a first attempt at deciphering the coming changes and their implications.

This book represents my attempt to understand what is happening to us as countries, societies and individuals. I have had the enormous privilege of developing these reflections in public, through a weekly article that appears in a good number of publications around the world. In your hands is the result of that exercise: a collection of columns written between 2016 and 2023. They are presented here as they were published.

This is the second installment after *Rethinking the World. 111 Surprises of the 21st Century*, published in 2016. In these columns I unpack, week after week, the events that sow so much anxiety in our times.

My work as an analyst and writer has also led me to publish several books that, in my opinion, help to understand important facets of what is happening to us. In *Illicit: How Smugglers, Traffickers and Copycats are Hijacking the Global Economy*, I explain that criminality is no longer what it once was: it is now global, cybernetic and, above all, political. In the early 21st century, it has taken over entire countries and become a transnational force.

16

Organized crime has taken over governments and entrenched itself in them, affecting international relations in ways we have not seen before. And those governments that have not been taken over by criminal groups are doing what they can to contain their assaults with little success.

Why are they not succeeding?

That is the question that encouraged me to write *The End of Power. From Boardrooms to Battlefields and Churches to States: Why Being in Charge Isn't What It Used to Be*. The key message of that book is that the weakening of power is a global and widespread phenomenon, and we find it in the Pentagon and the Vatican, as well as in governments, businesses, trade unions, in the world of education, science and culture, in investment banks and non-governmental organizations, among so many other spheres. In all of them, power has become easier to obtain, harder to use and easier to lose.

But this weakening doesn't just go one way. Those who aspire to exercise unlimited power have adapted to the new conditions of the 21st century. Just as there are centrifugal forces that dissipate power, there are other centripetal forces that concentrate it. They manifest themselves in new tactics and strategies that have been exploited by autocrats and those who aspire to be autocrats. That is why, in *The Revenge of the Power*, I explain how populism, polarization and post-truth — the 3Ps — have become the go-to tools for a new breed of autocrats that threaten democracy around the world: they ape democrats, but rule like autocrats.

In each of these books I have tried to reveal new trends and realities that will change the world. But I try never to forget the famous phrase of Rose Bertin, Marie Antoinette's dressmaker and pioneer of French haute couture in the 18th century: "There is nothing new but what has been forgotten." I know, like Bertin, that the world is full of what seems new but is not, as well as of things forgotten as old that suddenly come back to life and shake society.

Sorting out this hall of mirrors between the new, the old, the forgotten and the misremembered is the essence of the work of the columnist.

Why? Because every day news and commentary are published about events that, as we are told, will change the course of history. Rarely is this true.

Sometimes — very seldom — news items appear that touch on issues that seem transitory, but in a few years, turn out to have caused profound and unusual changes. Remote work or distance education are good examples of fundamental human activities whose changes seemed transitory but which, as we now know, are much more permanent than we knew, and the curious thing is that this data goes almost unnoticed. It comes to us buried in the inside pages, often placed toward the end of an article that few will read.

Think, for instance, of the joint communiqué issued by NATO heads of state and government at the end of their summit in Bucharest, Romania, in that distant early April of 2008. A reader would have had to reach paragraph 23 of that dense and bureaucratic text signed by George W. Bush, Nicolas Sarkozy, Angela Merkel and José Luis Rodríguez Zapatero, among others, to learn the detail that would end up leading Europe into its worst war in eight decades: the declaration that NATO would open accession talks with Ukraine. Newspapers barely noticed the fact at the time, and none of them interpreted it correctly. On the contrary: a Reuters report on the summit was headlined, simply, "Putin tells NATO: 'Let's be friends.'"

What was new at that time was what had been forgotten: that for more than a thousand years the Russians had considered Ukraine a spiritual cornerstone of their empire and, therefore, that remote 23rd paragraph would one day shake history. I always remember this when I ponder what to write in next Sunday's column. I am convinced that somewhere in the world a paragraph 23 of some kind appears almost every day. The challenge is to find it.

Unfortunately, in the world of social media what we get is the opposite, the endless repetition of what is already known. While the public sphere devotes itself to covering a few flashy events, the real forces of history plod along without anyone paying much attention to them. This is how societies form their blind spots, which then leave them defenseless against the vicissitudes of history.

The columns that are combined here are the result of my dissatis-faction with this situation. They respond to my conviction that faced with the din of the front page, what we lose is the most important thing: sensitivity to the weak signals that might tip us off to a tectonic change.

These pages present significant aspects of an alternative history of recent years. My goal is to find the fleeting detail that will end up turning the world upside down, the underlying trend that gradually reverses certainties, the forgotten footnote that in the end transforms everyone's life. Or perhaps to reinterpret what is already known in order to make visible its implications in seemingly unrelated fields.

Sometimes the details may seem trivial. The global shortage of bicycle parts that made itself felt in the wake of the Covid-19 lock-downs looked like an isolated and unimportant fact. The cognitive damage suffered by Italians who grew up watching junk TV produced by Mediaset — Silvio Berlusconi's media company — can be inter-preted as a purely Italian problem. The increasing willingness of dic-tators to organize mock elections is treated as a common practice.

They are not. If this is the data and circumstances to which my analysis returns time and time again, it is because I sense that they carry within them the seeds of great transformations. They demonstrate, at an incipient moment, the issues that will dominate our future: new technologies — from artificial intelligence to the manipulation of genes — conflict within a society or between countries, the deterio-ration of the public sphere and the rise of new forms of disguised authoritarianism.

Of course, tectonic shifts are not easy to forecast, and that is pre-cisely what we mean by tectonic. The earth's crust moves only once the underground forces that drive continental shelves reach a critical threshold, enough to overcome the resistance generated by inertia. But the forces that set it in motion are there all along, accumulating quietly until one day a catastrophe reveals them in all their might. They are forces that go from invisible to unmissable in an instant. It is no surprise that geologists are obsessed with searching for the slightest hint of them before they cause an earthquake.

The same thing happens to me. I am always on the lookout —

with how much success, you will have to be the judge — for the slightest sign, the detail that leads the forgotten to become new once more. And I look for those weak signals because I believe they are the key that opens and unlocks answers to that initial question: what is happening to us?

Because understanding what is happening to us is a vital task, the first step if we're to push back against the paralyzing anxiety that defines our era.

MOISÉS NAÍM
Washington, D.C.

2023

A World Without Precedents

This is new. Nothing like this has ever happened before. Many of us shared these thoughts last week after first — and correctly — recoiling horror and indignation at the barbarity of Hamas.

Despite the countless tragedies that Israel has suffered in its 75-year history — ranging from full-scale wars to terrorist attacks — it has never experienced a military assault on this scale targeting its civilian population.

The scenes of murderous terrorists calmly roaming the streets and indiscriminately killing or kidnapping their victims are both cruel and unprecedented. Never before has terrorism struck so fiercely at the heart of Israeli society.

The horror that Hamas's brutality produces in us should not, however, cloud our vision to the other unprecedented situations arising in Israeli politics. Even before the attack, the country was mired in an unparalleled political crisis. The polarization in Israel is so deep that in order to form a government, Prime Minister Benjamin Netanyahu was willing to accept the radical conditions demanded by fringe political groups.

Before now, he'd never included the most virulent far-right politicians nor the ultra-Orthodox religious groups in his government. These extremist minorities have now managed to impose radical policies that affect the entire population. Until now Israel has never had to go to war with such a divided society.

But it is not only in the Middle East where this feeling of "never before" reigns. The same is happening in the United States. There, too, a tiny group of far-right Republicans managed to remove the head of the House of Representatives, Kevin McCarthy, midway through his term — something that had also never happened before. In Spain and other democracies, tyrannical minorities are causing a wave of unprecedented situations.

But we should remember that this wave of unprecedented situations goes beyond politics, war and the economy. The most important of them is, of course, climate change. Never before has the planet's temperature risen at the rate it is climbing today. Scientists are reporting with genuine alarm that things are moving quickly, which will certainly cause more and more novel scenarios.

The list goes on: Never have we experienced a migration crisis of the magnitude that we are seeing on the southern border of the United States nor in Mediterranean Europe. And we are only beginning to understand the ways in which environmental degradation fuels never-before-seen levels of migration.

Fortunately, in the realm of the unprecedented, not everything is bad. Never before have so many people — at least those privileged with easy access to technology — been able to work from home. The number of remote workers is simply enormous and their impact unparalleled. The number of empty offices in London and the United States has reached its highest point in 20 years. The same is happening with distance education and health care. Never before has physical distance been so inconsequential to the lives of so many people.

And in science and technology, never before have breakthroughs come at this pace. Never before has humanity had the ability to precisely edit the genetic code of organisms, as we are doing with cutting-edge technologies such as CRISPR/Cas9, which allows for the precise altering of the DNA of any organism.

And never before has our ability to alter the genetic code been subtle enough to allow the manipulation of messenger RNA for therapeutic purposes. This was achieved by Katalin Karikó, the winner of the 2023 Nobel Prize in medicine, for research that allowed the development of modern vaccines against COVID-19. And it is already beginning to be understood that artificial intelligence is not just another piece of software, but rather constitutes in itself a historic "never before" that could end civilization as we know it.

In this unprecedented world, more and more of everything is happening, and faster. Fragmented geopolitics and a battered global ecosystem give rise to existential risks for humanity, while advances in science and technology empower us in unimaginable ways. We tend to celebrate the latter, but it has its dark side: Hamas committed its crimes by combining medieval tactics with cutting-edge technologies.

And for those of us who live through these times, this makes it much more difficult to think about the future. That's because as human beings our tendency is to always try to predict what is coming based on what has already happened. But when so many of the things that happen are new, our old tactics tend to fail.

As we stare in the rearview mirror, the future overwhelms us.

October 16, 2023

The Stealth Recession

Much has been said about the "democratic recession," meaning democracy is retreating in many parts of the world. But there is another recession, less well-publicized, that goes hand in hand with the first and could be more damaging: the global rule of law recession.

What exactly is the rule of law? Well, it's a group of institutions that guarantee that society functions based on explicit rules that are impartially enforced. The concept encompasses many things: limits on government power, transparent government decision-making, checks on corruption, the protection of fundamental civil rights, public order and personal security, compliance with rules and regulations and, in general, the proper functioning of justice.

Democracy without the rule of law is hollow. One can live in a country where the government is chosen by elections, but if that government repeatedly violates the limits on its power, is corrupt, opaque and tramples the fundamental rights of individuals, it can hardly be said that its citizens are free. It is of little use to hold an election every few years in a country where there is no order, laws are not followed and the courts are rigged.

Hence the gravity of the sprawling study recently published as the *Rule of Law Index,* by the World Justice Project (WJP). This study gathered together the perceptions and experiences about the rule of law in 142 countries based on surveys of some 149,000 households and more than 3,400 experts.

26

What they discovered is deeply worrying. The rule of law is in decline. "Our data shows that, in the last year, the rule of law has worsened in 82 countries, or 59% of the countries included in the index," says Daniela Barba, a researcher at the WJP. "In Latin America and the Caribbean, we see that 18 of the 32 countries in the region experienced a degradation in the rule of law," she adds.

And these are not isolated data points. The decline is a global phenomenon. For the sixth year in a row, more countries are getting worse than better.

It will surprise no one to see that the countries where the rule of law is strongest are the nations that provide an excellent quality of life for their citizens: Scandinavia stands out, with Denmark, Norway, Finland and Sweden taking the first four places in the index, and countries such as Germany, New Zealand, the Netherlands and Ireland also in the top ten.

At the other end we have a series of countries devastated by conflict and corruption: Cameroon, Egypt, Nicaragua, Haiti and Cambodia are among the ten worst in the world, but all of them achieve a better score than my beloved and ill-fated Venezuela, which appears dead last in the world ranking for having no limits on the power of the government and a weak and often co-opted judiciary.

In Latin America, Uruguay, Costa Rica and Chile lead the index, all of them placing themselves above 60% of the ideal score. (Denmark hits 90%.) But scores are falling across almost the entire region: Nicaragua, El Salvador, Ecuador and Mexico saw sharp declines in the strength of the rule of law this year. Honduras shows the greatest improvement in the region, although its score has only risen to 41% of the ideal score.

The rule of law is not the same as democracy, and the two should not be confused. There are countries like Singapore, where it is almost impossible to change the government through the ballot box, but where the rule of law is respected. Indeed, Singapore ranks 17th in the global index, ahead of consolidated democracies such as France, Spain and even the United States.

But Singapore is an exception. Much more common are cases

where, little by little, the rule of law is eroded, and then democracy collapses because — by that point — it no longer has any way to defend itself. And that is why the sustained trend over time confirmed by the World Justice Project is so worrying. Because as the rule of law is weakened across more and more countries, their democracies become increasingly vulnerable.

Cases like Argentina, which went from occupying the 46th place in the world ranking in 2019 to 63rd place this year, should give us pause. As does Colombia, which fell from 71st to 94th in seven years, and Peru, which went from position 60th to 88th, and also Mexico, which fell from position 79th to 116th. In each of these countries the erosion of the basic institutions that defend democracy has been gradual and almost imperceptible. But its long-term consequences are incalculable.

This may explain why we so seldom here of countries transitioning to democracy anymore. Because traveling the path to democracy where the rule of law is not in force is much more difficult than doing so where complying with the rules is already an established custom.

October 31, 2023

Modi: from Prime Minister to King of Bharat

Once upon a time, a king was bathing in the river when a badly wounded deer came down to the water to give birth. Overwhelmed with compassion, the king adopted its newborn fawn as his pet. Over time, he became so attached to it that at his death, his last sensation was his boundless affection for the animal. For this reason, the legendary King Bharata — the first ruler to unite India — was to be reincarnated as a deer. We are here, of course, in the world of myth and legends, but also of reality. King Bharata's name comes from Bharat, India in Sanskrit, meaning "the lands of King Bharata."

Bharat is the name that Narendra Modi, the Prime Minister of India, wants to adopt as his country's official name. There are many ways to practice populism, and this is one of them. It's a way to demonstrate power, to nourish narratives that demonize the country's recent past and commemorate the glorious days of the distant past. It also serves to create debates that distract public opinion from the government's mounting list of daily failures. Persia became Iran, Burma became Myanmar, Venezuela became the Bolivarian Republic of Venezuela and so on.

Modi's political party is the Bharatiya Janata Party, the Bharat People's Party, or in other words, the Hindu People's Party. And this whole family of words — Bharata, Bharat, Bharatiya — have the same religious origin: they all come from the sacred writings of Hinduism, starting with the *Mahabharata*, something like the Old Testament of that religion, which is essentially the epic of the Bharat kingdom.

29

And here's the problem: today's India, the most populous country in the world, is a much more diverse nation than it was in the times of legend. It contains a staggering 950 million Hindus who form the support base of Modi's Hindu Nationalism. But it is also home to 170 million Muslims — more than in Iran and Saudi Arabia combined — as well as 28 million Christians, 20 million Sikhs, eight million Buddhists, and many smaller groups. Trying to impose a purely religious term like Bharat to designate the entire country is an aggressive act of chauvinist populism. In short, ignoring the national identity of the more than 200 million non-Hindu citizens of India is a dangerous provocation.

None of this is surprising because religious chauvinism has been Modi's stock in trade since his career began. In 2002, when a series of riots between religious communities shook the state of Gujarat, then-governor Modi stood by while more than 1,000 Muslims were murdered by hordes of angry Hindus. The lesson that Modi took from this tragedy was manifested in his political behavior: the more cruelty he showed toward the Muslim minority, the more electoral victories he was able to rack up.

Modi's BJP government has never stopped inflaming religious tensions because it knows it's a tried-and-true method of clinging to power. Through a gigantic social media machine, the BJP and its sister organizations fuel tensions between religious communities every time an election looms. WhatsApp chains spread explosive rumors about sexual abuse perpetrated by Muslim pedophiles against Hindu girls, and of course they underline Muslims' voracious appetite for beef, since cows are considered sacred in Hinduism.

And Hindu vindictiveness doesn't just target Muslims. In June, Indian secret agents allegedly murdered Hardeep Singh Nijjar, a well-known Sikh community leader, in broad daylight in a quiet suburb of Vancouver, Canada. The Canadian government's outrage and the ongoing volley of accusations between the two countries have created a diplomatic incident that is expanding across the globe, introducing unprecedented tensions between India and Western partners that, until recently, were friends.

Modi has perfected the techniques of populism, polarization, and post-truth, and continues to use them to hold on to power. Trying to change the name of India to a purely Hindu term like Bharat fits perfectly into this pattern of behavior that is endangering Gandhi's democratic legacy. And all this in the name of King Bharata, who just wanted to take care of an orphaned fawn.

September 30, 2023

Dictators Without an Exit

One of the critical debates of our time is how to deal with dictators. In dozens of countries there is a fierce clash between those who will only accept the unconditional defeat and the eventual prosecution of a dictator and his cronies and those who are willing to accept horrible concessions in order to establish a democracy.

It is an issue whose urgency has become impossible to ignore. Vladimir Putin's invasion of his democratic neighbor, Ukraine, amplified the world's attention to this difficult problem. But it is not just a problem in Russia: from Chinese President Xi Jinping's concentration camps in Xinjiang to the tight control over dissent that Teodoro Obiang has maintained in Equatorial Guinea since 1979, the world today is governed by no less than 39 dictators (and that's without counting the eight kings, emirs and sultans who rule single-handedly).

Of those 39 dictators currently in power, 20 of them rule with impunity in Africa, 14 more in Asia, three in Latin America and two in Europe. Three command nuclear arsenals — Vladimir Putin, Xi Jinping and Kim Jong-un. Others are the despots of countries with significant international influence, such as Egypt, Cuba and Vietnam. Several rule the poorest countries in the world: Burundi, Laos, Nicaragua and many others whose misery stems in many cases from the dictator's incompetence and corrupt leadership.

Getting rid of a dictator today is far more difficult than it was a couple of generations ago. Back then, a common solution was exile.

Tyrants like Idi Amin of Uganda or Baby Doc Duvalier of Haiti knew that, if push came to shove, they could discreetly board a plane with suitcases full of money and retire in a luxurious mansion, preferably in the south of France. Those days are over.

On October 10th, 1998, General Augusto Pinochet was arrested in the name of universal jurisdiction during a stay in London, on charges of genocide and torture during his regime (1973-1990). Although he was finally released for health reasons and returned to Chile, his arrest marked the beginning of the end of exile as a solution to removing entrenched dictators from power. Years later, in 2006, former Yugoslav president Slobodan Milosevic died in a cell in The Hague while awaiting the verdict in his international trial for crimes against humanity, genocide and war crimes.

The intentions of these international prosecutions were undoubtedly good, but their unintended consequences continue to shape politics worldwide. By substantially increasing the cost a dictator faces for relinquishing power, these cases have paradoxically hampered all subsequent attempts at removing entrenched despots.

When the alternative offered to dictators is a long prison sentence and the loss of the vast fortunes they and their cronies have amassed, it is not surprising that they will do whatever it takes to avoid losing power. For dictators, staying in government is no longer about politics: it becomes an existential requirement. Partly because of this deeper entrenchment, the process that took place in past decades, when dictators left power and were replaced by democratic leaders and their followers, is now infrequent.

Of the last five countries which ousted their dictators, only one — Armenia — seems to have had any success in its transition to democracy. The others have seen their democratization process regress (Tunisia), collapse (Myanmar, Egypt), or degenerate into civil war (Sudan). In the latter case, there is an open war between military factions while the former dictator, Omar al-Bashir, sits in prison awaiting a trial that will likely carry the death penalty.

There are few cases in which massive street protests, combined with the support of the armed forces and parts of the international community, succeed in ousting a dictator. But this is happening less frequently. Much more common is the experience of countries such as Belarus, Cameroon, Cuba, Hong Kong, Iran, Thailand, Nicaragua or Venezuela, where large protest movements have been repressed by their dictators, in most cases brutally.

The world has lost the ability to remove dictators from power. The lack of attractive options and tolerable risks that result from losing power has led autocrats to redouble their efforts to repel the attempts to remove them. Dictators today are overthrown less frequently than in the past. And when they leave, what is often left is a country that is difficult to democratize or even govern.

The world needs to relearn the art and science of ousting dictators. Or get used to the dismal reality that tyranny and anarchy, not democracy, are the world's most common form of government.

June 13, 2023

A Gold Rush In Space

While the world is preoccupied with climate change, war and artificial intelligence, another profoundly transformative phenomenon is in full swing: space exploration. And getting to where we are today is just part of a long and fascinating history. In 1957, the Soviet Union launched a rocket into space. It carried a polished 23-inch metal sphere that weighed 185 pounds and had four antennas. This first artificial satellite, Sputnik, sparked a fierce race between the United States and the Soviet Union to achieve technological dominance in space. A lot has changed since then.

Just last week, for example, SpaceX, Elon Musk's aerospace company, carried four private passengers to the International Space Station on one of its rockets. As this was happening, Blue Origin, Jeff Bezos's company, finalized a $3.4 billion contract with NASA to develop a spacecraft capable of taking people to the Moon. And Richard Branson's Virgin Galactic sent its "space plane" to the edge of space, carrying two pilots and four company employees.

These are just three of the audacious — and expensive — ongoing efforts to explore the universe in what is shaping up to be a renaissance for space travel. Superpowers — the United States and the USSR— used to be virtually the only players. Today, several other countries — like China and India, for example — have launched their own space programs and private investment is booming.

In addition to privatization and commercialization, there are other forces that will influence and shape the new space race, including militarization, managing the space pollution caused by thousands of inoperative satellites still floating in orbit, as well as the insuppressible human passion to explore.

Private companies are taking the lead and developing the new technologies needed to conquer this growing market. The space industry was valued at $469 billion in 2021. SpaceX and Blue Origin are the top competitors. But these giants are not alone: they are supported by a vast ecosystem of some 10,000 small- and medium-sized companies in what is known as the New Space economy. This network of providers ranges from the producers of components for satellites and ground control systems to the designers and manufacturers of rockets, as well as those who want to profit from the rise of space tourism.

Another significant trend is the militarization of space. The major powers are developing orbital weapons and, simultaneously, defense systems against this type of attack. Anti-satellite weapons and surveillance systems are just a few examples of how space is becoming a theater of geopolitical conflict. In an incipient way, some of this is already happening.

The surprising success of the Ukrainian resistance to Russia's invasion owes much to its access to satellite technologies that allow it to dominate the battlefield, aim its weapons with pinpoint accuracy and attack enemy supply lines. We have yet to witness the first war where an adversary's orbital infrastructure is directly attacked, but that day will inevitably come. And when it does, the international system could be seriously destabilized.

A third aspect of the new space boom is space junk. It is made up of debris from previous satellite launches that no longer serve any function but continues to float haphazardly through space. This has created a thick layer of flotsam that no one knows how to remove. It is a growing problem because many of the new technologies require a large number of satellites to function. Proposals such as that of entrepreneur Greg Weiler of OneWeb — a company that intends to launch 100,000 satellites into space by 2030 — have raised serious concerns. As OneWeb has acknowledged, there are already almost a million pieces of orbital junk moving around the Earth at over 16,000

36

miles per hour, and the technologies to recover this debris are still in their infancy. Although these satellites are small, their numbers are enormous, and when they go out of service, they will still be in orbit, putting at risk all the systems that are still operational.

Why is all this happening? Two motives: profit and curiosity. Many technologies, such as global positioning systems (GPS) and projects like Elon Musk's Starlink, can only be commercialized with a vast space presence.

In Silicon Valley, entrepreneurs and technologists sense that there are great fortunes to be made in the cosmos, fueling the gold rush into space. On the other hand, human beings are innately curious. Space represents an unknown horizon, an irresistible challenge for our species. Our desire to discover and explore new frontiers will continue to drive interest in space as a market and as a battlefield.

When the great British explorer George Mallory was asked in 1924 why he wanted to climb Mount Everest, he replied, "because it's there." It sounds silly, but the challenge of what is there that we have not yet managed to conquer will always have a special attraction for humans. The thirst to be the first to conquer a challenge is one of the main factors that defines our species. We want to know what's out there. And space... is there.

May 31, 2023

How Our Language Got Disrupted

Changing times infuse new importance into some words, while marginalizing or completely transforming others. "Platform" is a good example of this. The word used to refer primarily to — according to Merriam-Webster — "a flat horizontal surface that is usually higher than the adjoining area." Not anymore.

Now Twitter, Instagram, YouTube and Facebook (now Meta) are called "platforms." They aren't alone. Thousands of entrepreneurs have begun calling their companies "platforms."

That's right, "platforms" are in, and "companies" are out. It turns out that platforms often are companies that want to dress up — or erase — the perception that they are corporations. But the reality is that behind the vast majority of platforms is a for-profit company.

Many platforms make money by drastically altering the way we work — changing existing products, introducing new ones,or making others more efficient. Cellphones are an example of this type of "disruptive innovation" because they have drastically altered the communication industry and many other "adjacent spaces." Of course, for every success of this magnitude, there are hundreds of thousands of platforms (based on some alleged or real disruptive innovation) that fail.

Another concept that has become very popular is "disruptive innovation." This is a term found in just about any presentation that seeks to promote an investment, restructure an organization, adopt a new technology, lay off employees or launch a new product — which nowadays is no longer called that but rather commonly referred to as a "solution." These solutions are preferably "green" and "sustainable" and operate within a "space" (formerly known as a "market").

The success of companies that, through a "digital transformation," seek to boost their competitiveness is commonly explained as the result of "organic" growth. This usually means increased sales or decreased costs that originate from efforts and initiatives that happen within the organization. All of this, of course, occurs thanks to the "team," the group of people formerly known as "employees." News about how things are going on the platform — both good and bad — are usually communicated on behalf of the "team." In some organizations, the role of the team leader is no longer to command but to evangelize, educate, persuade and encourage the team so that its members are "aligned" with the platform.

In fact, there are business executives who have changed the name of their position to "Chief Evangelist." According to indeed.com, an online company that seeks to connect job seekers with employers, a Chief Evangelist is "an active ambassador of a business, product or service. They spread a positive message about a brand to advocate for others to use a service or buy a product. [...] While customers can be decent brand evangelists, hiring someone to do the job full-time might bring in more sales. That is why it might be better for brands to hire evangelists that are dedicated to promoting their products."

All these activities must "generate synergies," "catalyze change" and "align" the size and culture of the organization to its mission and the financial realities of the platform. It should also foster the "resilience" of the platform and those who work on it. Resilience, of course, is the ability to recover from a misfortune and to adjust to the new situation. Some trees that survive strong gusts of wind are good examples of resilience. They bend, but they don't break. For some time now, there has been a proliferation in the use of resilience to refer to the ability of organizations and human beings to recover from negative events.

The new phraseology is strongly imbued with the cult of change. It follows, then, that the magnitude of change which inspires and justifies this plethora of new words must be unprecedented, or at least is promoted as such. We know, however, that unprecedented changes are rare. Rose Bertin, Queen Marie Antoinette's seamstress, famously explained in the 1770s that: "There is nothing new except what has been forgotten."

Our language continues to evolve, as it always has, and this serves to help people express new values with every phrase, sentence and paragraph. This, of course, is nothing new. But today we are seeing how our allergic reaction to authority and hierarchy leads us to hide power relations behind a series of euphemisms that obscure more than they illuminate. And it will continue to be so, until we are saved by some new disruptive platform in the language space, catalyzed by a resilient team that manages to achieve organic synergies!

May 17, 2023

This Time It's Different

New scientific discoveries and technological innovations are often exalted as harbingers of sweeping change. However, few of these "breakthroughs" live up to the hype. Instead, they are overtaken by other discoveries or technologies that go beyond what had initially been seen as a life-altering historic contribution.

That's why it's always a good idea to be skeptical of any new technology that, we're told, will "change everything." Typically, it's just a lot of hyperbole and exaggeration, and the world doesn't really change much after all. But sometimes — rarely — a new technology comes along that does set off profound and permanent changes in the lives of billions of people. Today, humanity finds itself facing one such moment. This time everything really will be different.

Recent innovations in artificial intelligence (AI) are not a passing fad whose consequences are being exaggerated. These are transformative technologies that will be with us for a long time. Indeed, the wave of innovation sparked by AI will change the world. It will affect rich and poor, democrats and autocrats, politicians and business leaders, scientists and dropouts, as well as singers, writers and journalists. It will also impact all kinds of activities, professions and lifestyles.

The so-called "large language models" — which are not limited to the high-profile ChatGPT from OpenAI — are a type of artificial intelligence that can understand and generate human language, as well as automate functions that until now have required human beings. Other forms of AI have learned to identify and turn huge volumes of text, images, sounds, voices and videos into perfect imitations. They can produce complete sentences, answer any type of question, and perfectly reproduce voices that cannot be detected as imitations. They are also able to learn a person's voice and use it in a conversation with another individual who does not know they are talking to an AI-powered computer.

These models have an infinite number of practical applications. The fight against climate change and the diagnosis and treatment of serious health problems are being tackled more effectively thanks to the use of AI.

All of this is happening very fast. A report from UBS Bank reports that ChatGPT reached more than 100 million active users just two months after its launch. It took TikTok nine months to reach that number, while Instagram needed two and a half years. ChatGPT is the fastest adopted technology in history.

Like all new technologies, AI is a double-edged sword: it will have a positive and a negative impact. All technology is dual: Gutenberg's printing press was used to print both the *Bible* and *Mein Kampf*.

In a short time, dictators, terrorists, scammers and criminals will be putting all their creativity to work exploiting AI, with dire consequences for humanity. Trying to stop them will not be easy.

Those who try these technologies are surprised by their immense possibilities. But those who know them intimately and understand the risks they carry can easily see the global chaos they could engender. Scientists, businesses and security agencies that are heavily involved in the development of AI are raising the alarm about the rapid spread of the new technology. In a recent interview conducted by Fortune's Alan Murray, Tom Siebel, the head of a major AI group, repeatedly called the risk associated with these technologies "terrifying." Elon Musk has said that AI could cause "civilization destruction."

History shows that efforts to contain the spread and misuse of new technologies don't work. Nuclear weapons, for example, continue to spread around the world despite the enormous efforts that have been made to limit their proliferation.

Once such a powerful new technology enters our species' toolbox, there is no getting rid of it. The recent initiative by a notable group of experts to put in place a moratorium on the research and development of artificial intelligence demonstrates that even leading experts share the same intuition as many of us: we're not ready.

Certainly, our society is not ready for what is about to be thrust upon us as a result of the birth of artificial intelligence. Our only alternative appears to be to adapt as quickly as we can, because now that the Pandora's box is open, there is likely no going back.

May 3, 2023

Russia's Population Shrinks and China's Ages

Can a military superpower maintain its global dominance even if its population is shrinking? What about when its population is aging and will soon be dominated by the elderly? These are not hypothetical questions; they are happening right now. Russia is depopulating and China is aging rapidly. And these are not the only demographic woes that are weakening these two nuclear powers.

Between 1994 and 2021 the Russian population decreased by six million (from 149 to 143 million people). According to the UN, if Russia follows the current demographic trend, its population will fall to 120 million by 2050. China is also shrinking. In 2022 — for the first time since 1961 — it had a net loss of citizens. But that's not all. On top of this, China's population is, on average, getting older, forcing a smaller and smaller percentage of the population to work to support the growing proportion of retirees.

These aging and shrinking trends in China and Russia will pose unprecedented challenges. Demographic decline not only threatens the stability of these military superpowers, but also brings labor shortages and amplifies disruptions to the job market. The decrease in the workforce simultaneously reduces the income that the government receives from taxes, which in turn reduces its ability to finance pensions and essential social services.

In this sense, demography can be just as destabilizing as any external shock. Similarly, a rapid increase in the population can be just as destabilizing as a sudden decline.

The Economist recently warned that "a demographic tragedy is unfolding in Russia. Over the past three years the country has lost around two million more people than it would ordinarily have done, as a result of war, disease and exodus. The life expectancy of Russian males aged 15 fell by almost five years, to the same level as in Haiti."

Naturally, the demographic situation in Russia, which was already bad, has been made worse by the war in Ukraine. According to U.S. and European security agencies, between 175,000 and 250,000 Russian soldiers were killed or wounded in 2022. And between 500,000 and one million Russians (many young and well-educated) sought exile abroad. War and the flight of human capital have added to Russia's chronic problems such as aging, low birth and fertility rates, high infant mortality, a weak health care system, and lethal levels of addiction to tobacco, alcohol and drugs. What's more, mortality rates worsened between 2020 and 2023 due to the Covid pandemic, which, according to The Economist, claimed the lives of between 1.2 and 1.6 million Russians.

Even setting aside the pandemic, China has been facing a sustained population decline. In 2022, there were half as many births as six years earlier. This is due, in part, to the "success" of the one-child policy that the Beijing government imposed in 1980 to limit population growth. In 2016, the government abandoned this policy, since by then Chinese leaders had realized that their problem was no longer rising birth rates but falling ones. The impacts are already apparent. In fact, the working-age population has been declining for the last eight years, which is raising concerns about China's anemic economy. In 2022, China's economy grew at its slowest rate since 1976.

The Beijing government currently sees population growth and population renewal as important means of stimulating the economy. To promote these goals, it has created all kinds of incentives to boost births, including cash payments, tax breaks and long periods of paid maternity — and paternity — leave.

Unfortunately, experience shows that attempts to boost the birth rate through government incentives are rarely effective. There are much stronger cultural, social and economic forces at work that have reduced the Chinese people's interest in getting married and having children. In 2022, for example, the number of marriages fell to its lowest level since 1985. The birth rate fell too. As the experience of countries such as Sweden, Italy or Australia shows, government subsidies aren't enough to reverse the trend.

The reasons for getting married and having children certainly include material calculations, but they are also determined by cultural factors and expectations about the future of the country and its ability to provide opportunities for its population.

Optimism about the future matters as much or more as the cash promised to each woman who has a child. And the data on marriages and childbirth show that a growing number of Chinese do not seem to be willing to bet on their country.

April 19, 2023

Bibi, AMLO and Freedom

Bibi, the prime minister of Israel, and AMLO, the president of Mexico, couldn't be more different. At the moment, however, their political strategies could not be more similar. Both are trying to change the politics of their respective countries in profound ways, and both are doing so using profoundly undemocratic means.

Benjamin Netanyahu (Bibi) and Andrés Manuel López Obrador's (AMLO) personal histories as well as the countries where they were born, live in and lead are radically different. So is the cultural, political and economic context in which they were raised. The territory of Mexico is 94 times that of Israel and its population is 14 times larger. Israel's per capita income is now at the same level as that of France or Germany, while Mexico suffers from chronic economic anemia. Since the 1970s, Israel's economy has been growing rapidly while Mexico's has been growing slowly. While Bibi boasts of the high-tech boom during his tenure, AMLO is using public funds to build a railroad and an oil refinery.

Another difference is that Bibi has lived his entire life in a democratic country, while AMLO was raised in a one-party state, where the PRI monopolized power from 1929 to 2000.

For Bibi, it is imperative that his government respond aggressively to attacks by internal and external enemies such as Hamas, Hezbollah and Palestinian militants. AMLO, for his part, will be remembered for taking on the Mexican drug cartels with a strategy he called "hugs, not bullets." (No, it didn't work.)

The surprise is that, despite their many differences, Bibi and AMLO have adopted exactly the same political strategy: a frontal attack on democracy. This attack is not being waged with soldiers and tanks, but with lawyers, journalists and political cronies. Bibi is trying to push a series of reforms through the courts that would dilute laws and institutions designed to prevent the prime minister and his allies from concentrating power.

While Bibi attacks the judiciary, AMLO attacks the electoral system. The Mexican president has launched an offensive against the National Electoral Institute (INE), the public body in charge of organizing elections in Mexico and preventing fraud. The INE is recognized worldwide as an independent institution that defends democracy and — unlike many countries these days — does not give a rubber stamp to elections rigged by the resident autocrat. Similar to Donald Trump and Jair Bolsonaro, AMLO has continually criticized the INE, calling it "rotten," "corrupt" and biased. His most recent attack has been to slash its budget. Lorenzo Córdova, the institute's president, told journalist Anne Applebaum that AMLO's reforms would force them to lay off 85 percent of their staff, severely limiting INE's ability to carry out its mission.

But the attack is not only on the electoral system. AMLO has also been attacking the media and specific journalists who criticize him or who have exposed his falsehoods. (A study by the consulting firm Spin found that AMLO has made 56,000 false or misleading statements on "Mañaneras," his daily morning news conference.) Another battlefront for the Mexican president has been the judiciary. He recently lashed out at Norma Piña, the president of the Supreme Court, a woman AMLO slams as soft on crime.

The U.S. State Department, journalists, academics, politicians and a wide range of non-governmental organizations have declared their firm opposition to AMLO's strategy. Tens of thousands of protesters have been filling the Zócalo, the streets of Mexico City and other cities to protest against him.

It is the same in Israel. More than 100,000 Israelis have taken to the streets in major cities to protest Bibi and his coalition of radical parties and leaders. Two countries that could not be more different turned out to be identical in their defense of democracy.

Isaac Herzog, the president of Israel, declared: "We are no longer in a political debate, but on the brink of constitutional and social collapse." Veterans of Unit 8200, an elite section of the Israeli military intelligence, have joined those who have publicly denounced Bibi's attempt to concentrate power. In a letter released to the public they said, "We will not volunteer for a country that unilaterally changed the basic social contract with its citizens."

What is happening in the streets of Mexico and Israel goes beyond a cry to stop undemocratic legal reforms and reducing the budgets of public bodies such as the INE or attacks against journalists and judges.

It is a reaction to the imminent loss of freedom.

March 7, 2023

The Other Deadly Pandemic

The world's governments are currently dedicating enormous resources to containing Covid-19 and its mutations. Fortunately, they are succeeding. What is less fortunate is that they are neglecting another pandemic that has been claiming millions of lives each year, as well as disabling thousands more — mental illness.

Pandemics are known to spread rapidly and attack a large number of victims. That's precisely the case with the current mental health crisis.

According to the World Health Organization (WHO), nearly one billion people suffer from depression, bipolar disorder, anxiety, isolation, dementia, drug and alcohol use, schizophrenia and eating disorders (anorexia and bulimia), among other problems. In fact, 14.3% of worldwide deaths each year — some 8 million people – can be attributed to mental disorders.

Depression, for example, is the world's leading cause of disability. And suicide ranks as the fourth leading cause of death for people between the ages of 15 and 29.

According to Project Hope, an NGO that specializes on these issues, someone somewhere commits suicide every 40 seconds. Men take their lives twice as often as women. In turn, depression is twice as common in women as in men. Although suicide is a global phenomenon, its highest incidence is in lower-income countries. In 2019, for example, 77% of suicides in the world occurred in low- and middle-income countries.

Covid-19 produced a 25% increase in the number of people suffering from anxiety and depression.

But the mental health crisis was already in full swing long before the pandemic. Jonathan Haidt, a renowned social psychologist, maintains that the rise in teenage mental illness in the United States began in 2012. According to him, the crisis "is related in large part to the transition to phone-based childhoods, with a special emphasis on social media."

The evidence in the U.S. is overwhelming. Between 2004 and 2020, the number of American adolescents suffering from major depression increased by 145% for girls and 161% for boys. Since 2010, college students suffering from anxiety have increased by 134% and those with bipolar disorders by 57%. Between 2010 and 2020, suicides among teenage girls increased by 82%. The U.S. Centers for Disease Control (CDC) reported that between 2011 and 2021 the number of young women who feel persistently hopeless and sad increased by 60%.

About 15% of the adolescent girls interviewed by the CDC revealed that they had been forced to have sex, an increase of 27% in two years. The American Academy of Pediatrics, the Children's Hospital Association and other U.S. medical institutions have declared a "National State of Emergency" regarding children's mental health.

On the other hand, the misuse and unhealthy abuse of digital technologies are not exclusive to young people. Middle-aged and elderly men and women also show the negative impact of social media on their lives when these technologies are used in an abusive or toxic way.

This is a global crisis. Statistics and studies around the world show similar trends. The Mental Health Million Project is a 2022 report based on surveys of more than 220,000 people in 34 countries. The study shows a decline in mental health across all age and gender groups. It also found that English-speaking countries have the lowest levels of mental well-being and that, in terms of age, the 18-24 age group has the worst mental health of all the groups surveyed.

Unfortunately, a shortage of psychiatrists, psychologists and other mental health professionals is the global norm. According to Project

Hope, two thirds of those who need help do not receive it, even though there are effective treatments available. Many lower-income countries have less than one mental health specialist for every 100,000 people.

Cultural and institutional factors make patient care difficult. In many countries and cultures, having mental health problems is stigmatized, so many keep their troubles hidden. Admitting you suffer from mental health problems can cost you your job, your partner and your friends. From the institutional point of view, the major challenge involves ensuring access to mental health coverage — which can be prohibitively expensive, especially when it is only available privately.

Fortunately, things are changing. Artificial intelligence and remote treatment via the internet will allow access to the health system for patients currently shut out from it. There are also promising advances in medication and treatments. In many countries, shame is being replaced by activism that encourages transparency and channels fresh resources to address these problems.

No problem can be solved until it has been recognized, studied and debated. The mental health pandemic is a crisis that needs to be pulled into the light where it can be examined, analyzed and, ultimately, cured.

February 22, 2023

Years That Define Eras

Just mentioning certain years in history like 1789 (the French Revolution), 1945 (the end of World War II) or 1989 (the fall of the Berlin Wall) is enough to bring to mind profound transformations. So, it's worth asking, what will we eventually look back on as the first iconic year of the 21st century?

Until recently, 2016 was a clear favorite. That was the year of Brexit (June 23) and the election of Donald Trump (November 8) as well as the starting point of a new wave of global populism, polarization and post-truth that continues to threaten many democracies. But what about March 13, 2020? That was the fateful day when the U.S. Centers for Disease Control officially declared that we were in the midst of a global pandemic. Could it be that Covid was just the first of a long string of outbreaks that could end up overshadowing the entire century? Only time will tell.

Another event in 2020 that symbolizes the revolutionary changes that are heading our way was the Nobel Prize in Chemistry, awarded to Emmanuelle Charpentier and Jennifer Doudna for the gene-editing technology known as CRISPR/Cas9. Manipulating our DNA using this technique promises tremendous progress in curing hitherto lethal diseases, but it also creates serious threats. CRISPR in the wrong hands is a danger to humanity.

And so is the development and dissemination of new artificial intelligence techniques. On November 30, 2022, the OpenAI company unveiled ChatGPT, a technology that finally, emphatically passes the Turing test. It's a robot that replicates natural language so fluently that its responses are indistinguishable from those of a human being. This was what the founder of modern computing, Alan Turing, had defined as "artificial intelligence" in a seminal essay published all the way back in 1950. Now, as of 2022, what once seemed like science fiction has become a reality. Because ChatGPT is not just another product release or app from Big Tech. Artificial intelligence is going to be as transformative to knowledge industries as the introduction of machines was to the Industrial Revolution. Perhaps even more.

But the young 21st century has not only brought pandemics, technological change and polarized politics, it has also brought us wars that resemble those of the last century, or the century before that. On February 24, 2022, Vladimir Putin ordered the invasion of Ukraine. This surprise was followed by others: instead of lasting a few days, Putin's war is about to reach its one-year mark. In response, Europe realized that it can act as a cohesive strategic unit. This newfound realization implies that, instead of limiting itself to speeches and exhortations, it can act as a first-rate military power. The ferocious cyberattacks expected from Russia never materialized or were neutralized. In addition, the ineptitude of the Russian military is only surpassed by the medieval savagery with which it operates. Barbaric daily attacks on Ukrainian civilians and the country's infrastructure seem to be the only response the Kremlin has.

As a result, in September 2022 Putin reintroduced an option that was long thought outdated or unthinkable: deploying nuclear weapons. "If the territorial integrity of our country is threatened, we will without a doubt use all available means to protect Russia and our people," Putin said. At face value, this seems like the kind of thing that any sovereign leader would say about the defense of his country. The important detail here is that this particular leader has the world's largest nuclear arsenal at his personal disposal. "This is not a bluff," Putin warned. Clearly, what happens in Ukraine has geopolitical ramifications of the most profound type.

Another important change in world politics occurred on October 23, 2022, when Xi Jinping, the Chinese leader, managed to break the rule that would have forced him to leave power at the end of his term, a precedent that every other Chinese leader since Mao was obliged to follow. On that day, Xi was re-elected China's president and Communist Party general secretary for the third time, clearing all obstacles to becoming China's first dictator-for-life since Chairman Mao's death.

Finally, so far this century, climate change has manifested itself with ferocious intensity. The frequency and magnitude of human suffering — as well as the material damage — that have taken place this century from climate change alone are profoundly and rapidly altering our planet. There is no symbolic date for this: climatic catastrophes have become everyday events.

February 1, 2023

2022

The Rapid Rise of Gaslighting

At the end of each year since 2003, Merriam-Webster's Dictionary announces its selection of the English word of the year. According to the respected dictionary founded in 1831, "gaslighting" was the most searched-for word on the internet in 2022. Peter Sokolowski, the dictionary's editor, told the Associated Press that this year searches for the word increased by 1,742%. The editor also noted that it was in the top 50 most searched-for words every day.

"Gaslighting" is a colloquial way of referring to the tactics and tricks used to make a person doubt their reality and question what they feel, believe and do. The purpose is to weaken the victim psychologically in order to influence their perceptions, behavior and decisions. This idea was originally used in a play that opened in London and New York in 1938 and was later brought to the big screen in 1940 in Great Britain and remade in America in 1944. The film, Gaslight, tells the story of an unscrupulous husband who sets out to manipulate his wife to the point where she begins to believe she is going crazy. Among his many tricks, the husband rigs the gas lights in the house to turn on and off when his wife is there alone.

The list of tactics used by the modern gaslighters is long and nefarious, but includes contradictions, confusion and skepticism about the validity of previously unquestionable truths, which are then replaced with false narratives. There are also attacks on the person's self-esteem and the exploitation of their insecurities, along with the concealment of information and the constant use of falsehoods.

The word had fallen into disuse until the mid-1990s, when it became popular among psychologists and psychiatrists.

But the explosive increase in the frequency of internet searches for the word does not only come from these areas, but also and in a massive way from politics, where gaslighting is shaping what entire societies believe. In fact, gaslighting is closely related to another word that, in 2016, was selected by the Cambridge Dictionary as the word of the year: post-truth. This is the propensity to accept an idea as true based on emotions rather than facts. In recent years and in many different countries, we have seen how public opinion has been influenced by leaders and groups that disdain data, evidence and even logic. A dramatic example of both gaslighting and post-truth is Brexit. Its promoters made intensive use of gaslighting tricks and managed to create a public opinion matrix dominated by post-truth. Famously, when Minister Michael Gove, one of the Brexit leaders, was asked about a study by respected experts showing how dire it would be for the UK to break ties with Europe, his reaction was simply, "People in this country have had enough of experts."

Attempts to influence the opinions and behavior of a society (or part of it) are, of course, nothing new. And propaganda has always been an indispensable tool in political contests. Today, however, propaganda, post-truth, large-scale dissemination of lies and gaslighting have acquired unusual power and toxicity. New technologies and a plethora of social media platforms allow individuals and groups to play a role that was previously only available to governments, political parties or corporations.

We have already seen the dire consequences of the use of social media to deepen divisions, spread lies and foment chaos.

It is urgent that we protect societies from the harmful use of these new platforms.

To achieve this, it is imperative that we impose high costs and serious consequences both on digital offenders and on those who facilitate their unacceptable behaviors. It is encouraging, for example, to see how U.S. courts have imposed multimillion-dollar fines on Alex Jones, a deplorable figure convicted of defamation against the families of the children murdered in the Sandy Hook school massacre. Likewise, there is very important ongoing litigation by Dominion Voting Systems against Fox News, a company that, according to Dominion, dedicated day after day of programming to lying about the unreliability of its voting systems and causing the company considerable harm. Even Donald Trump is finally beginning to pay the political costs for gaslighting the American public with his lies about electoral fraud, which have most recently included his request to suspend the U.S. Constitution. Only by imposing high monetary, legal and reputational costs will society be able to defend itself against the modern manifestations of large-scale use of gaslighting.

December 19, 2022

When Doing the Obvious Is Impossible

Why do societies and their governments passively tolerate bad ideas? Why are so many obviously failed public policies impossible to reform? The list of countries whose governments cannot or dare not confront their policy taboos is long and varied. Take drug policy as an example.

On June 18, 1971, then-U.S. president Richard Nixon declared a war on drugs. Drugs are "public enemy number one," he said. According to the Drug Policy Alliance, a non-governmental organization that opposes the prevailing policies in this field, the United States spends $51 billion a year on the war against drug trafficking and consumption. In 2015, the Global Commission on Drug Policy, formed by a respected group of former heads of state, studied the issue in-depth and concluded that "the global war on drugs has failed and has had devastating consequences for individuals and societies around the world."

By now everyone realizes that tackling this serious problem mostly through prohibition, eradication and incarceration does not work. Even though in recent years some reforms, like the legalization of cannabis, have spread, the war on drugs as formulated by Nixon more than half a century ago is still being waged.

The rigid, automatic defense of the current regime closes off the possibility of exploring other alternatives. None will be perfect but, surely, alternatives that improve on the status quo are out there, waiting to be tried.

Fossil fuel subsidies are another example of a destructive policy that's impossible to reform. While the world is embarking on an unprecedented effort to decarbonize by reducing oil, gas and coal consumption, governments are spending unimaginable sums of money to reduce the price of gasoline and electricity — encouraging its consumption. According to the International Monetary Fund, the world annually spends the equivalent of 6% of the global economy to keep the prices of fossil fuels artificially low. Experts believe that these subsidies will exceed 7% by 2025. Governments are stepping on the brake that slows fossil fuel use at the same time that they are keeping their other foot on the accelerator.

Or take the U.S. embargo on Cuba, in place since 1962. The original goal of the embargo was, and still is, to bring about regime change in Cuba. The idea was that it would weaken the Cuban economy and the resulting popular protests would pave the way for the establishment of a democratic regime. Obviously, this has not happened, and Cuba remains the oldest dictatorship in Latin America. Each year since 1992, the UN General Assembly has adopted a resolution demanding that the U.S. lift the embargo. However, instead of weakening the Castro dictatorship, the embargo has served as an excuse used by the Havana government to justify its catastrophic economic policies.

There are plenty more examples. Immigration policy, Europe's common agricultural policy, labor rules that inhibit the creation of new jobs, easy access to firearms in the United States, bad education policies, outdated UN governance and the ballooning of U.S. military spending are all terrible policies that cannot be changed.

Behind every bad idea exist strong political, economic, cultural or religious interests. For example, we know that energy policy is heavily influenced by large corporations. A recent and revealing fact in this regard is the number of lobbyists representing the interests of fossil energy companies participating in the UN summit on the environment (COP27). This year, there are 25% more "fossil lobbyists" (as the NGO Global Witness calls them) than there were at last year's COP26 in Glasgow. Only one country (the United Arab Emirates) has a larger delegation than the lobbyists.

The war on drugs has created a huge and well-financed political bureaucracy and powerful global criminal networks that after more than half a century have learned to cohabitate. The economic embargo on Cuba is defended by politicians in the United States who covet the votes of Cuban exiles living in Florida.

Those who benefit from these policies are few, but well organized and amply funded. Those who are harmed are many more, but regularly fail to leverage their numeric advantage to eradicate the bad policies that affect them. But we are living in an age of surprises. In the near future, doing the obvious may not always be so impossible and some of these bad ideas may finally be buried.

November 15, 2022

When Organized Crime Is the Government

Mohamed bin Salman, the crown prince of Saudi Arabia; Xi Jinping, the president of China; and Tsar Vladimir Putin have plenty of things in common. Add this one to the list: all three have championed anti-corruption drives. Dictators all over the world have. Not surprisingly, they found plenty of corruption. Some of the accused were sentenced to death, and most others received long prison sentences.

Yet, there is no evidence that global corruption declined as a result. Rather, these anti-corruption campaigns are the preferred pretext for autocratic governments to get rid of their opponents. And while victories in the fight against corruption are few, its mutations are increasingly visible. Along with what we perceive as "normal" corruption, we must now add kleptocracy and, on top of that, mafia states.

"Normal" corruption is transactional. It occurs when a private citizen or an organization bribes a public official to gain an advantage. It is the traffic policeman who, in exchange for a payment, skips the speeding ticket, or the real estate developer whose secret kickback to a city official allows him to add a few more floors to the building under construction, or the contractor who promises the finance minister a 10% cut of a big government contract. This is classic corruption, version 1.0, to be found in a greater or lesser degree almost everywhere from Austria to Zimbabwe.

Classic corruption is harmful, of course, and must be kept at bay. It is a chronic disease that weakens society.

Unfortunately, in many countries, corruption goes much further. These are the nations governed by kleptocrats (from the Greek *klepto*, for theft, and *cracy*, government). It is a system where the president, prime minister or monarch uses the resources of the nation as if they were his or her own and distributes them among their relatives, associates, political allies and high-ranking military officers.

We have seen kleptocracies on all five continents: from "Baby Doc" Duvalier's Haiti to Nursultan Nazarbayev's Kazakhstan. Many of these kleptocrats keep their people destitute while stealing the nation's wealth. But not all. The classic contrast is between Mobutu Sese Seko, the bloodthirsty kleptocrat of Zaire (now the Democratic Republic of the Congo), between 1965 and 1997, and Suharto, the dictator of Indonesia, between 1967 and 1998. Their periods in power very nearly match, and it was hard to tell who was the bigger thief. But Suharto allowed Indonesia to develop under his rule, while Mobutu did the opposite. The real per capita income of Indonesians increased 20-fold during Suharto's term, while that of the Congolese fell 25% in those same 30 years.

As devastating as kleptocracy may seem, it is not the type of corruption we should be most worried about. Certain countries go further to become mafia states. In those countries, corruption goes from being a source of illicit enrichment for the rulers and their cronies to being used as an additional tool for statecraft. In Putin's Russia, Maduro's Venezuela and El Sisi's Egypt, rulers use corruption as a lever to increase their power both domestically and abroad. Mafia states are the maximum expression of Corruption 3.0. It is no longer about criminal groups influencing the government from the outside to make money, but about the seat of corruption shifting to the seat of government itself.

Vladimir Putin, for example, uses characters like Yevgeny Prigozhin, head of the Wagner Group — a mercenary army — to do the Kremlin's dirty work all over the world. From his humble beginnings as Putin's cook — or, well, head of the catering company that handled the job — Prigozhin rose in power and wealth alongside the Russian leader until he became a key accomplice. The grim record of human rights violations perpetrated by the Wagner Group has now left Putin's cook no choice but to continue his support to the corrupt leader in perpetuity.

When we talk about corruption, then, it is important to specify which of these manifestations we are talking about. All three are harmful, but the second is far more harmful than the first, and the third much more than the second.

Corruption 3.0 deployed by autocratic governments in support of their geopolitical strategies is a threat to which the world has no effective response. Mafia states are not only a problem for judges, prosecutors and police officers, but a threat to the world's democracies and to international security.

November 1, 2022

Where Is the NEXT Big Boom Going to Be?

Which economy will grow fastest in the next few years? Try to guess. Perhaps you are thinking of Vietnam, which has been steadily taking market share from China, which has hamstrung itself through its draconian zero-Covid policy. Or the African champion of growth, Rwanda, whose economy has quintupled since 1995. Or Bangladesh, whose export sector is the catalyst for Asia's biggest boom.

The answer is none of those. The world champion in economic growth in the coming years will be Guyana. That's right. The miniscule, seldom-heard-of strip of tropical forest on South America's northern coast is in the midst of a giant oil boom.

Since 2015, Guyana has led the world in offshore oil discoveries, with 11.2 billion new barrels discovered, almost a third of all new oil discoveries worldwide in that period. Researchers at Nexus Group, a consulting firm, expect the country to become one of the world's top five offshore oil producers within a few years, ahead of oil giants like the United States, Mexico and Norway. By the middle of the next decade, Guyana is expected to produce more oil per capita than any other country. Just the government's oil revenue could top $21,000 per capita, nearly double today's total GDP per person.

This year, the Guyanese economy could grow 58%, an unheard-of figure. Oil sector GDP-growth could average 30% a year between 2023 and 2026. What has historically been one of the poorest countries in the Americas has already surpassed the world average per capita income, and the boom is just getting going.

But while this is good news for Guyana, is it bad news for the environment? Not necessarily. Guyana's oil emissions intensity — that is, the amount of carbon released per barrel produced — is only half the world's average, and it continues to fall. If Guyanese oil displaces its dirtier competitors, Guyana's oil boom could actually drive down carbon emissions.

Another area of concern is the boom's socioeconomic impact. Will the bonanza really help the Guyanese people? The country is getting richer, certainly, but many of its inhabitants remain poor. It ranks a lowly 108th out of 191 countries on the UN's Human Development Index. The Economist Intelligence Unit classifies it as a "flawed democracy": elections are competitive but not always fair. A disputed election result in 2020 gave rise to a bitter brawl that lasted for months and triggered several waves of violence between the supporters of the contending candidates.

Ethnic tension has long defined politics in a country divided by the legacy of the British empire: 40% of Guyanese trace their ancestry to India, 30% to Africa, while 10% are indigenous and the remaining 20% are mixed. Guyanese voters tend to vote by ethnic bloc, a practice that rarely goes hand in hand with political stability. And corruption, unfortunately, is deeply entrenched.

For decades, we have seen how oil booms almost always end in tears. Rival groups fight fiercely for control of oil revenues instead of working together for a better future for all. The phenomenon is so common that it has its own name: the resource curse. Given its ethnic divisions and history of corruption, Guyana has already ticked off two risk factors for the resource curse. Will the Guyanese be able to break the cycle?

They might because they also have a couple of trump cards up their sleeves. Flawed as it may be, Guyana is still a democracy, and this helps inoculate countries against the resource curse. And the sheer size of this oil boom, coupled with Guyana's tiny population, might make it possible to satisfy everyone's aspirations without having to get embroiled in the impoverishing cycles that come when rival groups are scrambling for their share of the oil loot.

Without wise and prudent political leadership, oil wealth can easily become a curse. Will the leaders of Guyana heed the lessons of other countries? The world will be watching.

October 19, 2022

Is Globalization Over?

They say that we have reached the end of globalization. Just look around. Trump's protectionism, Brexit, supply chain problems created by Covid-19 and Putin's criminal aggression in Ukraine have all helped derail the wave of global integration that was triggered by the fall of the Berlin Wall in 1989. Surely, with the stock market crashing, interest rates on the rise and a looming global economic slowdown, we have arrived at globalization's funeral and the bells are tolling.

While this perspective has become very fashionable of late, it is wrong in almost every way. Mainly from the point of view of the economy, but also from a social and cultural standpoint. Indeed, the surprise of the last two years has been how resilient globalization has turned out to be. In an exceptionally turbulent period, the strength and variety of the connections between countries has been more surprising by its durability than by its fragility. In fact, the data suggests that the global financial crisis of 2008-2009 and the great recession that it triggered had a bigger negative impact on the world economy and politics than any other event in the past decade.

The volume of international trade grew a lot during the period of hyper-globalization (1985-2008), going from around 18% to 31% of the total value of the world economy. With the 2008 crisis, that figure fell to around 28%. And that's where it has been, more or less, ever since: holding steady despite all the economic shocks and political upheavals of recent years.

Trump's protectionism reduced the integration of the United States with the rest of the world. In the U.S., trade fell from 28% of gross domestic product (GDP) in 2015 to 23% in 2020. UK exports to the European Union fell by a hefty 14% in the year after Brexit. But these swings, large as they were, have been offset by greater economic integration in East Asia and Africa, where the connections and inter-dependence between countries continue to deepen and expand.

Economic integration seems to have its own inertia that resists even blows as big as the trade wars started by Trump or the UK vote in favor of Brexit. Uri Dadush, an international economics expert, has found that the protectionist barriers erected in recent years have had a negligible effect on global trade. Of course, supply chains have come under stress and these disruptions have spurred companies to move some of their manufacturing facilities closer to end markets. Europe is now undoubtedly experiencing the painful economic consequences of its energy dependency on Russia. But, according to the available data, the net global effect, even considering these momentous changes, has not been a reduction in economic integration.

It is also important to keep in mind that globalization goes far beyond trade and other international economic flows. Globalization is based on the global spread of knowledge, ideas, philosophies, politics and people as much as it is based on the trade of goods. And in this broader sense, globalization seems to be speeding up, not slowing down. TikTok has 1.4 billion users spread over 150 countries, for example.

Science is another example of the power of globalization. Scientists from all over the world compete with their colleagues in other countries. But they also collaborate as often as never before. The number of scientific collaborative efforts located in different countries is booming. The speed at which scientists were able to create the Covid-19 vaccines, then produce them on a large scale and distribute them around the world in record time, saving millions of lives, is an important example. If this successful instance of globalization could happen once, it can happen again and again.

Naturally, globalization is not invulnerable and not all its conse-quences are positive. The levels of inequality that coexist with globalization are unacceptable, for example. If the war in Ukraine drags on much longer or — tragically — goes nuclear, it could cut off key supplies of energy, food and fertilizer that form the backbone of economic globalization. Worse still, a Chinese military assault on Taiwan could wipe out much of that country's microchip-making capacity, crippling a world increasingly reliant on digital technologies. In the near future, quantum cryptography could make all the encryption that currently exists on the web obsolete. That would cause a severe cyber-security crisis that would limit digital globalization.

These threats exist. They are real and serious. But they are conjugated in the future tense. At the moment, the world is more deeply integrated than it was a decade ago. Despite its costs, problems and accidents, integration between countries has not died. The challenge ahead is how to protect ourselves from its defects and make the most of the doors it opens for us.

October 5, 2022

Latin America, quo vadis?

Colombia has just elected its next president, Gustavo Petro. Despite his long political career, the president-elect presents himself as an outsider who is out to dislodge the long-ruling elites from power. That's the same promise made by Andrés Manuel López Obrador of Mexico, Gabriel Boric of Chile, Pedro Castillo of Peru, Alberto Fernández of Argentina, and several other Latin American presidents. On October 2, Brazil will hold elections and it is almost certain that the current President Jair Bolsonaro will face off against former president Lula da Silva.

In addition to aggressively confronting their opponents, all of these leaders have promised sweeping institutional changes and economic reforms. All of them have also committed to reducing poverty and inequality.

Will they succeed?

No.

For several decades, barely any out of the long list of leaders who have tried to make sweeping changes to their respective countries have succeeded. The only exceptions to this trend were Hugo Chávez and his anointed successor, Nicolás Maduro. The two did indeed drastically transform Venezuela. They destroyed it.

The new Colombian president is the latest member of this club of leaders coming to power on the back of alluring populist promises that they either won't be able to keep or, more ominously, will impose in spite of dire consequences. They will lead societies that suffer such extreme levels of political and social polarization that reaching the necessary agreements and compromises between rival groups will be next to impossible.

As in many other parts of the world, important decisions in Latin America are held up by a new form of polarization that feeds on group identities such as religion, race, gender, region, age, economic interests, ideologies and more. This polarization, which has always existed, has now been supercharged by post-truth: the rise of disinformation, fake news, and the manipulation and dissemination of messages that create distrust, fear and anger.

These are the three "Ps" that define the current political environment across much of the world: populism (divide and rule, promise and win), polarization (the use and abuse of discord) and post-truth (who, what, to believe?).

All signs point to the global economy experiencing a sharp contraction, and Latin America is bound to be seriously affected.

Governing successfully in this context becomes even harder in the difficult economic situation facing Latin America. The region's economies depend on the price of their main exports: raw commodities. When global demand and prices rise, Latin American governments are able to spend freely, and smooth over political and social frictions. When prices fall, political and social conflict intensifies. It is a long-standing pattern.

All signs point to the global economy experiencing a sharp contraction, and Latin America is bound to be seriously affected. While conventional wisdom is that recessions tend to depress demand and contain rising prices, Latin America is likely to experience the double whammy of a recession and rising inflation, the much-dreaded phenomenon of stagflation.

Runaway inflation, a phenomenon hitherto unknown to the vast majority of people in the region, especially those under 30, will impose itself on the agenda as a pernicious source of hunger, impoverishment, inequality, economic stagnation and social conflict.

The political effects of inflation will be compounded by a terrible pre-existing condition: disillusionment with democracy. Millions of

Latin Americans hard hit by the pandemic, unemployment, bad public services, food insecurity, corruption and crime have lost hope that elections and democracy will bring the solutions they desperately need.

This is the context in which President Gustavo Petro will have to govern Colombia.

He has three alternatives: The first is to try to implement his agenda piecemeal by opportunistically working with some of the leaders, parties and social groups that oppose him. That would inevitably require the president to make concessions. Broadening his base of support in this way will require messy compromises.

The second alternative is that Petro pushes for a vast and inclusive national accord that allows important decisions to be made on the basis of a broad consensus. Again, this involves making concessions that may be hard to swallow for the president and those who supported him in winning the presidency.

The third option is to behave as other 3P presidents have done around the world: stealthily weakening the institutions, the norms, and the checks and balances that define democracy by demonizing his opponents on the basis of a fire hose of lies.

Let's hope that the Colombian democracy will survive the allure of the 3Ps.

June 30, 2022

Democracies In Danger of Extinction

This past decade has been rich in world-changing events. Some were impossible to ignore, but others were more gradual and went almost unnoticed. Among the most important of these is the global crisis of democracy.

On all continents, democracies are dwindling while undemocratic systems are on the rise, currently accounting for 70% of the world's population, that is, affecting 5.4 billion people. According to studies by the V-Dem Institute at the University of Gothenburg, a decade earlier the percentage of people without democracy was 49%. Not since 1978 has there been such a low number of countries in the process of democratization.

There are two reasons why this democratic backsliding didn't cause alarm or provoke a significant reaction. The first is that there were just too many other urgent problems that made it difficult for champions of democracy to successfully compete for the attention of leaders, the media and public opinion. The pandemic and the global financial crisis are just two examples of a long list of events that left no room for less immediate concerns. The second reason is that most attacks on democracy were deliberately opaque and difficult to perceive, which, as a consequence, made it much more difficult for people to fight back.

Let's consider the primary cause of this global neglect of democracy, a phenomenon that Larry Diamond, a respected professor at Stanford University, calls "the democratic recession": how could you mobilize the population to defend democracy while the pandemic was causing millions of deaths around the world? According to the World Health Organization (WHO), between 2020 and 2021 alone, 15 million people died from Covid-19 and its variants.

In the past decade, the effects of global warming have also intensified. Wildfires, extreme heat, floods, hurricanes, typhoons and melting ice caps became more frequent, deadly and costly.

There were also financial problems. Between 2007 and 2009, a deep financial crisis was unleashed in the United States, caused serious damage to that economy, then infected other countries and left enduring political repercussions. Perhaps the most important of these is growing economic inequality.

This problem has worsened in the past decade and continues to be a major source of political conflict and social instability. One of the countries where it has been most acute is China, which has emerged as one of the most lopsided societies in the world. But the world's attention has not been focused on China's inequality, but rather on its rapid economic growth. Between 2010 and 2020, the Asian giant's economy more than doubled in size and — depending on how you calculate it — is now the first or second largest economy in the world. In that same period, the Chinese regime deepened its authoritarianism. In 2018, President Xi Jinping managed to remove the rule from the constitution that, since 1982, limited the presidency to two five-year terms. Thanks to this constitutional reform, Xi can be president until he dies.

The past decade also saw Brexit, the unexpected and traumatic withdrawal of the United Kingdom from the European Union. It was also the period in which there was an explosive increase in the economic, political and social influence of social medias such as Facebook, YouTube, Instagram, Twitter and TikTok. And, of course, the decade of Putin's many wars. The Russian military fought in Georgia's Abkhazia and South Ossetia, Ukraine's Crimea and Dombas, as well as in Syria. Those ten years we also saw the rise of Donald Trump, his conquest of the Republican Party and his rise to the Oval Office.

Many of these events were shaped and driven by the rapid rise of smartphones. Today more than six and a half billion people (84% of the world's population) own one.

While all this — and much more — distracted our attention, a group of authoritarian leaders took over a large number of the world's democracies.

The evidence of the deterioration of democracy in the world is surprising and worrying. But even more surprising is the shocking lack of a response in the face of these attacks by anti-democratic forces.

This is because many of the assaults on democracy are happening in such a stealthy way that they are practically invisible. And of course, a problem that is never detected will never be solved. The world's democracies are facing a dangerous problem, but a problem we've not fully awakened to. We need to acknowledge it, publicize it and confront it.

May 17, 2022

How Are Putin and Musk Alike?

They can't be more different. Putin is a genocidal dictator, and Musk is a brilliant inventor. The Russian leader is responsible for the deaths of tens of thousands of innocent people. Elon Musk is responsible for the world's best-selling electric cars, for pioneering innovations in battery technology and for technological advances such as PayPal that allow for digital payments. He's also behind SpaceX, which builds rockets that can be launched into space, recovered and quickly reused. Then there is the hyperloop — a pneumatic mass transit system that will be able to carry people and goods very fast over long distances. And don't forget Neuralink, a company whose mission is to develop technologies that will allow the brain to communicate wirelessly with a computer.

Both Putin and Musk want to change the world: Putin by destroying and Musk by creating. They both have the power and the money to finance their ambitions. According to Fortune magazine, Musk is the richest person in the world. According to the estimates of several intelligence services, Vladimir Putin is secretly the richest. In addition to his personal fortune (estimated at perhaps $200 billion), Putin is also free to use Russian state funds to finance his ventures.

In this, the dictator and the entrepreneur show some parallels. Putin wanted Ukraine and Musk wanted Twitter. The first illegally invaded the neighboring country and the second legally bought a company for $44 billion.

Both decisions were made by a single person. The protocols and processes that normally influence the making of such important decisions were irrelevant.

Naturally, the invasion of Ukraine and its aftermath of death and destruction is infinitely more serious than the purchase of a very expensive company whose operation has enormous political and social implications. But both the invasion and the acquisition happened because these two men wanted it. Period.

Putin justifies the invasion with arguments from the past, while Musk explains his interests in terms of the future and the challenges facing our civilization. The Russian dictator maintains that Ukraine was always part of Russia and should become so once again, and that his military incursion is simply seeking to correct a geopolitical blunder made after the collapse of the Soviet Union. For him, the Kremlin should have never allowed its Russian-speaking satellites to become independent countries.

Musk instead thinks that a revamped Twitter may be the best instrument for protecting freedom of speech throughout the world: "My strong intuitive sense is that having a public platform that is maximally trusted and broadly inclusive is extremely important to the future of civilization," he said.

The billionaire innovator has been worrying about the world's future for years. In one of his talks, he made this bold prediction: "The future of humanity is going to bifurcate in two directions. Either it is going to become multiplanetary, or it's going to remain confined to one planet and eventually there is going to be an extinction event."

The contrasts between the brilliant visionary out to transform our civilization into a multiplanetary one and the bloodthirsty dictator trying to return the world to the 19th century could not be more sobering. But the invasion of Ukraine and the takeover of Twitter illustrate how weak accountability is in authoritarian regimes and among the ultra-rich tech titans. In both cases, the boss makes the decision without showing much concern for the opinions of those who disagree with them, or for the fact that they might not know what they don't know: one of the most common reasons why dictators fall and companies fail.

Let's hope that, at least in this regard, Musk and Putin are different.

May 3, 2022

Putin's Next Move

Would he actually do it? Is Vladimir Putin really such a nihilistic sociopath with so little regard for human life that he would use nuclear weapons against his enemies? Or is he, rather, a clever negotiator who uses the nuclear threat to extract concessions from his rivals? These are the questions that are keeping America's diplomats, generals and spies — as well as America's allies — up late at night.

For decades, the doctrine of Mutually Assured Destruction (MAD) served to deter any world leader who might be tempted to use nuclear weapons. That's because if they did, it guaranteed a retaliatory nuclear strike and, therefore, the death of hundreds of millions of people and the devastation of entire cities. There would be no winners. But now things seem to have changed.

A few days ago, Bill Burns, the respected director of the CIA, publicly acknowledged that the United States is concerned that Russia might use tactical nuclear weapons in Ukraine. Burns said that "given the potential desperation of President Putin and the Russian leadership, given the setbacks that they've faced so far, militarily, none of us can take lightly the threat posed by a potential resort to tactical nuclear weapons or a low-yield nuclear weapon." The CIA is "watching very closely," Burns said, though he also clarified that they have yet to detect any signs that Russia is preparing to take such a step. It is obviously worrying that the future of humanity depends on the decisions of a single person. Recognizing this, and taking into account Russia's unacceptable behavior in Ukraine, and its equally reprehensible performance in Chechnya and Syria, it is only natural that much effort is being made to understand Vladimir Putin's thinking.

Bill Burns, who had served as U.S. ambassador to Russia from 2005 to 2008 and as the Deputy Secretary of State under Barack Obama, is the U.S. official who has had the most personal interactions with Vladimir Putin. In his memoirs published in 2019, Burns reveals that the most notable characteristic of the Russian leader is "his passion for control, founded on an abiding distrust of most of those around him, whether in the Russian elite or among foreign leaders." Burns speculates that the worldview that now defines Putin's way of thinking was nurtured both by his training as a KGB officer and by his experiences as a child and teenager on the mean streets of Leningrad in the postwar years. Putin himself has said that in this urban context "the weak get beaten up."

Andrew Weiss is another renowned expert on Russia who as early as 2014 was decrying that "Putin is far more isolated from major foreign counterparts than at any point in his tenure. After nearly 15 years at the helm and lately at the center of the world's attention [after annexing Crimea], Putin sees himself as a giant among weaklings who don't measure up to him and can't compete with him." Eight years later, how much has Putin changed? Surely his recent military misadventures have opened his eyes to the shortcomings of his military and the surprising strengths of the Ukrainians, not to mention the resilience of the growing coalition of countries opposing him. But there are aspects of Putin's personality that do not seem to have changed. CIA Director Burns recently said: "Putin has been stewing in a combustible combination of grievances and ambition for many years."

It is difficult to know what Putin may be planning. But he himself has explained publicly how he thinks. We know that his worldview comes straight out of the 19th century: an anarchic international order where the only thing that ultimately matters is military power. His enemies, meanwhile, live in the 21st century. President Zelenskyy, for one, looks more at home giving a speech at the Grammys than in a suit and tie with his own cabinet. While Zelenskyy walks around in an olive drab T-shirt, Putin clearly prefers to be seen in a business suit.

Zelenskyy greets his constant visitors with relative informality in his sandbag-fortified offices, while Putin instead forces them to sit at the other end of a 20-foot-long white table.

It's difficult to wrap our minds around Putin's 19th-century geopolitical thinking. The idea that the only thing that really matters is who has the most firepower is old and outdated. We'd prefer to not look at the world that way. But unfortunately, it appears that Vladimir Putin isn't going to give us any other option.

April 20, 2022

The Dictator in His Mousetrap

Early in his presidency, in 2000, Putin gave a long televised interview. He spoke of his vision for the future of Russia, shared memories of his youth, and reflected on what he had experienced, including a lesson he'd learned from a rat. When he was very young, Putin and his parents lived in a small apartment in a run-down building in Leningrad (now Saint Petersburg) that, among other problems, was infested with rats. The young Putin used to chase them with a stick. "There, I received a quick and lasting lesson in the meaning of the word 'cornered,'"

Putin said in the interview. And added: "Once I spotted a huge rat and chased it down the hall until I drove it into a corner. It had nowhere to run. Suddenly it lashed around and threw itself at me. Now the rat was chasing me. Luckily, I was a little faster and I managed to slam the door on its nose."

From an early age, Putin understood that a cornered animal can be dangerous. It's a lesson we should all heed. But what if instead of being cornered, it gets caught in a trap?

A typical mousetrap consists of a box in which there is a door that the mouse can enter. Inside, there is a mechanism tripped by a piece of cheese. By taking the cheese, the mouse triggers a spring that shuts the trap door and leaves it stuck inside. It's trapped. The same thing happens to contemporary dictators. They enter the presidential palace attracted by the cheese — which in this case is power — and before they know it they are trapped there. If they leave power, they endanger their freedom or even their lives, as well as those of their relatives and accomplices. Their high position also allows them to better preserve the enormous fortunes that have been stolen. Naturally, dictators have no desire to give up power.

The metaphorical mousetrap that traps dictators in power illustrates one of the great challenges of today's world. What should be the fate of deposed dictators? In the past, those who weren't killed or imprisoned and managed to escape with their ill-gotten loot often wound up in idyllic places frequented by European royalty. Now tyrants who lose power end up in Europe, but not in Monaco or Biarritz, but rather in the International Criminal Court of The Hague.

The impunity enjoyed by a number of earlier dictators disappeared when Chile's former president, Augusto Pinochet, was arrested while visiting London in 1998. This move was an expression of the new human rights doctrine of "universal jurisdiction." It marked the beginning of a new era of accountability for serious human rights violations. For a dictator like Venezuela's Nicolás Maduro, for example, resigning means going to jail. Vladimir Putin now faces a similar predicament.

Naturally, this reality makes dictators even more reluctant to give up power. They have no reason to believe that the immunity they may be promised by other governments will last. Circumstances, alliances and governments change, and new rulers may decide that they are not bound by the commitments of their predecessors. For these dictators, the only reliable government is the one they preside over and the only armed forces that will defend them are the ones they command.

This is one of the thorniest problems of our time. Should an agreement be sought with dictators responsible for the deaths of thousands of innocent people? Or should ethics, justice and geopolitics force us to try to overthrow these dictators?

There are no easy answers. How many deaths would be avoided if a ceasefire were reached in Ukraine? Is it acceptable to make a deal with Putin to withdraw his troops in exchange for agreeing to some of his demands? For many, this would be immoral; they argue the only acceptable outcome is for Putin to lose power. Others maintain that the priority is to stop the killing of innocent civilians.

There are no obvious answers to these questions. But at least today we know that the answers can be shaped by countries where democracy reigns. Of all the horrible news that Putin's invasion has brought, there is a piece of good news that should give us hope: democracies have shown that they can work in concert and collectively confront the ills that affect the planet. This is an opportunity for the defenders of liberty to set the agenda instead of the tyrants.

March 22, 2022

Ukraine and the Other Great Crisis

For months, Russian President Vladimir Putin said that he had no intention of invading Ukraine, but on February 24 he did just that. Since then, surprises have been the norm. Putin himself was surprised since it is now obvious that things have not turned out as he had planned. The dictator overestimated the effectiveness of his armed forces and underestimated those of Ukraine. A devastating cyberattack by the Russians, for example, has yet to take place and Putin's army shows unexpected signs of disorder and has been forced to improvise.

We have also been surprised by President Volodymyr Zelenskyy, who has become an international symbol of courage, patriotism and leadership. In turn, the Ukrainian people have demonstrated exactly what it means to defend their homeland from the clutches of a blood-thirsty dictator.

Unfortunately, all this does not mean the Ukrainians will be able to repel the Russian attack. Russia's armed forces greatly outpower those of Ukraine. It is to be expected, however, that Ukraine will be able to prolong its insurrection against its invaders, an effort that will surely garner the sympathy of the world and the military and financial support of many countries.

Putin not only got the Ukrainians wrong, but he also underestimated the world's democracies. This is without a doubt the biggest surprise so far. The European Union responded in a united and effective way, which is certainly not the norm. We saw European leaders, politicians and bureaucrats reacting quickly and making decisions that, until recently, were unimaginable. The United States has allied with Europe, Japan and other countries to inflict economic pain on Russia for Putin's aggression. The world's democracies reacted with unusual speed and some discarded principles that for decades had been fundamental pillars of their foreign policy. Germany, for example, decided to increase its military spending and send war materiel to the Ukrainian armed forces. Switzerland abandoned what had been a defining factor of its foreign policy and even of its national identity: neutrality in the face of international conflicts.

The invasion of this tyrant is an unacceptable crime, but the world urgently needs to develop the capacity to respond to more than one crisis at a time.

The severe sanctions adopted by this international alliance have disconnected Russia from the world economy. As a result, Putin has condemned his population to poverty and isolation. Sadly, we will also see more terror and repression directed at Russians who dare to confront the government and demand a better future. As the economic situation worsens, the Kremlin will likely feel more threatened by its own citizens protesting in the streets and public squares than they will by democrats abroad.

As Russia's isolation deepens, many of the world's democracies have shown an unprecedented capacity to cooperate and defend the values they share. Swiftly designing and imposing the most severe sanctions in history and coordinating their adoption among many countries was not easy, but it got done. This is one of the most welcome side effects of the invasion: discovering that democracies can successfully tackle big problems. This experience can serve as a guide when facing the other global threats that lie ahead for us.

Coincidentally, four days after the invasion of Ukraine, a panel made up of the world's most prominent scientists published a report warning about the unprecedented human and material damage that we can expect from climate change, as well as the alarming rate at which these catastrophes are increasing. The report of the Intergovernmental Panel on Climate Change (IPCC) is based on the research of thousands of scientists from around the world. According to the report, we are at risk of adverse conditions becoming so extreme that vast areas of the planet will be uninhabitable, as will some of the most populous urban areas.

The climate crisis is at least as threatening as Vladimir Putin. The invasion of this tyrant is an unacceptable crime that cannot be tolerated, and we must support those who oppose it. But the world urgently needs to develop the capacity to respond to more than one crisis at a time. Ukraine should not be abandoned, but neither should the fight against global warming. The latter is very difficult, but now we know that, acting together, the world is capable of achieving difficult things.

The leaders of the world's democracies have shown that, in the face of an existential threat, policies can change decisively and quickly. It is time for them to boldly use this newly discovered superpower to attack the other great crisis facing humanity.

March 8, 2022

Why We Drag Our Feet When
It Comes to Climate Change

As images of Russian troops surrounding Ukraine grab headlines, the United States National Oceanic and Atmospheric Administration has published an important report. Its main conclusion is that, in the next 30 years, sea levels along the U.S. coast will rise as much as they did during the entire 20th century. To put that into context, consider that in the last 100 years sea levels rose faster than in the previous 2,000 years. Another fact: 40% of Americans live in coastal areas, and a significant portion of the country's economic activity occurs therein. It's a global problem and, of course, the rise of sea levels is just one of the many manifestations of climate change.

So why is it taking so long for humanity to deal effectively with a crisis that could end civilization as we know it? Why do politicians fail to make the necessary decisions to reduce emissions of carbon dioxide, the gas that contributes most to global warming?

One possible explanation is the sense of powerlessness. After all, what can a normal citizen do to prevent rising sea levels or the droughts, floods and forest fires that are becoming increasingly frequent, destructive and lethal?

It is a task that requires that multiple governments coordinate their policies on a large scale. And while it may seem that there is little that individuals can do, they can have a big impact, collectively, by electing politicians who will mobilize society and build support for the difficult decisions that must be made to contain the climate emergency. The task at hand is unprecedented, but with enough political will, strong popular support and new technology, it can become a reality.

Unfortunately, popular support for these tough decisions is often undermined by the sense of powerlessness that grips us as we consider the scale of the problem and meditate on the confusion surrounding possible solutions. Is the threat as serious as they make it out to be? Are the proposed remedies correct? Can the experts be trusted?

The duality between tangible costs now and hypothetical benefits in the future makes it politically difficult to stomach the measures that tackling climate change requires.

These are valid questions. But, in some cases, all they do is muddy the waters. Skepticism and confusion about how to deal with the problem have been made worse by the politicization of the issue by those who benefit from the status quo. Two researchers, Doug Koplow and Ronald Steenblik, have just published a study showing that governments that say they are doing their best to reduce their CO_2 emissions are, at the same time, spending $1.8 trillion (€1.59 million), or 2% of global gross domestic product (GDP), to subsidize the very industries that contribute most to climate change: coal, oil, gas and agriculture.

Large companies know how to shield themselves against initiatives that threaten their profitability. Decades ago, the tobacco industry funded so-called "experts" and research centers that questioned the link between tobacco use and cancer. For years, they managed to postpone the government's acceptance of what had long since been a scientifically proven fact. Tens of thousands of smokers lost their lives in the interim.

Oil companies also finance skeptics who question the global climate emergency. In 2019, ExxonMobil paid $690,000 (€608,000) to eight groups of activists and scientists who deny the crisis. In addition, the company continues to fund U.S. lawmakers who oppose the adoption of a carbon excise tax, an initiative that ExxonMobil publicly supports.

Another difficult obstacle to overcome in the attempt to prevent the planet from becoming uninhabitable for us is the paucity of intergenerational solidarity. "I don't care, I'm not going to be here when the catastrophic climate crisis comes." It's a comment we've all heard. In fairness, it can be said that this lack of interest in the health of the planet that our descendants will inherit is also fueled by the lack of a clear political consensus about what to do.

The solutions currently available, such as the elimination of subsidies for highly polluting companies or the payment of a carbon-consumption tax, would raise the cost of electricity, gasoline, heating and, therefore, many manufactured products. These increased costs are immediate and concrete. On the other hand, the benefits promised by solutions to global warming are long term and difficult to quantify and guarantee. It's just a bet. This duality between tangible costs now and hypothetical benefits in the future makes it politically difficult to stomach the measures that tackling climate change requires.

New energy technologies currently in the pipeline will surely help us fight the climate emergency. But technology alone will not be enough to fix the problem. We will also need major innovations in the way we govern ourselves.

February 23, 2022

The War On Death

We all know that a Rolls-Royce is one of the most expensive cars in the world. What you may not know is that last year they sold more cars than ever — 49% more than the previous year — making it the best year since the company was founded in 1906. And they aren't the only automaker that had a bumper year. Ferrari also reported record profits in 2021.

So what happened? Well, the pandemic made many rich people realize that life is short. That, at least, is the explanation given to the Financial Times by Torsten Müller-Otvös, the head of Rolls-Royce: "Quite a lot of people witnessed people in their community dying from Covid, and that made them think that life can be short and you'd better live now than postpone it to a later date."

Obviously, the "many" rich people who became aware of their mortality are not that many. The very lucrative year that Rolls-Royce had was on the back of just 5,586 vehicle sales worldwide. But while a few wealthy people now know that life is short, there are others who have decided to pour vast fortunes into finding treatments so we can all live healthier and longer lives. On January 23, the company Altos Labs opened for business. Like many biotech startups, their mission statement claims sweeping ambitions to transform the field of medicine. But unlike most other startups, they just might pull it off.

According to the U.S. National Cancer Institute, about 40% of Americans will develop one of the 200 different known types of cancer in their lifetime.

Rick Klausner, who was the director of the U.S. National Cancer Institute, is the founder and chief scientist of Altos Labs. Klausner managed to recruit several Nobel Prize winners and a large group of the most prestigious scientists in the world for the nascent biotech company. He also raised $3 billion from major investors. And all this is just the beginning of a vastly ambitious scientific and commercial research project.

The company will be dedicated to finding treatments to rejuvenate cells that have been affected by genetic abnormalities, injuries or the effects of aging. The goal is to restore cells to health and make them more resilient. If they succeed, it will not only improve the quality of life of those suffering from chronic diseases, but it could also add several years to their lives.

Recently, Joe Biden also declared war on death. Last week the president announced the creation of a "cancer cabinet" within the White House dedicated to speeding up research and coordinating the government's different efforts in this area. As Obama's vice president, Biden was also in charge of launching an anti-cancer program that made some progress but fell short of its promised goals. Now as president, Biden — who lost one of his children to brain cancer — recalled that, although the coronavirus pandemic claimed 800,000 American lives, during that same period 1.2 million people died of cancer.

According to the U.S. National Cancer Institute, about 40% of Americans will develop one of the 200 different known types of cancer in their lifetime. In turn, the American Cancer Society estimates that this year there will be almost two million new cancer patients in the country, of whom 600,000 will succumb to the disease. Biden wants to reduce the number of cancer deaths and emphasized that the program aims to cut fatalities in half within 25 years. According to the American president, during the last five years there have been many important scientific advances that, in combination with those that are in the pipeline, will make it possible to achieve the proposed goal.

The pandemic has brought us many surprises. One of these is a greater awareness of our own mortality and the reactions that this awareness provokes. For those who have the means, the response to the virus and its lethal threat is to enjoy what they have here and now. Obviously facing the pandemic by buying a Rolls-Royce is an option only for a privileged few, but you don't have to be a millionaire to refuse to postpone gratification. Millions are doing so.

The pandemic has whetted an appetite in some people to help others. Some do it individually and modestly and others ambitiously and on a large scale. The scientists who launched Alton Labs are a good example of those who have captured the sense of urgency, discerned the new scientific opportunities and are acting upon them on a large scale.

But what is perhaps most notable is the way the pandemic and its dire aftermath have fueled a surge of introspection that led many to rethink — or perhaps think for the first time — about their life's purpose, values, hopes and frustrations. It is with this new vital charge that some are dedicating themselves to defeating cellular aging, others to conquering cancer. They have reacted to this global shock with a dose of idealism that's been sorely lacking. And that will undoubtedly leave a legacy far greater than a Rolls-Royce parked in the garage.

February 7, 2022

2021

An Uninhabitable Earth?

"Friends of the Earth warn that we have lost precious time in the race to bring climate change under control." "The UN secretary-general expresses disappointment with the inconclusive outcome of the climate change conference." "The South criticizes the North for failing to keep its promises on climate change." "The agreement was weak, even if we meet each goal, we will not get to where we need to be."

These are not reactions to COP26, the recent climate conference in Glasgow. No, these are some of the headlines that appeared after COP meetings in Buenos Aires in 1998, in The Hague in 2000, in Lima in 2014 and in Paris in 2015. Activist Greta Thunberg's opinion on Glasgow echoed them: "It is no secret that COP26 is a failure. It should be obvious that we cannot solve the crisis with the same methods that got us into it in the first place."

Why is it that despite the overwhelming consensus for the need to act urgently to protect human life on our planet we are still unable to muster the necessary changes?

The results of every one of the 26 climate change conferences held over these 26 years have been disappointing. Yes, in Kyoto, in 2005, developed countries set out goals to reduce emissions, and in Paris, in 2015, they agreed to do what it takes to keep the average temperature from rising more than 1.5 degrees Celsius. But most of the promises have not been kept. In fact, things aren't getting better, they are getting worse: since the first conference, carbon emissions have increased by 60%.

Naturally, this frustrating track record left expectations for Glasgow at rock bottom. Nonetheless, the meeting produced three important decisions: the United States announced that it would double its budget to tackle climate change; China pledged to cease construction of coal-fired energy plants in other countries, and more than 100 countries committed to reducing their methane gas emissions by 30% by 2030. But, as the UN Secretary-General António Guterres observed, the Glasgow conference was "an important but insufficient step" which "reflects the interests, contradictions and the state of political will in the world."

Why is there this inaction in the face of such an obvious threat? One important factor is the lack of political will, which, in turn, is due to the unpopularity of measures that increase the cost of energy and other products. Another difficulty is deciding which countries should start a strict diet that limits their consumption of hydrocarbons while others maintain or even increase theirs. And, of course, there's the thorny matter of deciding which nations should finance the enormous investments necessary to mitigate the impacts of climate change and adapt to the new reality. The list of obstacles is long and overwhelming.

Many of these impediments can only be overcome with a massive global production of "public goods." These are items that can be consumed by any person or entity, even if they did not pay their share of the cost of producing or using them. The classic example is a lighthouse that helps ships navigate safely at night. Ships that have not paid for its construction still benefit from it like all the others. Another characteristic of a public good is that it can be consumed by multiple people or organizations at the same time. The fact that someone is consuming the services of the lighthouse does not prevent other ships from doing so as well. But no private party would invest in a good that anyone can use without paying. This is why the provision of public goods falls fundamentally on the state; it is the one entity with the capacity and the incentives to finance public goods through tax revenue.

Examples of public goods are many and range from street signs to national defense. Naturally, most of the investments in public goods are made by governments within their national territory — which is also where their citizens live and pay taxes. But how do you finance public goods in supranational spaces such as the oceans or space, where there are no citizens who pay taxes? The demand for public goods is always greater than the supply, a situation that becomes more dramatic in the case of global public goods. And reducing CO_2 emissions is a classic example of a global public good, perhaps the public good that the world needs most urgently right now.

This is the central problem facing humanity in its battle to control climate change, since the bulk of the investments necessary to achieve, the objective will have to come from taxpayers in rich countries. Will the most developed nations be able to put their financial power behind building public goods across the planet — and not just in their own territories — in order to maintain a climate that sustains human life as we know it?

The survival of civilization as we know it depends on the answer to that question.

December 7, 2021

Why Dictators Love Elections

The proliferation of autocrats who love to stage presidential elections is a surprising political phenomenon. Of course, we're not talking about free and fair elections that a dictator might lose. Oh, no. What they want is an exercise that gives off the illusion — or at least the passing aroma — of democracy, but where their victory is securely guaranteed. And the strange thing is that, even though people both inside and outside the country know it's all a sham, autocrats near and far continue to put on these threadbare electoral shows.

Rigged elections have a long history. Saddam Hussein, Muammar Gaddafi, or the leaders of the Soviet Union and its satellites loved to hold elections they would always win with 99% of the votes, or, when it was tight, 96.6%. More recently, the likes of North Korea's tyrant Kim Jong-un, Hugo Chávez and Nicolás Maduro in Venezuela, Vladimir Putin in Russia, and Aleksandr Lukashenko in Belarus have all "won" fraudulent elections.

An extreme case of these is Daniel Ortega of Nicaragua. A few years back he argued before the Nicaraguan Supreme Court that term limits injured his fundamental human rights. This absurdity was accepted by the justices who, obviously, were his lackeys. Inevitably, the international courts that considered this aspiration declared it void. That didn't stop Ortega. In 2011, the president violated the Constitution and ran for a third term. He won that election using all sorts of tricks and traps. A few weeks ago, he did it again. He was declared the overwhelming winner, making him president for an unprecedented fourth term.

Ortega, an erstwhile Marxist who in the 1970s joined the armed struggle to overthrow the dictatorship of Anastasio Somoza, has now, at the age of 75, become a classic tyrant himself, a strongman who has misruled one of the poorest countries on Earth with an iron fist for two solid decades. The idealistic Marxism of his youth contrasts jarringly with the opulent lifestyle that he and his family now enjoy.

Ortega loves elections, especially when he can imprison the main opposition leaders, including businessmen, journalists, academics, social activists and student leaders. He throws them all in jail, including seven presidential candidates. He also brutally repressed street protests against his government's corruption and authoritarianism. The abuse of state resources to support the autocrat's re-election campaigns, the coercion of public officials who are forced to vote in favor of the incumbent, the censorship of social media and the tight control of the armed forces are the familiar ingredients that tyrants like Ortega use to steal elections.

Rigged elections keep people under the sway of leaders and policies that deepen their misery, perpetuate inequity and enshrine ongoing injustice. They also underscore that the international community lacks the tools and strategies to punish those who do away with democracy in a given country. The United States, the European Union and most countries in America have denounced the abuse and illegality of Daniel Ortega's government. The United States has imposed ever tougher sanctions on the leaders and main beneficiaries of the monstrous Nicaraguan regime.

Unfortunately, none of this will make Ortega give up his ruinous hold on power. The Nicaraguan dictator embodies George Orwell's observation that "we know that no one ever seizes power with the intention of relinquishing it."

Paradoxically, democracy is based on just the opposite principle: on the premise that the power of rulers who are freely chosen by the people in fair elections must be held for a limited time only. The longest-lived and best consolidated democracies in the world have managed to establish laws, institutions and rules that stop leaders from perpetuating themselves in power. Other countries, however, have become victims of Orwell's insight: their leaders increasingly take it for granted that, once obtained, power is not to be let go.

In the early 21st century, more and more leaders begin to look for ways to extend their terms and weaken the checks and balances that limit their power from the moment they're first elected.

Daniel Ortega, his family and his accomplices must be celebrating their make-believe win. Nicaragua's election shows why dictators love such electoral shams so much.

November 19, 2021

Two Letters From China

At the end of July, Wendy Sherman, the U.S. Deputy Secretary of State, paid an official visit to Tianjin, in northwest China. There she met with her counterpart, Vice Foreign Minister Xie Feng. The purpose of the visit was to reduce tensions between the two countries.

It didn't work.

Xie Feng had two letters for her. One was titled "List of U.S. Wrongdoings that Must Stop," the other, "List of Key Individual Cases that China Has Concerns With." The first states that Washington must unconditionally remove visa restrictions on senior government officials and members of the Chinese Communist Party and their families who wish to enter the U.S. It also calls for eliminating U.S. sanctions on party and government leaders. The second letter expresses "serious concerns" about the way certain Chinese citizens who have been banned from the U.S. have been treated, as well as the bullying and harassment of diplomats and the growing anti-Chinese sentiment in the U.S.

A day later, Deputy Secretary Sherman responded via Twitter: "We will continue to press the PRC [People's Republic of China] to respect international norms and its international obligations."

Since that meeting, things have only gotten worse. China has carried out tests of a new hypersonic missile that flies at more than five times the speed of sound. Swarms of up to 150 fighters and bombers have penetrated Taiwan's air defense identification zone. China is building 119 underground silos to house ballistic missiles with global reach. A Pentagon report warns that the Asian giant is increasing its nuclear arsenal faster than was previously believed. China could have 700 nuclear warheads in 2027 and more than 1,000 by 2030. (The United States has 3,750.)

In Washington, it is now a given fact that a second Cold War has already begun. American planners realize that a prolonged conflict with China is imminent, even in the absence of direct military confrontation. Instead, conflicts will be settled in the economic, political, communications and cyber arenas, as well as in the world of espionage and sabotage. It will also likely play out in limited armed confrontations between countries allied with one or the other of the superpowers.

There are dozens of bills under consideration in the U.S. Congress intended to limit, counter or sanction China. A survey conducted in early 2021 by the Pew Center found that 89% of Americans viewed China as a competitor or enemy. Sophisticated observers wring their hands over the Thucydides Trap, which posits that when a rising power threatens the dominant role of an established power, conflict is almost inevitable.

Surely, the United States and China are destined to compete. But what should be equally obvious is that they must also collaborate. Worldwide threats and problems threaten the national interest of both superpowers and cannot be mitigated or eliminated by either of them acting alone. The most obvious example is the fight against global warming. The very nature of the problem, as well as the policies to deal with it, require close collaboration between Beijing and Washington. And this coordination is not going to happen out of altruism, international solidarity or because it is simply the most reasonable solution. No, it will happen because it suits the powerful. It is in the national interest of these two giants to slow temperature rises, because the disasters that will follow will have no regard for oceans or borders.

Another example of an area in which collaboration between China and the United States is essential is global health. We know that Covid-19 is not the first nor will it be the last pandemic to affect the world. We also know that, in this pandemic, collaboration between governments — including the U.S. and China — has been lousy. But the speed and efficiency with which scientists developed vaccines, and with which laboratories and companies in multiple countries produced billions of doses in record time, show that cooperation can still trump competition.

The list of areas in which the U.S. and China will be forced to cooperate is long and urgent. The fight against nuclear proliferation — especially that of Iran and North Korea — and against the proliferation of chemical and biological weapons, Islamist terrorism, cyberattacks, the instability of the world financial system, piracy and the chaos of mass migration are just some of the items. But the list goes on: drug trafficking and the trafficking of weapons and people, as well as how to properly regulate the internet.

Xi Jinping, the Chinese leader, posed what he described as a fundamental question: "Whether China and the United States can properly handle mutual relations is a question for the century that concerns the fate of the world, and both countries must answer it."

He's right.

November 9, 2021

What Was Colin Powell Doing
On September 11, 2001?

Having breakfast. In Lima, Peru.

Powell, who was the U.S. Secretary of State at the time, had accepted an invitation from Peru's then-president, Alejandro Toledo, to a breakfast at the Presidential Palace. But Powell had not traveled to Lima just to meet Toledo. He was representing his country in what promised to be a historic meeting: on that particular September 11, 34 countries in the Americas were about to commit to strengthening and defending democracy. The document to be signed — the Inter-American Democratic Charter — enshrined the principle that "the peoples of the Americas have a right to democracy and their governments have an obligation to promote and defend it."

Democracy was flying high at the time. In a wide range of countries, opinion polls revealed that it was broadly perceived as the best political system. It was, after all, the system that had confronted and defeated a despotic Soviet Union, ending the ruinous and inhumane communist system that the Kremlin wanted to impose on the rest of the world.

Before meeting the dignitaries, who would sign the Democratic Charter, the former general — who at the time was perhaps the most-admired politician in the United States and regarded as a possible future president — paid a formal visit to the president of Peru. He was accompanied by five senior officials from the State Department and Toledo received them in the company of Roberto Dañino, the president of the Council of Ministers, the minister of foreign affairs and the nation's drug czar. None of the attendees imagined, on that promising morning of September 11, that the world would change in ways that still touch us all to this day.

As they sampled Peru's celebrated cuisine, one of Powell's aides handed him a note and whispered in his ear. Recalling the moment, Roberto Dañino, whom I interviewed for this piece, says that Powell read the note, frowned, and briefly informed the group that a plane had lost its way and crashed into a building in Manhattan. Talks continued until, minutes later, the aide came back and gave Powell another note. He read it, and without losing his composure, told the diners that a second plane had crashed into a building, and that everything suggested a terrorist attack was underway.

"Who is behind this?" Dañino asked. "Al Qaeda," Powell quickly replied, but then corrected himself. "The truth is that I don't know. But my military experience has taught me to react calmly to big events. Hopefully the dust will settle, and we will be able to see things more clearly." They asked him if he would fly back to Washington right away, leaving one of his deputies to sign the document. "Not at all," Powell replied. "I'll stay and sign. Democracy is the best weapon against terrorism. The only thing I ask is that you move up the signing ceremony so I can fly back as soon as possible."

And that's what they did. The Democratic Charter was signed by representatives from every government in the hemisphere, except Cuba, binding the signatories to promote and protect democracy.

A lot has changed in these 20 years. A recent IPSOS survey of 19,000 people in 25 countries (including Argentina, Brazil, Chile, Colombia, Mexico and Peru) showed that many of these Latin Americans view their own country's democracy as the worst in the world. Even more worrying is that 44% of respondents want "strong leaders willing to break the rules." What's more, the perception that society is fragmented is higher among Latin Americans (64%) than the rest of the world (56%).

Polarization within Latin America is inevitably reflected in the polarization of governments in the region. It is not surprising, then, that in the last 20 years the Inter-American Democratic Charter Powell signed has not been successfully invoked even when it was flagrantly violated, such as by Hugo Chávez and Nicolás Maduro in Venezuela, and Daniel Ortega in Nicaragua.

Colin Powell passed away on October 18 at the age of 84. In the media's exhaustive recounting of his life, there was talk of many successes and failures. Yet his signature gracing the bottom of the Democratic Charter was all but forgotten.

I know that even in his retirement the general and diplomat was deeply concerned about the precarious state of world democracy. I wonder if Powell ever imagined that if things continued on the road they are now, perhaps the document that he signed in Lima 20 years ago would have to be applied to the United States.

November 3, 2021

¿*Bye, bye*, Democracy?

"The United States is heading into its greatest political and constitutional crisis since the Civil War, with a reasonable chance over the next three to four years of incidents of mass violence, a breakdown of federal authority and the division of the country into warring red and blue enclaves."

Thus begins an explosive article recently published in The Washington Post by Robert Kagan, who, until 2016, was one of the most influential foreign policy strategists in the Republican Party. His analysis deals with issues that we typically associate with the weak democracies of Latin America, with their well-known propensity for political self-destruction. Indeed, Kagan's analysis marks a milestone in the latinamericanization of U.S. politics.

His analysis has two pillars. First, that former U.S. president Donald Trump is the inevitable candidate for the Republicans in the 2024 elections. The initial belief that his power and influence would fade after his 2020 loss has proved illusory. Trump has the money, the political machinery and millions of passionate followers. Plus, in 2024, he will face politically vulnerable opponents. Yes, Trump could face legal or health problems that prevent him from running, but placing stock in these assumptions is wishful thinking, not political strategy.

According to Kagan, the Republican Party is no longer defined by its ideology but by loyalty to Donald Trump. Party leaders who do not unconditionally support the former president are summarily marginalized and mercilessly attacked. The second pillar is that Trump and his allies are working hard to guarantee electoral victory through undemocratic means, should it be necessary to resort to them. The clumsy and doomed attempts to use lawsuits to give Trump the votes he lacked to beat Joe Biden, as well as the media blitz to persuade the country that Trump's election was stolen, will no longer be so clumsy or hastily improvised. Rather, a sophisticated, fierce and well-funded project is underway to control the electoral process in key states, with a focus on vote tallying as well as empowering elected state officials to make the final determination as to who won the election in their state. "The stage is thus being set for chaos," writes Kagan, who continues: "Imagine weeks of competing mass protests across multiple states as lawmakers from both parties claim victory and charge the other with unconstitutional efforts to take power. Partisans on both sides are likely to be better armed and more willing to inflict harm than they were in 2020."

Kagan sounds the alarm about dangerous trends that are new to the United States, but not to Latin America. He deserves credit for perceiving that strongmen like Trump do not engage in politics like other democratic leaders, but rather employ asymmetric tactics to achieve their goals.

Let's look at it this way: Osama bin Laden taught the world the meaning of asymmetric warfare, while Donald Trump showed us the meaning of asymmetric politics.

Asymmetric warfare is an armed conflict in which one of the parties has many more resources and military capabilities than its opponent, forcing the weaker side to resort to unconventional strategies, tactics and moves. In 2015, Donald Trump did not have a party willing to nominate him as its presidential candidate, but he was willing to break all the traditional rules and norms of politics, surprising and disorienting his rivals. Plunging into asymmetric politics not only allowed him to take over the Republican Party but also lay claim to the U.S. presidency. And although he failed to win reelection in 2020, his success as the leader of a movement that thrives on political asymmetry is unquestionable.

So, what do we do about it? How do we strengthen American

democracy and prevent leaders with undemocratic tendencies to undermine democracy from within? Paradoxically, the best way to confront the asymmetric politics that give electoral advantages to demagogues, populists and charlatans is not to imitate them. Attacks on democracy must be fought with more and better democracy. The world's democracies — and America's most urgently — need to be repaired and reformed so that they can respond to new realities (like pandemics) or old malignancies (like inequality). But before discussing concrete initiatives to defend democracy and combat the asymmetric attacks to which it will be subjected, it is necessary to create a broad consensus about how serious this threat is. The asymmetric attack on democracy is not "more of the same." It is a different political phenomenon with grave potential consequences. To defeat it, we have to understand it, raise awareness about its toxicity and give it the priority it deserves.

Hopefully, democracy will rise to the challenge.

October 12, 2021

Two American Surprises

Dramatic international developments that affect us all are becoming more frequent. Some touch us directly and others reverberate around us. But the daily news leaves us with the feeling that we are in a time of great change.

In some cases, we don't need the media to tell us about the magnitude and severity of change. We live them daily. The coronavirus is one example. It is inescapable, global and, in many ways, unprecedented. Another example is the record number of climate refugees who have fled their homes due to devastating wildfires, hurricanes and cyclones. Heat waves with temperatures that in the pre-industrial era occurred every 50 years now occur every ten years.

But the changes that affect us are not only due to climate change and the pandemic. Global politics is also catching us off guard. Nobody expected that a mob of Donald Trump's supporters would storm the U.S. Capitol or that the U.S. withdrawal from Afghanistan would be so ineptly handled by the Biden administration. On the other hand, frictions between the United States and China have become so frequent that it is now normal to hear that a cold war is already underway between the two superpowers. Global warming is changing the world, but so is geopolitics.

In addition to these pressing and much discussed trends and events, there are others that — without being so visible — will have enormous consequences. Two are worth noting.

One of the under-reported trends has to do with the demographics of the United States: the current growth rate of its population (0.35% per year) is the lowest in 122 years. This is partly due to America's rapidly falling life expectancy. This decline actually preceded the Covid-19 pandemic, the disease that has already claimed the most lives in United States history. These increases in mortality mainly affect the poorest citizens, specifically workers and, in particular, the 52% of the population who do not have a college degree. This inequality has been exacerbated by Covid-19. From the outbreak of the pandemic in 2019 to 2020, life expectancy among Hispanics and African Americans in the United States fell three years. Among the white population it dropped 1.2 years. These changes in American demographics will have a huge impact on the politics and economy of the whole country.

One of the area's most directly affected by this demographic shift will be fiscal policy: who pays taxes and at what rate, as well as what programs the government will spend those tax dollars on. America's long-running tolerance for its high levels of economic inequality is finally ebbing, and Joe Biden aims to reduce the gaps even more. To do this, he plans to take advantage of the state's ability to collect taxes and to use public spending to catalyze social change. An example of this is his decision to increase the corporate tax rate on large multinational corporations. In addition, he decided not to do so unilaterally, but to create a broad coalition of countries that would act together.

The objective of making this an international initiative is to prevent companies from moving their operations abroad to reduce their tax bills. The purpose is to stop the "race to the bottom" among countries which compete in their bid to attract foreign investors by lowering their taxes. The proposal by Biden and his Treasury Secretary Janet Yellen is to impose a global minimum tax of 15% on all companies with revenues above $890 million.

According to the Organization for Economic Co-operation and Development (OECD), large multinationals have been able to avoid taxes for amounts ranging from $100 million to $240 million each year, that is, 4% to 10% of their total taxes. Between 1985 and 2018 the tax rate paid by the largest multinationals fell by half, from 49% to

24%. In 2017, which is the last period for which there is reliable data, multinationals placed 40% of their earnings, approximately $700 billion, in tax havens where they paid little or no taxes.

With this agreement, the United States managed to get 132 countries to commit to charging the global minimum rate. The countries that participate in the agreement represent more than 90% of the global economy, which means that companies that try to move their profits to other countries to avoid paying taxes will have very few options.

It is not clear whether this agreement will survive, at least in the form it was originally put forward. Presumably, companies will use their enormous financial resources and political influence to bring the final agreement into line with their interests. But in any case, it shows that international cooperation is possible.

And that's a change worth celebrating.

September 28, 2021

Two Ideas Defeated in Kabul

What was defeated in Afghanistan was not just the most expensive and technologically advanced army in the world, but also two ideas that had deeply influenced the Western world. The first is that democracy can be exported, and the second is that the U.S. military is the best in the world.

Since the collapse of the Soviet Union, one of the most popular and enduring policies in wealthy democratic countries has been to promote democracy in places where it doesn't exist or where it's precarious and dysfunctional. Unfortunately, diplomacy, money, technology and military interventions have not yielded very substantial and sustained results.

It turns out that transitions from dictatorship to democracy are more likely to succeed when brave and talented local political leaders play a leading role in convincing the people to protest, take to the streets and paralyze the country if necessary. Or, even better, when there are splits within the dictatorship and the military refuses to massacre and repress its own people.

At best, foreign support for democratic transitions has played a secondary role. Sadly, in some cases, foreign intervention, rather than accelerating transitions to democracy, slows them down or derails them altogether.

The export of democracy is not just an abstract idea, a moral obligation or a political promise. It has also become an industry that moves huge sums of money. It is estimated that the United States, the

European Union, Canada, Australia, the Scandinavian countries and others spend about $10 billion a year to support programs that seek to strengthen democracy around the world.

This immense amount of money is only a fraction of what the U.S. has devoted to Afghanistan. In the past 20 years, and in that country alone, the U.S. government spent $145 billion on "reconstruction" activities, which does not include, among others, the costs of the war. A Brown University study found that between 2001 and 2021 the U.S. government spent a total of $2.2 trillion dollars on Afghanistan.

The case of Afghanistan illustrates — painfully — how two decades of multinational military intervention, broad global political support, hundreds of thousands of deaths and unimaginable amounts of money were not enough to consolidate democracy.

The U.S. withdrawal from Afghanistan also makes another long-held belief difficult to defend: that the United States has the most competent and powerful armed forces in the world. It is, without a doubt, the most technologically sophisticated army on the planet. And the most expensive. But that does not make it the most successful.

The contrast between a Taliban in sandals and a turban with an assault rifle slung over his shoulder, and a marine with a bulletproof vest, communication equipment, night-vision goggles, high-tech explosives, multiple weapons and support from drones, helicopter gunships, planes and satellites could not be more revealing. Equipping a single Taliban fighter likely costs a few hundred dollars. Outfitting a Marine costs $17,500, not counting the costs of air, cyber and logistics support. That the Taliban were able to defeat this supremely well-armed and super-trained American force is a fact that will be studied for a long time in the world's military academies.

It is interesting to note that the two ideas that were defeated in Kabul share a common factor: a lot of money often distributed in haphazard, wasteful and, at times, corrupt ways. Clearly, spending massively and freely didn't help to achieve the desired goal. In some cases, it distorted the effort and, ultimately, contributed to its failure.

It is crucial that the right lessons be drawn from these defeats. It would be a mistake to conclude that the countries that are the bulwark of world democracy must give up their efforts to protect and fortify the weak democracies that we see proliferating today. The important thing is to understand which areas foreign aid can usefully address, and what form that aid should take. What is clear is that the way the West has been promoting democracy is not working.

The same goes for the U.S. military. Of course, they must have the best available technology and their troops must have the best training and equipment. But does that really need to cost $740 billion per year? Should U.S. military spending exceed the sum of all military spending of the next 11 top-spending countries combined? Aren't these virtually unlimited budgets a source of strategic errors? Would the war in Afghanistan have lasted two decades if the military had faced real budget constraints? My answer to these four questions: No.

September 9, 2021

The Great Divide: Science Booms
While Politics Bomb

Scientists never had any doubts that we would get a vaccine against Covid-19. And they were right. Very few, however, predicted that such a vaccine would be available so quickly. History suggested that the vaccine would take years to develop and produce in large quantities. Yet, scientists who began researching Covid-19 in January 2020 were soon ready to begin phase 3 clinical trials to evaluate its effectiveness. Typically, it takes years for any drug or treatment to be ready for phase 3 trials. In this case, it took six months.

Correctly predicting an outcome but overestimating how long it will take to achieve it has become common. We've seen it in climate change, in the digital revolution and genetic engineering. In these three cases, the experts correctly anticipated the nature of the changes, but not the extraordinary speed at which they are occurring.

Scientific discovery and technological innovation define humanity. And we know that new technologies tend to have unanticipated consequences for society, the economy and politics. And of course, on governments, which normally lag in adapting and responding to conditions created by technological change.

What has happened with the Covid-19 vaccine — its invention, production and distribution — is a telling example of the dangerous gap between technology and politics. While the scientific effort to create and produce the Covid-19 vaccine was global, the response from governments has been local. Although laboratories in different

122

countries shared data and expertise, important governments, such as China's, hid or misrepresented it. Scientists showed vision, flexibility and speed; governments have been shortsighted, rigid and slow.

All this is not to say that there have not been rivalries between some scientists and fierce competition between pharmaceutical companies. But we all saw how scientists responded effectively to the crisis, while politicians and governments in many places denied the very existence of the pandemic or downplayed it. Some ridiculed social distancing policies and the use of masks, promoted fraudulent treatments and encouraged the use of amulets with magical powers. In India, Brazil and Mexico, the pandemic is wreaking havoc. Narendra Modi, Jair Bolsonaro and Andrés Manuel López Obrador are not responsible for the pandemic, but they are guilty of reacting badly and much too slowly to the tragedy that their countries are experiencing.

The norms, rules and values that guide politicians are, of course, very different from those that guide scientists. While for scientists merit is key, politicians prioritize the loyalty of their collaborators and tolerate their ineptitude. For scientists, decisions must be based on evidence, while traditional politicians weigh heavily on their previous experiences, anecdotes and intuition. While scientific research seeks change through the creation and adoption of new knowledge, politics tend to privilege ideas and ways of acting that are comfortable and well-known — even though in their speeches all politicians present themselves as agents of change. Finally, the scientific method is based on reason and the empirical verification of claims whose validity can be verified and replicated by others. In politics, on the other hand, personal passions and beliefs prevail, not to mention religious beliefs and, in some cases, faith in magic.

All of the above does not mean, of course, that some scientists aren't influenced by passions, interests and prejudices, or that politicians never endorse meritocracy, rationalism and the promotion of change. But what this contrast reveals are some of the sources of the divide between science and politics.

The backwardness of politics is brutally manifested in the stagnation of governments, in their systemic dysfunction and especially in the abysmal quality of the decision-making processes in matters of public policy. Politicians would do well to adopt the spirit of experimentation that has always distinguished science. This, together with the openness to new ideas, the dispassionate evaluation of the evidence and the force of empirical reality could begin to rebuild the credibility of democracies in the face of the multiple crises that threaten them.

Bridging the divide between today's booming science and bombing politics is no easy feat. But it is also imperative.

May 5, 2021

Arab Youth

It was once jihadists, now it's white supremacists. For years, Islamist terrorism was seen as the major threat to Europe and the United States. But not anymore. Now our worries have shifted to Covid-19 and to white extremist violence.

Terrorism from white supremacists is very real and on the rise. According to FBI Director Christopher Wray, "racially motivated violent extremism, specifically of the sort that advocates for the superiority of the white race, is a persistent, evolving threat." The FBI has officially raised the threat level assigned to these groups, putting them at the same rank as the Islamic State. Wray also revealed that while the FBI investigated 850 cases of white supremacist terrorism in the U.S. last year, it now had 2,000 open cases. This terrorism is not just an American phenomenon. In recent years, its presence and violent actions have also increased in Europe and Oceania.

Of course, the fact that jihadists have stopped making headlines does not mean that the conditions that fueled their violence have diminished. Frustration and despair are still all too common among young Arabs. One indicator of the extent of young Arab frustration is that about half of this group has considered emigrating from their home country. In some Arab nations the number of young people wanting to leave is overwhelming — 77% in Lebanon, 69% in Libya and 56% in Jordan, for example.

This data comes from a telling opinion poll conducted by ASDA'A-BCW, a public relations firm in Dubai. For 12 years, the company has carried out an annual survey of young people between the ages of 18 and 24 living in 17 countries in the Middle East and North Africa. The results of these opinion polls often clash with deep-rooted perceptions.

The backlash against corruption is one of the factors driving support among young people for the wave of anti-government street protests that have become frequent in countries such as Lebanon, Algeria, Sudan and Iraq.

For 40% of those surveyed, religion is the main driver of identity — more than their family (19%) or their nationality (17%). But that religious identity does not translate into support for governments that also define themselves religiously. The young people surveyed want governments that are less corrupt and more efficient, capable of creating jobs, and improving the quality of education. Eighty-seven percent are concerned about unemployment, and more than half do not believe that their current government is capable of solving the problem.

Forty-one percent of those surveyed said that corruption is widespread in their country, and 36% believe that there is government corruption. This backlash against corruption is one of the factors driving support among young people for the wave of anti-government street protests that have become frequent in countries such as Lebanon, Algeria, Sudan and Iraq, among others. As in other parts of the world where the streets have become an important scene of political protests, in the Arab world these have been fueled by social media. Five years ago, 25% of young people surveyed reported that social media was their main source of news. Now that percentage has rocketed to 79%.

The near-universal use of the internet by young people makes one of the poll's findings especially surprising. When asked about the main determinant of their individual identity, only a tiny 5% said that their gender was the most defining factor. Since the sample of the interviewees was designed so that there was an equal number of women and men, the small weight the respondents gave to their gender identity is striking. However, this is consistent with another surprising result: 64% of the young women surveyed think that, in their country, women have the same rights as men and 11% believe that women enjoy more rights than men. Unfortunately, the survey doesn't offer an explanation for this unusual finding.

Finally, another interesting revelation from this survey is the huge appeal the United Arab Emirates has for the young. Thirty-four percent of respondents think the UAE has increased its influence in the region, second only to Saudi Arabia (39%). The Emirates are — for the ninth year running — the country where most young Arabs want to live: 46% declared it their favorite destination to emigrate to, more than the 33% who prefer the U.S. This is perhaps the most striking result: it shows that these young people don't want to live in the West, necessarily. They want to live in a country that works.

The frustrations and expectations of these young Arabs present formidable challenges to their respective governments. Even before the pandemic and its devastating economic consequences, these 200 million young people faced the highest unemployment rates in the world and governments that were intolerably corrupt and incapable of undertaking the necessary reforms. Now the situation is much worse.

As a consequence, in many Arab countries, young people will take to the streets to protest. In others they will take planes, boats and cars to migrate to new countries, because they feel that they cannot change the useless and corrupt governments they are now stuck with.

We will have to see what the polls of young Arabs tell us next year.

April 7, 2021

The United States, a Dangerous Ally

"America is back," declared an excited Joe Biden. He was speaking to a group of mostly European political leaders, via video link, at the Munich Security Conference. The new president emphasized that "the transatlantic alliance is back." Naturally, the message was well received. Angela Merkel, Emmanuel Macron and Boris Johnson all applauded America's new stance. In his remarks, Biden also renewed America's commitment to NATO's Article V, which obliges the military alliance's member nations to respond collectively to an attack against any one of its members. During Donald Trump's presidency, he repeatedly refrained from publicly acknowledging that, as a member of NATO, his country would accept that obligation. Naturally, Trump's reluctance produced a great deal of anxiety in the capitals of Europe... and glee from the Kremlin.

That changed when Biden entered the White House. The U.S. president used his speech at the Munich conference to leave no doubt about his administration's position on Article V. "An attack on one is an attack on all," Biden said, and promised that his country would honor its commitment.

As president, Donald Trump disdained multilateralism, alliance-building and diplomacy, which he considered a waste of time. Instead, he prioritized the development of personal relationships with the leaders of countries such as China, Russia, Saudi Arabia and North Korea. He didn't accomplish much and, in general, U.S. relations with many of the countries he sought to seduce deteriorated.

128

It is fascinating to see high-level diplomats emulating the strategies of many multinational executives.

For their part, both Biden and his officials repeat, whenever possible, that alliances will be the central pillar of the administration's foreign policy. They see diplomacy as the main instrument to further U.S. national interests. According to them, successfully attacking the pandemic, climate change and the economic crisis, and preventing Iran from having nuclear weapons, would all be impossible without coordination with allies. From the perspective of Biden and his administration, Trump's slogan "America First" ended up meaning "America Alone." According to them, Trump's position only served to isolate the country, including unilaterally ceding geopolitical spaces that were quickly filled by China and Russia. It also proved that while America's military and economic power is important, it is not enough to accomplish the nation's international objectives.

Potential allies are keen to work with the United States in pursuit of their common interests. There is no doubt that repowering these alliances is necessary. Global problems that cannot be solved with local responses are proliferating and with them, the need for countries to act in a coordinated manner.

Unfortunately, Washington's attempts to build a much-needed network of international alliances will have one major obstacle: the volatility of U.S. politics.

Why? Consider what would happen to a country that enthusiastically embraces Biden and dives into an alliance with the United States only to find four years later that the U.S. elections have ushered in a new president who has no interest in upholding Biden's agreements. That issue is very much on the minds of foreign policy leaders of the very countries that Washington needs as allies. In the virtual corridors of the Munich conference, the most pressing question was not whether the United States was back. The burning question was — and still is — how long it will stay "back." They realize that the United States is not a politically stable country.

It is fascinating to see high-level diplomats emulating the strategies of many multinational executives. Since the late 1990s, business leaders have built complex and highly efficient supply chains that start in China and flow to markets around the world. These supply chains allowed companies to drastically reduce their inventories. Just-in-Time (JIT) logistics practices became universal in inventory management. In order to minimize costs, supplies arrive with speed and precision at their destination, just when they are needed for the manufacture of the final product.

The trade war that Trump set off with China created all kinds of headaches in global supply chains. Companies that depended on JIT logistics discovered that it was dangerous to put all their eggs in one basket. To mitigate the risk, executives were forced to balance the principle of "Just-in-Time" with that of "Just-in-Case." Many were forced to invest in finding new suppliers, at considerable cost, just in case.

Business leaders understood that as much as they want the United States to create stability and limit imbalances, this will not always be the case. Political leaders will likely emulate them. The politics of alliances promoted by Joe Biden will be shaped by the diplomacy of "Just-in-Case."

March 3, 2021

Political Surrogates

Despite being home to the Galapagos Islands as well as 32 majestic volcanoes — several of them active — and being the world's largest producer of bananas, Ecuador rarely attracts international media attention. It is not Brazil, Mexico or Argentina, the giants of the region. Its political instability is not as problematic as that of neighboring Peru, nor has it been looted top to bottom like Venezuela. In short, it is a normal Latin American country: poor, unequal, unjust, corrupt, and full of decent and hard-working people. Its democracy is flawed but competitive, its institutions are weak, but they are there, and its economy — the eighth largest in the continent — depends on the export of oil, bananas, shrimp and gold. And, of course, on the money that Ecuadorians abroad send back to their families.

These days, Ecuador is making headlines more often. The country is in the midst of electing a new president, and that is always newsworthy. But, according to analysts, this time the Ecuadorian election results will reveal trends that we will likely see repeated in the rest of Latin America.

One trend is that while the left will likely regain power, it is no longer obvious what that will mean in terms of the actual policies it will implement. Between the end of the last century and the beginning of this one, leftist presidents have been proliferating. From Lula da Silva to Hugo Chávez, from Evo Morales to the Kirchner couple, and from Michelle Bachelet to Rafael Correa, just to name a few. Their policies varied significantly.

131

In the first round of the Ecuadorian elections, no candidate obtained enough votes, forcing a second ballot on April 11. The most-voted-for candidate in the first round was the leftist Andrés Arauz, who was mentored and supported by former President Rafael Correa. Which candidate came second in this election is the subject of a fierce battle between the conservative businessman Guillermo Lasso and the indigenous candidate Yaku Pérez, who claims there was a fraud.

The businessman promises efficiency, economic growth and jobs; the leftist offers equality, less poverty and more justice; and the indigenous leader vows to vindicate the rights of the indigenous people and protect the environment. This menu — of the businessman, the leftist and the indigenous leader — is something we have seen in other countries, too. The result is usually unpredictable. Brazil is currently headed by a right-wing populist, and Mexico by a left-wing populist. We have seen right-wing presidents adopt left-wing policies and vice versa. And this trend will likely continue.

But in Latin American elections there is another important trend — what Michael Reid, a journalist and commentator on Latin America, has called "Presidents by Proxy." Think of them as political surrogates. These are individuals close to a president who is not eligible to run for office again but uses surrogates to continue to wield power.

Arauz, the Ecuadorian candidate with the most votes in the first round, got where he is thanks to the support of former President Rafael Correa, who could not run as a candidate since he was declared ineligible following a corruption trial. Cristina Kirchner was President of Argentina thanks to her husband Néstor Kirchner (and reelected after she was widowed). In Mexico, Deputy Margarita Zavala, the wife of former President Felipe Calderón, was a candidate in the 2018 presidential elections where Andrés Manuel López Obrador was the winner. In Colombia, Juan Manuel Santos and Iván Duque reached the presidency thanks to the support of former President Álvaro Uribe. In Brazil, Dilma Rousseff was President thanks to Lula da Silva, and in Bolivia, Lucho Arce won the election thanks to the popularity of his former boss Evo Morales, who gave him all his support.

Populism — both on the right and on the left — with its chronically unfulfilled promises, its fixation on policies already shown not to work, and its authoritarian propensities, is always a major threat. But *continuismo* — when a leader continues in power beyond their term limits — is an even greater threat. If a populist president is incompetent or corrupt, but democracy works in his or her country, then the voters will take care of removing them from power. Countries can overcome a term under a bad president, but the damage can be enormous and irreversible if that bad president remains in power for long stretches of time. Or if once their term of office is over, they do step down but in practice continue to exert power through another politician who acts as their political surrogate.

It is important to set legal limits on a president's continuity. Ideally, they should be elected for a term of no more than six years and no less than five. At the end of that single term, they should not be able to run again for president. Ever.

This solution might seem drastic and imperfect. It is. But its defects are more tolerable than the consequences of having "forever presidents" who end up defining a nation's politics for decades. Unfortunately, the *continuismo* that relies on political surrogates is more difficult to uproot. But it is critically important to fight against it and to ensure that candidates are not beholden to former presidents but are genuine, autonomous leaders whose decisions are not dictated by their political mentors.

February 17, 2021

Joe's Dilemma: Peace or Justice

Susan Bro embodies the dilemma that may very well define Joe Biden's presidency: can there be peace without justice? Bro is the mother of Heather Heyer, a 32-year-old woman who was killed in Charlottesville, Virginia, in 2017 by far-right activist James Alex Fields. Fields deliberately ran his car over a group of peaceful protesters who were marching in opposition to a group of neo-Nazis, Klansmen and white supremacists who had gathered from around the country for what they called Unite the Right Rally. In commenting on these tragic events, the U.S. president at the time, Donald Trump, famously stressed that there were very fine people on both sides of the protest. Joe Biden has said that what happened in Charlottesville convinced him to run for president.

Susan Bro worries that, in the pursuit of unity, Joe Biden may sacrifice justice. She told The New York Times that healing requires holding perpetrators accountable. Unity follows justice.

Biden offers another perspective: "We can join forces, stop the shouting and lower the temperature. For without unity, there is no peace — only bitterness and fury."

The list of emergencies that the new president must deal with is overwhelming. The pandemic, its catastrophic economic consequences, climate change, a deeply unequal and polarized society, and dozens of international crises are just some of the urgent problems facing the Biden administration. If responding effectively to just one of these challenges is immensely difficult, tackling them all at the same time is daunting. But there is no alternative: the threats are real, they have been getting worse and they demand immediate attention. Biden has rightly divined that progress in fighting any of these threats requires that the divisions that now fragment the country and block important decision-making be curtailed. Unity was the theme of President Biden's inaugural address and is the message he reiterates every time he addresses the nation.

Biden is an experienced politician and knows how difficult it will be to unite partisan Democrats and Republicans. Moreover, leading Americans to cut the vitriol and coexist in more harmony with their compatriots who support leaders and causes that they find unpalatable is as urgent as it is difficult.

Biden also knows that while 82 million Americans voted for him (or against Trump) another 74 million did so for Trump (or against the current president) and that more than a third of Americans believe that he is an illegitimate president. Clearly, the national unity that Biden advocates is necessary. But, is there a contradiction in aiming to bring polarized Americans together while at the same time arresting and jailing those who invaded the Capitol, or the Republican politicians, lawyers and bureaucrats who actively engaged in staging a coup that aimed at keeping Trump in power?

The political tension between peace and justice is already causing problems in Washington.

Just one day after the start of the Biden administration, and in reaction to the decision to proceed with the impeachment of Donald Trump, Republican Senator Ted Cruz urged Democratic Party leaders to put aside what he described as their "partisan hatred" of Donald Trump, and added: "It seems that Senate Democrats [...] want to start the new Congress [...] with a vindictive and punitive impeachment trial."

That same day, a journalist asked Speaker Nancy Pelosi, the Democratic head of the House of Representatives, if prosecuting Donald Trump did not contradict the calls to unify the country. "The fact is that the president of the United States committed an act of incitement, of insurrection," replied Pelosi, adding, "I don't think it's very unifying to simply say 'let's just forget it and move on.' That's not how you unify. It is our responsibility to protect and defend the constitution and that is what we are going to do." Referring to Trump, the Democratic leader affirmed: "You don't say to a president, 'Do whatever you want in the last months of your administration and you're going to get a get-out-of-jail card free,' because people think we should make nice-nice and forget that people died here on January 6, that the attempt to undermine our election or to undermine our democracy, to dishonor our Constitution. No, I don't see that at all. I think that would be harmful to unity."

The peace versus justice debate is not new in the United States or the rest of the world. In fact, it is frequently found in many of the societies that are beginning to recover from war, prolonged periods of violence and serious human rights violations. "Truth and Reconciliation commissions" played an important role in South Africa, Sri Lanka and Colombia.

This, of course, is not the case in the United States. Nonetheless, recent events show that it is not prudent to take for granted that America's institutions (Congress, the media, the military and especially its judicial system) have the strength, resources and tools needed to cope with a political environment where those who demand redress and justice constantly clash with those who advocate magnanimously looking ahead for the sake of social peace.

January 28, 2021

How Will We Remember January 6?

January 6 was a very bad day for President Donald Trump and a very good day for American democracy. The dead and wounded will be remembered as a tragic outcome of the president's violent rhetoric. But what happened that day — and I'm not just referring to the take-over of Congress by Trump's supporters — could very well mark the beginning of an important period of renewal and strengthening of American democracy.

On January 6, the laws, institutions and norms that limit presidential power in the United States were stress-tested. Fortunately, they survived Donald Trump's attempt to stay in the White House despite losing the election.

This is not to say that American democracy has passed through this crisis unscathed. It had already been weakened, and although the coup failed, Trump and his accomplices have left the country even more vulnerable and divided. What's more, the blow to America's international prestige is enormous.

But, as we have seen, Trump, along with some Republican members of Congress and the anti-democratic forces that actively participated in the coup attempt, were discredited even more. The seizure of the Capitol building by violent rioters incited by the president was, obviously, a historic event. Something like this hasn't happened since British forces set fire to the Capitol in 1814. Fortunately, this time the occupation was short-lived.

But other very important things happened for U.S. democracy on

January 6. That morning we learned that the two Senate candidates running for office in the state of Georgia — Raphael Warnock and Jon Ossoff — had defeated their Republican rivals. Warnock will be the first black senator from Georgia — a southern state with a long history of segregation and racial discrimination. Jon Ossoff, 33, will be the first Jewish senator elected in a southern state since the 1880s and the youngest senator in the Democratic Party since Joe Biden was elected half a century ago.

The electoral wins of these two candidates mark a milestone that goes beyond the historic nature of their election. With those two additional votes, the Democratic Party, which already has a majority in the House of Representatives, will also have a majority in the Senate. This hasn't happened since 1995. Control of Congress will give Joe Biden more freedom and accelerate the appointment of government officials that require Congressional approval and that of the federal judges whom the president proposes and the Senate can approve or reject. Of course, Biden also has much better chances of initiating meaningful and long-lasting economic and political reforms.

On a day that was full of surprises we also got a letter and a speech that — albeit not as dramatic as the televised occupation of the Capitol — changed the course of history.

Mike Pence, who as vice-president also serves as president of the Senate, sent a letter to his fellow senators. In the letter, the until-then submissive, obedient, adulating and, surely, long-suffering Mike Pence informed senators that he would rigorously comply with the limited duty mandated by the Constitution in the process of certifying the electoral college votes for the president and vice-president. What Pence did not say in his letter, but everyone knew, is that this was not what his boss, the president, had ordered. Trump publicly reiterated that he expected Mike Pence ("who owes me so much") to support the electoral fraud that he had mounted in collusion with senators Ted Cruz and Josh Hawley and other Republican operators. Perhaps for the first time in four years, Mike Pence put his country's democracy before Donald Trump's personal interests. Had the opposite happened, the coup would have had a better chance of success.

138

The other surprise was the speech by Mitch McConnell, the Republican leader of the Senate. For four years, McConnell had loyally supported Donald Trump. On January 6, he stopped. When the counting of the electoral votes began in the Senate, and before the invasion of the Capitol prevented further debate, McConnell gave a devastating speech that exposed, and effectively defeated, the coup that Trump and his allies were trying to perpetrate. If McConnell had aligned himself with the coup plotters that day, we would now be speaking in a different tone about American democracy.

The defects of this democracy are in plain sight, as are all the challenges it faces. The reforms it urgently needs are also known. But will they be implemented? Will they be successful? We don't know. But we do know that January 6, 2021, will likely go down in history as the day the United States began to reshape its democracy.

January 12, 2021

2020

Trump's Ghost Will Hunt America

What do Leninism, Maoism, Peronism, Gaullism, Castroism and Chavism have in common? They're political movements that long outlasted their charismatic founders. Some, like Leninism, went global. Some, like Cuba's Castroism, were mostly regional. Others, like Gaullism in France and Peronism in Argentina, are purely national.

Donald J. Trump will be the first American leader who can boast of having an influential political movement named after him. Trumpism — his brand of nostalgic nationalism, autocratic bullying and egotistical manipulation — resembles other movements named after their leaders. Like those, it will have a long shelf life.

The men who founded these movements have plenty in common. Each discovered an untapped political market. Each reached into reserves of public rage that more conventional leaders had not registered — or preferred to ignore. Each connected powerfully with people's intimate sense of identity and converted these feelings into engines for political engagement. Each ignited devotion in their followers, a devotion so ardent that it outlived them. And each remade their country's politics for a generation or more.

The movements they founded share important traits: an eagerness to transgress political norms, unbridled opportunism, a marked authoritarian streak, anti–intellectualism, nationalism, a hostility toward rules and institutions that check executive power, and a fierce enmity against rivals, who are not treated as compatriots but as enemies who pose an existential threat.

These movements' ideologies have proven peculiarly malleable. Maoism has been applied to everything from the original vintage of

143

totalitarian communism to today's state-led Chinese hypercapitalism. Gaullism was applied to the prickly nationalism of General Charles de Gaulle himself and to the technocratic centrism of Jacques Chirac. Argentina's Peronism has become famous for its plasticity, attached variously to the soft-touch fascism of Juan Domingo Perón, to the neoliberal reforms of Carlos Menem, and to the leftist populism of Néstor and Cristina Kirchner. While Venezuela's Chavism converted the once-rich nation into one of the world's poorest, polls show that almost half of the population still supports Hugo Chávez, who died in 2013.

Today, Trumpism seems poised to join this list, regardless of what happens to Trump personally. Why? Because his politics of grievance, rage, race and revenge worked, winning a presidential term, vast power and fanatical support. Also, Trumpism is not rigidly beholden to any specific ideology. All this will stimulate new political leaders to run on platforms that could, once again, lure the voters whom Trump activated.

Trump himself may still run for the presidency in 2024. But his ideological incoherence will prove an advantage to politicians who aspire to succeed him at the helm of Trumpism. Like Perón, whose ideology was a mishmash of left and right, Trump has advocated so many positions, including contradictory ones, that a successor could sell any number of policies in his name.

It is possible that, in coming decades, center-right politicians in the United States will honor Trump's name while not really championing his disastrous ideas, much as Democrats kept attending "Jefferson-Jackson" dinners long after the party had abandoned Jacksonian nativist populism. But that will take decades, and in the nearer term much worse could be in store.

Commentators have often noted that America's next authoritarian populist could be a defter tactician than Trump, who made one unforced error after another in his efforts to retain power. In the hands of a smart, disciplined, media-savvy demagogue, Trumpism could return, and pose an existential threat to the Constitution.

Much depends on how Republican elites respond. For four long years, they've been riding the Trumpian tiger. The ride provided huge rewards — three conservatives appointed to the Supreme Court! Enormous tax cuts! But their enjoyment has been tempered by the panicked realization that, when they do dismount, the tiger will try to eat them. The post-election period has shown that the Republican Party lacks the road map to extricate itself from this position — and with protesters at Stop The Steal rallies now chanting, "Destroy the GOP! Destroy the GOP!" it's little wonder they are scared to try.

Just as Maoism did during China's Cultural Revolution — empowering young zealots to humiliate old Communist Party stalwarts, and strip them of power — Trumpism could destroy the party that brought it power. Or, as Maoism did starting in 1979 — when Deng Xiaoping honored Mao's name, while dismantling his legacy and introducing market-oriented reforms — Trumpism could end up saving the GOP. It's even possible that, as in China, it will end up first destroying, then rescuing, the party. Alternatively, it could divide Republicans and draw Trumpists into a new political machine.

To Americans, this will doubtlessly feel new. But it's not. What we know is that when an -ism attaches itself to a family name, disaster often follows — and that disaster never seems to blunt the -ism's appeal. Perón devastated Argentina's economy, turning a country whose prosperity once rivaled western Europe into a political and economic basket case. Mao, Castro and Chávez left broken countries in their wake. Yet calamity never buried their -isms. Any hope that the damage Trump has done to America will help bury Trumpism is probably misplaced.

Trumpism will be around much longer than Donald Trump.

December 18, 2020

A World With Three Internets

The global, decentralized, non-governmental, open and free internet that we all know is vanishing.

Today's internet is neither global nor open. More than 40% of the world's population now lives in countries where internet access is controlled by the authorities. The Chinese government, for example, restricts access to Google, YouTube, Facebook, Instagram, Twitter, WhatsApp, CNN, Wikipedia, TikTok, Netflix and The New York Times, among others. There are, of course, Chinese versions of those digital products. In India, Iran, Russia, Saudi Arabia and many other countries, the government blocks websites and censors their content.

The internet is no longer decentralized either. While it is true that the internet has empowered many individuals and groups by giving them a better chance of being heard and influencing others — including their governments — it has also evolved in a way that gives other governments and the Tech Giants — Google, Microsoft, Amazon and Facebook — ever-greater control over the internet. As a result, in many countries, the technology of political liberation has become a tool of repression.

The internet is not free. Google searches, Facebook meetings, Twitter messages and WhatsApp chats may appear to be free, but they're not. We pay for them by letting those who provide these services know virtually everything about us. That information enables them to dominate the lucrative market for global advertising.

But perhaps the most important trend transforming the internet is the way it is fragmenting into three distinct blocks. The world is on its way to having a Chinese, an American and a European internet.

The Chinese internet is closed, censored, protectionist and has high barriers to entry for companies from outside its digital borders. These cyberborders transcend the geographic borders of the country and include allies like North Korea and others. Its main competitive advantage is the almost one billion internet users in China. Its most influential protagonist is the central government and its national security, intelligence and citizen control services. Its great weakness is trying to use barriers from the past (protectionism and censorship) to contain the high-speed arrival of 21st-century digital innovations.

Then we have the United States version of the internet, which is anarchic, innovative, aggressively commercial and with strong monopolistic tendencies. The central players are the giant technology companies. With their huge war chests, large pools of technological talent and their unmatched prowess for innovation, they have a dynamism that their foreign counterparts simply can't rival.

But the vulnerability of the American system is that a business model based on the bartering of free digital services in exchange for users' personal data is not sustainable. Nor is the monopolistic control the tech companies enjoy. Or their indifference to the malicious use of their platforms by some actors that seek to sow social chaos, polarization and to influence elections. This is already beginning to change.

Europe, on the other hand, is the epicenter of an alternative internet approach that addresses the flaws of the American model and the abuses of the Chinese one. The European internet is more regulated, tries to protect users, confronts monopolies and defends democratic values. The European Commission has imposed billions of dollars in fines on Google, Apple, Microsoft and other tech companies. In 2018, the European Union adopted the General Data Protection Regulation (GDPR), setting strict guidelines for the collection, storage and management of personal data. This regulation is the concrete manifestation of a legal approach that treats the protection of personal data as a fundamental human right. While the Chinese system is based on an autocratic regime's need to control the country's huge population and the U.S. system on its business and technological dynamism, Europe is trying to influence the others by exporting its philosophy and system of rules based on democratic and humanistic values.

These three blocks are already fighting fiercely to gain full control over their respective areas of digital sovereignty, and the frictions between them are obvious. In addition to applying their antitrust and tax laws to American companies, the Europeans threaten to restrict Big Tech's access to their market if they don't conform to their rules. For its part, the United States is imposing sanctions and blocking companies like Huawei. China, naturally, is fighting back.

We will eventually have three internets, but the defining battle will be between the United States and China. And the confrontations of these digital superpowers will not be restricted to cyberspace and to the protection and expansion of their digital sovereignty. We already see this in the efforts of Washington and Beijing to ensure that their companies dominate 5G technology, the new generation of mobile telephony that will revolutionize communications and transform the internet. However, these are just skirmishes. The real clash will be over who will gain leadership in the field of artificial intelligence, an emerging technology that will remake the world.

That revolution is just beginning.

December 8, 2020

Seventy-four Million

The recent U.S. election had its highest voter turnout in 120 years. More than 80 million people voted for Joe Biden and 74 million for Donald Trump, making them the most-voted-for politicians in the history of the country. It was initially thought that the pandemic — along with President Trump's early claims that there would be fraud — would dampen voter turnout. This was not the case. Sixty-seven percent of the electorate voted either in person or by mail.

The other surprise was that 74 million people voted for Trump — 10 million more than voted for him in 2016. This was surprising because of what those voters didn't care about as well as for what mattered to them and motivated their support for Trump.

They didn't mind, for example, voting for a president who consistently lies and is exposed for it, too. Shouldn't compulsive lying be enough to get you defeated at the polls? Seventy-four million Americans don't think so. They don't believe Trump is a liar, or they don't mind, or they have goals, needs and hopes that are more important to them than the honesty of the president.

And shouldn't the fact that 26 women stepped forward to publicly accuse Trump of sexual misconduct — including, in some cases, rape — be enough to lose the female vote? Isn't the Access Hollywood video enough to alienate female voters who heard and saw Trump tell host Billy Bush that, when you're a star, they let you do it. You can do anything. Grab 'em by the pussy"? Well, no. About half of white women voted for Trump.

But if the 74 million don't care about the multiple complaints of sexual harassment against the president, shouldn't they care about the health of the planet? It seems not.

Trump has denounced the fight against global warming as a ruse by China to weaken the U.S. economy. President Trump's decisions have been devastating for the environment. Not to mention very lucrative for the companies that pollute the most, as well as the lobbyists who represent them. Do Trump's supporters care that he has filled the top positions in regulatory agencies with the very lobbyists that represent the industries that they are supposed to regulate?

Obviously not.

Do they care that the Trump administration has been both chaotic and inept and that it bungled the pandemic so badly? What about his disdain for experts, scientists and the professionals that run the complex machinery of government? Apparently not. The 74 million Trump voters also don't care that two important documents remain secret: Donald Trump's tax returns and his health care policy. What's in Trump's taxes that has made the president willing to go to such great lengths to keep them out of public scrutiny? Shouldn't voters know what financial obligations the president has and to whom? Shouldn't it be known if the president is a tax evader?

The other document that still hasn't surfaced is Trump's proposed health care plan. The president has been very explicit about his intention to undo Barack Obama's Affordable Care Act. He has repeatedly promised that he will replace it with "something much better." The president's political operators have offered voluminous and confusing documents, but so far, they have not disclosed the details of what that "something better" is. What is clear is that repealing Obamacare without giving the public some alternative will cause a lot of harm to a lot of people, including, of course, millions of those who voted for him. Either they don't know, or they don't believe it, or they don't care.

The list of reasons that disqualify Trump from leading the nation for another four years is long. His reluctance to denounce white supremacists. His disinterest in confronting institutional racism. His meager achievements in foreign policy and the fact that, in important matters, he has ceded America's international influence on China and Russia. His extensive conflicts of interest. His authoritarian tendencies and the myriad corrosive ways in which he has undermined American democracy. None of that seems to matter enough to the 74 million.

But then what do they care about? What moves them to support Trump so unconditionally? Many things. They range from the very material ("don't raise my taxes") to the highly spiritual ("Trump understands how I feel"). From the positive ("Let's make America great again") to the negative ("If Biden wins, African Americans will invade the suburbs"). From the defense of rights ("the right to bear arms") to the defense of values ("I am against abortion"). From blocking illegal immigration ("a big, beautiful wall") to opposing economic globalization ("China and Mexico are stealing our jobs").

The demographics of the 74 million are diverse and confusing. It includes significant percentages of Hispanics, the rural population, white men with no college education, evangelical groups, businessmen, workers and many other groups. The economic geography of Trump's supporters is also striking. According to a study by Brookins scholars, "the Biden's winning base in 477 counties encompasses fully 70% of America's economic activity, while Trump's losing base of 2,497 counties represents just 29% of the economy."

Moreover, the fact that polling organizations failed to anticipate the behavior of these 74 million voters confirms that we still don't know what really drives their unconditional support for Donald Trump.

We have four years to find out.

November 30, 2020

The Dress Rehearsal

How will the world look once the Covid-19 pandemic is contained?

This question is as urgent and important as it is difficult to answer. Every day, we are surprised by news of important and unprecedented developments in politics, the economy, society, culture, business, science and more. Many of these changes were unimaginable even a few months ago. Yet, while it is impossible to reliably project what the world will look like in a decade or two, we can probe the present to find changes that are harbingers of things to come.

Market valuations help predict the future.

Take the bike boom, for example. Worldwide demand for bicycles has soared to hitherto unseen levels. The surge in demand took manufacturers, mostly in China and Taiwan, by surprise and shortages ensued. The sudden, global appetite for bikes was due to people trying to mitigate the risk of Covid-19 contagion by avoiding public transportation and biking instead. Also, to the fact that there are more unemployed people with the time to enjoy a bike ride. Streets and roads with dramatically lower automotive traffic are also more welcoming for cyclists. Once the pandemic abates, bicycle use will surely decline from the current levels, but it is reasonable to expect that the number of regular bikers will be greater than it was before the outbreak. The growing appetite for "green" transportation options is also a component of the new demand for bikes. And, not just for bikes: a soaring market for electric cars, buses and trucks has emerged. One small, but revealing, recent event is that Tesla is now the world's most valuable carmaker. This ten-year-old company boasts a market capitalization that is higher than those of Toyota and Volkswagen combined. Just in the past year, the price of Tesla'sshares has increased almost fivefold. While stock markets value Toyota at 16 times its profits, Tesla's is valued at a whopping 220 times earnings. Even Elon Musk, Tesla's CEO, was surprised by his company's extravagant valuation. Indeed, it is safe to assume that Tesla's skyrocketing stock market performance was also driven by speculative behavior.

Stock market valuations are driven by many factors — including market bubbles — and may not accurately reflect the true value of a company. But they do suggest how investors are valuing not just its current performance, but also its future potential. From this perspective, it is interesting to realize that Zoom, the video conferencing company, is valued by the markets four times higher than Delta Airlines. In fact, buying the world's entire U.S. airline industry would be substantially less costly than acquiring Amazon. Another interesting signal is that Netflix is now 25 percent more valued by the markets than ExxonMobil. These two companies are iconic examples of two important global trends: cocooning and decarbonization. Cocooning refers to protective behavior, the preference to stay inside one's home, insulated from perceived danger, rather than going out. Netflix epitomizes this preference, while the decline in the value of ExxonMobil reflects the drop in the world's demand for hydrocarbons. The lower demand for oil and gas has a cyclical component and price fluctuations are normal. But the currently depressed price of oil, for example, is not only driven by a weak global economy that consumes less crude.

Decarbonization is still accelerating.

Prices are also being pushed down by the widespread expectation that decarbonization — the movement toward phasing out the carbon dioxide emissions that result from the use of fossil fuels — will be an accelerating trend. Most analysts expect global demand for oil to peak around the year 2030 as renewable sources of energy continues to grow at a fast pace and the mass adoption of electric vehicles becomes a reality. Fossil fuels will continue to be the main source of energy in the foreseeable future, but increasingly severe climate emergencies will create enormous social and political pressures to accelerate efforts toward decarbonization.

Scientists, policymakers and the public continue to be surprised by the speed at which climate is changing and creating extreme weather events. Most recently, Siberia was the location of these unprecedented climate accidents. In June, the temperature in the town of Verkhoyansk reached 100.4 degrees Fahrenheit, the highest temperature ever recorded anywhere north of the Arctic Circle. Siberia has experienced an unprecedented heat wave. In the first semester of 2020, the region's temperature was nine degrees Fahrenheit warmer than the average temperature recorded between 1951 and 1980.

Antarctica, the earth's other pole, is also warming up. Scientists are concerned that the enormous Thwaites Glacier, also known as the doomsday glacier, is melting at a quick pace and perhaps becoming unstable. The Financial Times reports that if the glacier, which is the size of Britain, actually melts, global sea levels are estimated to rise by two to three meters. Among all the uncertainties about the world after the pandemic, there is a certitude that looms large: in the future, climate change will change the world more than Covid-19. Will this coronavirus pandemic be remembered just as a dress rehearsal for a global and unprecedented climate accident that alters civilization as we have known it?

October 30, 2020

The Three Amigos

In 1986 Hollywood released the comedy *The Three Amigos*. It's the story of three traveling comedians (Steve Martin, Chevy Chase and Martin Short) who, dressed as Mexican cowboys, arrive in the town of Santo Poco to put on a show. Instead, they find a Mexican town besieged by a gang of bearded ruffians on horseback commanded by "El Guapo." Naturally, the three friends (with the help of the beautiful and long-suffering Carmen) manage to free Santo Poco from El Guapo and his henchmen. The script for *The Three Amigos* indulges every cliché and stereotype that Americans have of Mexicans. In fact, El Guapo and his gang fit perfectly with Donald Trump's description of Mexican immigrants: murderers, rapists, bad *hombres*. And, let's not forget, animals.

When Trump first began his anti-immigration rhetoric, and before Andrés Manuel López Obrador (AMLO) became president, the Mexican politician reacted indignantly: "Trump and his advisers speak of Mexicans the way Hitler and the Nazis referred to the Jews. We cannot consent to a state policy that undermines the dignity of the legitimate interests of Mexicans and the nation." AMLO also denounced the wall that the U.S. is building along the Mexican border as "a monument to hypocrisy and cruelty." In contrast, Trump said, "It's beautiful" and added that "Mexico is not our friend."

That was then. Now, as President of Mexico, López Obrador recently visited the White House and, staring President Trump in the eye, acknowledged that: "We have received from you, President

Trump, understanding and respect." AMLO also said he appreciated the way Trump and his government treat Mexico and Mexicans. Trump was not far behind in his praise of Mexico, its president and the millions of Mexican immigrants who work in his country.

Grandiose, vacuous and clearly mendacious statements are business-as-usual in meetings between heads of state. In fact, the most interesting thing about the meeting between AMLO and Trump is not the falsehoods they said, but the truths they left unsaid. Perhaps the most important of these unmentionables is that they both preside over nations where Covid-19 is wreaking havoc. The United States is the world champion in terms of absolute number of infections, while the runner-up is Brazil, led by Jair Bolsonaro. But very close behind them, near the top of the tragic list, is Mexico.

Unfortunately, it appears that the "remake" of *The Three Amigos* is going to be a tragedy rather than a farce. The three stars in the current version are at once very different and very similar. Their origins, careers and ideologies could not be more different. But they are identical in terms of their narcissism, populism and irresponsibility.

Initially, all three minimized the severity of the pandemic. All three were slow to react and spurned the recommendations of experts.

Face masks and social distancing just aren't their style. "With the coronavirus, there is this idea that you can't hug," the Mexican president said on TV. "You have to hug. Nothing happens. What protects us is not allowing corruption." Then he displayed several amulets and religious images that, according to him, are his "protective shield." For their part, Trump and Bolsonaro (who is referred to by his followers as "the Trump of the Tropics") also recommended the use of amulets. Theirs, however, are not religious but pharmaceutical. Trump was the first to recommend the use of hydroxychloroquine to treat victims of Covid-19. In fact, he announced that he himself was testing the drug. The same with President Bolsonaro (who tested positive for the virus last week). Both ordered the purchase of massive quantities of this controversial drug whose healing properties have not been scientifically validated, despite the overwhelming evidence that it has dangerous side effects. And, of course, we cannot forget President

Trump's display of medical scholarship when, at a press conference, he speculated that taking bleach might be a good remedy for the virus, as well as bombarding it with ultraviolet rays.

The three amigos share a deep-rooted disregard for science and experts. Another feature they share is a willingness to use the health emergency to deepen the divisions that fragment their respective societies. Who would have thought that the use of a mask could be transformed into a wedge issue? Well, the three amigos did.

Certainly, some of the most iconic photos this pandemic will leave behind will be of these three presidents and their loyal followers defiantly exposing their faces without protective masks. These will be contrasted with the photos of people wearing their masks, illustrating a world divided between pro-mask and anti-mask groups.

We can be sure that the approach of these maskless Covid-19 leaders is not sustainable and that the pandemic itself will eventually undermine the power that the three amigos wield today.

July 16, 2020

Four Ideas Damaged by Covid-19

Covid-19 kills not just people, it also kills ideas. And when it doesn't kill them, it discredits them. For example, received ideas about office work, hospitals and universities will not be the same when the dust settles from the pandemic. Nor will some of the more universal ideas about economics and politics. Here are four cases in point:

1. The United States is a source of global stability. False. The truth is that Washington has become an epicenter of geopolitical instability. The Bush administration's response to the 9/11 terrorist attacks, for example, sparked long and costly wars. In 2008, the U.S. exported a serious financial crisis to the rest of the world. But no war or economic crisis has so eroded America's influence in the world as the deeds of Donald Trump's administration. Since his election in 2016, the president has shown, almost daily, that instead of calming the world and his country, he prefers to set off conflict and stir discord. America's reaction to the pandemic has only confirmed that the White House is a volatile, accident-prone and unreliable ally.

That the United States now radiates instability is particularly ironic because the greatest beneficiary of the international order that Trump is unraveling is the very nation that he presides.

2. International cooperation. The pandemic has also shown that the international community is incapable of coming together to respond effectively to global threats. The tragedies of Syria, Yemen, Venezuela and the Rohingyas are just some examples of the ineffectiveness of the international community. Covid-19 has demonstrated

conclusively that a strong international community that works in coordination with its member nations does not exist. The response of most countries to this health emergency has not been to act jointly, but to entrench themselves behind their borders. The pandemic, for example, should have strengthened the World Health Organization (WHO), a flawed but indispensable multilateral entity. Instead, the White House — convinced that the WHO had been co-opted by the Chinese government — said it would withdraw from the organization. This came at the very moment that the Trump administration should have been leading an international coalition to support and reform the organization. Distrust of international cooperation has also contributed to ineffective coordination between countries with regards to safety standards as well as the production and distribution of medicines and medical supplies. And this is another irony: the rejection of international collaboration has led to an essentially local and inadequate response to a global threat.

3. Fiscal austerity. This idea, once the obligatory remedy for dealing with a financial crisis, is now toxic. Before, when faced with an economic crash, the government moved to severely restrict its spending and lower its indebtedness. Now it's the opposite: spending more and increasing debt is the latest macroeconomic fashion. Everywhere you look, governments are increasing public spending to unprecedented levels. The fiscal deficit, which is the difference between tax collection and other government revenue and public spending, has shot up to levels that have never been seen before outside of war time. In the U.S., for example, this year's fiscal deficit will reach a sum equivalent to 24% of the total output of the entire U.S. economy. The indebtedness of almost all countries has also increased. Japan has the world's largest debt relative to the size of its economy. But the United States is the world champion in absolute numbers: it owes $20 trillion (€117.8 trillion). In the coming years, deciding when and how these debts will be paid (and by whom!) will surely spark a fierce and furious global debate.

4. Globalization. This is another idea that was previously lionized and is now demonized. As is often the case, the idea wasn't so great

before, nor is it so bad now. For many, globalization is expressed in terms of the flow of products and money between countries. For others, its main and most worrying manifestation is immigration. In practice, globalization is much more complicated. It includes, of course, the enormous increase in the international flow of products, services, money and information. But it also includes the activities of terrorists, traffickers, criminals, scientists, artists, philanthropists, activists, athletes and non-governmental organizations. And, of course, it also includes the diseases that can now move at great speed across the globe.

Governments can hinder some of these manifestations or stimulate others. What no one can do is completely end the multiple ways countries intertwine. The pandemic and its economic consequences will encourage the adoption of policies that cushion the external shocks that periodically shake countries. There will be more protectionism. But the advantages and attractions of some facets of globalization will not disappear.

What do these discredited ideas have in common? All four are important pillars of the world order that emerged after World War II. Although all four pillars are damaged, it is possible to repair and improve them. This will be a major challenge in the years to come.

June 30, 2020

Parking Lots, Coughing and the Pandemic

What do cars in a parking lot have to do with online searches for terms like "diarrhea" and "cough"? And what do these data points tell us about the pandemic that is raging across the globe? As it turns out, a great deal.

Researchers at Harvard Medical School have used satellite imagery to track the number of cars parked at six major hospitals in Wuhan, the city of 11 million inhabitants in central China where Covid-19 originated and then spread to the rest of the world.

Who would have thought that counting the cars in a parking lot could reveal an incipient pandemic?

The Harvard scientists tracked the parking lot photos from January 2018 to April 2020. By analyzing the images, the researchers discovered an unusual increase in the number of cars parked between August and December 2019. In those months, the number of cars was above average and also higher than during flu outbreaks. But that is not all. In China, Google is blocked. The go-to search engine is called Baidu. In September and October, Baidu searches for the terms "cough," "diarrhea" and "breathing problems" originating from Wuhan skyrocketed.

The researchers came to a shocking conclusion: "Increased hospital traffic and symptom search data in Wuhan preceded the documented start of the pandemic in December 2019."

The conclusion is explosive because, according to the data, the outbreak began months before the Chinese government told the world what was happening, which wasted time other governments needed to prepare for the onset of pandemic. Not surprisingly, Beijing has denied this and questions the study's validity.

The authors acknowledge the limitations of their methodology and of the data they used. However, despite these limitations, it is obvious that the research provides a useful perspective. And not just about the pandemic.

Bureaucracies tend to hide their mistakes and authoritarian bureaucracies even more so. Take the Soviet reaction to the Chernobyl nuclear meltdown in 1986. The disaster scattered radioactive material across the Soviet Union, parts of Europe, and even reached Canada. Everything indicates that the "Chernobyl effect" — the desperate scramble to conceal the problem in fear of political blowback — shaped the Chinese government's response when it was clear that what was happening in Wuhan was serious, massive and unprecedented.

The truth finds a way to come out. As hard as they tried, Soviet leaders couldn't prevent the world from learning about Chernobyl. The same is true of China. First, there was a deliberate delay by the local government in Wuhan and then by the authorities in Beijing in acknowledging the magnitude of what was happening. It has always been difficult for governments to hide their secrets. Sooner or later the truth gets out. Today secrets are exposed faster than ever. Even the secrets of dictatorships.

Everything can be measured. Who would have thought that counting the cars in a parking lot could reveal an incipient pandemic? Or that a spike in internet searches for certain words might forecast an epidemic? In these times, the mere fact that we exist as individuals generates a mountain of data that can be captured and processed — whether we like it or not. Mobile phones, cameras, computers, sensors and platforms such as Facebook, Instagram, Twitter and Flickr are ceaselessly collecting data about our behavior and transforming it into information that can be used — for good or bad.

Everything is politicized. The Harvard study comes at a time of extreme tension between the United States and China. Trade, technology, finance, military superiority and geopolitical influence are just some of the arenas in which the two superpowers are facing off. Another important arena is international prestige. After the initial delay in recognizing and communicating the extent of the pandemic, Beijing has launched a broad propaganda campaign. It is emphasizing its success in containing the pandemic and contrasts it with the chaos-prone White House response. For its part, the United States government has launched a broad smear campaign against China, emphasizing the opacity of its approach and pinning responsibility for the crisis on Beijing. Attacks on China will certainly be a central theme of Donald Trump's re-election campaign. China will undoubtedly respond.

In a world without secrets, conflicts can be managed, but not suppressed.

June 16, 2020

Pandemic Reactions, Exaggerations and Confusion

"The world has changed forever!" "A new international order will emerge from this catastrophe."

These were common refrains after the terrorist attacks of 9/11 and the Great Recession of 2007 to 2009, but also following just about every security emergency and international economic downturn that has routinely shaken the world. An analysis of the major international crises since the 1980s reveals several recurring factors. The Covid-19 pandemic is different and far more menacing than the crises that preceded it. Still, we are now seeing some of the common factors present in past crises. Here are five worth noting:

1. The impact of the crisis is exaggerated, and predictions of change are overstated. After previous crises, the world didn't change, either forever or for everyone. Of course, terrorism and economic problems have had serious repercussions, but, in practice, there has been more continuity than change.

2. The way governments react to a crisis has a much bigger impact than the events that precipitated it. The 9/11 attacks resulted in nearly 3,000 deaths and $100 billion in initial losses. The ensuing conflicts in Iraq, Afghanistan and Pakistan left more than 480,000 dead, including 244,000 civilians. The same happened after the last financial crisis. The massive stimulus that governments disbursed to save companies from bankruptcy had a greater impact than the crisis itself. Many governments prioritized relief to large private companies at the expense of the middle class and workers. This exacerbated economic inequality

and stirred social discontent, which, in turn, fueled a populist wave that has disrupted the status quo in many countries.

3. Crises are not global. The Great Recession was so severe and the developed economies' reaction to it was so massive that it was natural to see it as a worldwide phenomenon. But it wasn't. China, Brazil and other emerging markets were not hit as hard. Instead, they became the new engines of the global economy and helped revive the United States and Europe.

4. Crises lead to the impassioned demand for reforms that never materialize. Another factor that's omnipresent in a crisis is the call to reform international institutions, democracy and capitalism. When a crisis breaks out, it is common for political and intellectual leaders to call for the elimination — or at least major reform — of the United Nations, NATO, the International Monetary Fund, the World Bank, governments and the private sector. As we well know, none of that has happened.

5. What we believe to be permanent turns out to be temporary, and vice versa. Another common element in crises is the surprising disappearance or sudden irrelevance of leaders and institutions that we assumed to be permanent and omnipotent, for example Saddam Hussein, Muammar Gaddafi, and some of the big banks such as Lehman Brothers and Washington Mutual or insurers such as AIG. At the same time, we often see how ideas, leaders and political agreements that seemed temporary, end up becoming permanent.

Not all of these lessons from the past apply to the Covid-19 pandemic. This crisis is different. The coronavirus has triggered a global emergency to which no country is immune. Technology, globalization, the digital revolution, the total absence of a known cure, and the fact that there are now more people living in cities than in the countryside are just some of the differences.

But despite these differences, there are patterns from the past that are being repeated today. In the long term, the exaggerated or inept reaction of governments to the pandemic is likely to produce as much or more damage than the pandemic itself. Nor has denouncing multilateral organizations been lacking in this crisis. The U.S. government recently stopped paying its dues to the World Health Organization and is demanding it be restructured.

The pandemic has also brought us new ways of living that started as temporary solutions but will likely be permanent, such as telecommuting. Finally, a common factor in all major crises is the proliferation of conspiracy theories to explain what is happening and the rise of quacks and charlatans out to take advantage of people's fear and confusion to sell them bad ideas or fraudulent products. As we have already seen in the news, this pandemic has revealed a prodigious number of charlatans.

Some of them are presidents.

May 20, 2020

The Secret Memorandum to President Trump

To: President Donald J. Trump
From: XXXX
Re: Election strategy

It is a great honor, Mr President, to be called on for advice on how to guarantee your richly deserved reelection. I share your disappointment with your current advisers, who have failed to turn your stellar leadership into an overwhelming electoral advantage. In fact, I feel that the only useful adviser you have is your brilliant son-in-law, Jared Kushner.

But the current situation cannot be ignored. The pandemic and its economic consequences will inevitably be politically costly for you come November. By Election Day there will be millions of people without jobs, tens of thousands of bankrupt companies, and tens of thousands of deaths from Covid-19. The gravity of the situation will surely be exaggerated by the liberal media. They have always refused to acknowledge your talent and the success of your administration. The most recent example being the very unfair way they reported your suggestion that we may be able to ingest or inject household disinfectants to deal with the virus.

Despite all this, I am convinced that you can still win the election. But in order to do so you must be willing to do whatever it takes. The most recent polls indicate that Biden is ahead of you in all battle-ground states. If the elections were today, he (and not you) would be the next president of the United States. But that reality does not daunt me. We have other ways to ensure that you remain in power.

One advantage, of course, is being the incumbent president of the United States and enjoying all the visibility and resources that your office entails. Another is money. You've already raised $187 million more than Biden. We also have more and better digital technology and cyber resources, which includes, of course, the invaluable help of your good friend Vladimir.

But we must accept that, even with these advantages, Biden may still have more popular support come November. If so, we will have to resort to another weapon in your arsenal: the judiciary. During your presidency, in collaboration with Majority leader Mitch McConnell, you have managed to appoint 158 judges, including two justices to the Supreme Court. They are, no doubt, very grateful to you. We know from history that the judiciary can be crucial in deciding elections. In the 2000 presidential race between George W. Bush and Al Gore, the Supreme Court intervened in a dispute over a vote recount in Florida. The court's decision favored Bush, pushing him beyond the finish line in the race to the White House. And it is on this precedent, on this historic example, that I base my optimism for your reelection.

Let me be brutally honest in my recommendation: if we cannot win through the ballot box, we will win in court. If it is not through votes, it must be through the bench. We must prepare now to create dozens of ambiguous and confusing situations at the polls, in the vote counts, and in any other aspect of the electoral process that will sow confusion and allow the judges you've appointed to settle the score.

In addition to preparing to unleash this judicial *Blitzkrieg* on the electoral system, we must make sure that those who do not intend to vote for you don't vote at all. It's that simple. We know which are the deeply contested, Biden-leaning places where you need to win. That's where we must make the process so slow, the voting machines so faulty, and the lines so long that people give up on voting altogether. We must also mobilize to prevent absentee and early voting — whether by mail or electronically — wherever democrats have an advantage.

We should also disseminate information that makes the location of the voting stations as confusing as possible. Absenteeism is our friend.

Preventing convicted felons from voting is another tactic we should explore. More than 7% of the adult African American population cannot vote because they have served time in prison. In the white population the proportion is only 1.8%.

The list of possible tactics to suppress voting is long and well known. We must use them all. The only difference is that this time I propose we make them the central pillar of your reelection strategy.

Mr President, I have left the most important thing for last. The battle will not be to win the votes of your fan base. They're in the bag already. The battle is to get the skeptics, the fence-sitters, the confused, the misinformed and the idle not to vote. We will have to use social media to spread mistrust, doubts and criticism about the elections and the democratic system. Luckily, in this regard, we also have the help of our Russian friend.

I remain at your disposal, ready to do whatever it takes to ensure that you remain our president for the next four years.

With great respect and admiration,

XXXX

Note to Readers: This memo is fake and the product of my imagination.

May 5, 2020

Big Problems, Small Leaders

Henry Kissinger thinks the world will never be the same after the coronavirus. "While the assault on human health will — hopefully — be temporary, the political and economic upheaval it has unleashed could last for generations." He warns that "the historic challenge for leaders is to manage the crisis while building the future. Failure could set the world on fire."

United Nations Secretary General António Guterres echoes this concern and says that the relationship between the great powers has never been as dysfunctional as it is now. "Covid-19 is showing dramatically [that], either we join [together]... or we can be defeated."

According to Martin Wolf, the renowned Financial Times columnist, the pandemic "is the biggest crisis the world has confronted since the Second World War and the biggest economic disaster since the Depression of the 1930s. The world has come into this moment with divisions among its great powers and incompetence at the highest levels of government of terrifying proportions."

There are many things we don't know. When will we have a vaccine? What will the impact be of the virus on poor countries where overcrowding is the norm and where working from home is not possible? What if Covid-19 comes and goes in waves? But the most pressing question is whether those who govern us will measure up to the test. Martin Wolf concludes: "We do not know the future. But we do know how we should try to shape it. Will we? That is the question. I greatly fear our answer."

Badmouthing our political leaders is normal, and so is criticizing their performance. It is a cathartic and popular habit that often has no practical consequences. But disdain for our leaders needs to be doled out with some care. By its nature, the struggle for power that defines any political contest highlights governments' dysfunctionality, ineptitude and corruption.

Let's face it, governing has always been difficult, and it is becoming even more so. Power has become easier to get, but also more difficult to use and, therefore, easier to lose. Sometimes it seems like there's no way for a leader to maintain high standing after coming into office. Instead, we frequently see honest and well-meaning leaders whose reputations have been shredded by their critics. As we know, in the 21st century partisan attacks are magnified by social media, bots, trolls and other online political weapons. It is therefore advisable to exercise caution in criticizing our rulers.

I try to keep all of this in mind as I think about the individuals who are in charge of the world today. Even so, it is hard not to conclude that, with a few exceptions, our current crop of world leaders falls dramatically short of what the moment demands.

When the global financial crisis broke in 2008, Gordon Brown, the then-British prime minister, was in charge of the Group of 20 (G20), a hitherto irrelevant multilateral entity that he brought back to life and used as an effective coordinator of the global response to the financial crash. This year, it is the turn of the King of Saudi Arabia to helm the G20. Yet, due to his advanced age and poor health, he has delegated the role to his son, Mohammed bin Salman. Yes, him. The guy whose security service killed and dismembered dissident journalist Jamal Khashoggi. Bin Salman is the leader who must convene, rally and coordinate the international community's response to the coronavirus pandemic and its economic consequences.

In the United States, the National Economic Council is the main body advising the president on economic policies. Since its inception in 1993 it has been led by some of America's most respected economists. Donald Trump's appointed director is Larry Kudlow, mostly known as a financial commentator on CNBC. Alas, this is not an isolated case. The Trump administration is in no way distinguished by the expertise and experience of its top policymakers.

In Europe, the panorama is little better. One of the things we need from rulers these days is good judgment. Today, we're meant to be reassured by the likes of Boris Johnson, Viktor Orbán, Pedro Sánchez, Pablo Iglesias, Matteo Salvini and Luigi di Maio. In the developing world, Jair Bolsonaro, Andrés Manuel López Obrador and Daniel Ortega are in the news for their pandemic denialism. Philippine President Rodrigo Duterte has threatened to shoot dead those who do not follow lockdown orders. And Narendra Modi of India is using the virus as an excuse to deepen discrimination against Muslims.

I don't want to romanticize the past, or to suggest prior leaders were always better. We have had a Hitler and a Churchill, a Mao and a Mandela. But there is no doubt that this pandemic has caught the world at a moment of great institutional weakness and poor leadership.

Crises close many doors, but also open others. This crisis will have any number of unexpected consequences. One of them may be a strong reaction against small-minded, myopic rulers and the heralding of leaders with the character and the vision to face the problems on the scale of the ones we face.

April 21, 2020

Unprecedented

"It took the world three months to reach 100,000 confirmed cases of infection. The next 100,000 happened in just 12 days. The third took four days. The fourth, just one and a half." Those were the words of Tedros Adhanom Ghebreyesus, the director general of the World Health Organization, in his recent warning to a group of world leaders.

In the days following this meeting, the United States Congress managed to overcome its now customary inaction and approved the largest economic stimulus package in history. More than $2 trillion will go to individuals, state and local governments, and private companies to alleviate the economic devastation caused by the extreme measures that will be necessary to combat the pandemic. How much is $2 trillion? Antony Bugg-Levine, the CEO of NFF, a financial NGO, explains it this way: If you add a dollar bill every second for 24 hours a day, seven days a week, then in approximately two weeks you will have a million dollars. Reaching $1 billion will take 40 years and reaching $2 trillion would take 80,000 years.

The magnitude of this economic initiative is astonishing. But even more surprising is that this unprecedented avalanche of cash won't be enough to save the U.S. economy from a recession. Most experts are still anticipating a deep economic downturn in the U.S. this year. This recession will cause record layoffs, corporate bankruptcies, as well as massive evictions for both private homes and commercial properties when residents and businesses can't make rent or mortgage payments.

Why are the experts so pessimistic? In large part because of the inevitable lags and problems in distributing the stimulus money, an effort that will, of course, be compounded by the continuing human catastrophe caused by the spreading virus. As long as there is no vaccine or treatment for Covid-19, the economy will remain weak. In addition, for many of the most needy, financial relief may come too late. The fear is that a large number of small- and medium-sized companies will be forced out of business before financial aid arrives.

Meanwhile, the consumers who would have kept those businesses running are now lining up to collect unemployment insurance. To get an idea of the magnitude and speed of the crisis it is worth noting that three weeks ago, 200,000 workers applied for these benefits in the U.S. Last week the number was 3,300,000, or 16 times more than the week before. By comparison, the previous record had been in 1982 when 650,000 workers applied for unemployment insurance.

The American economy is not the only one that's in trouble. China, for example, is experiencing the second most severe economic contraction since the 1970s. Its economy is highly dependent on its exports to the rest of the world, and that demand has fallen dramatically. A large number of countries are already, or will soon be, facing unprecedented economic crises. Emerging markets, which were already going through difficult economic times before Covid-19 made its appearance, are now facing even tougher challenges.

The fight against the coronavirus is going to be enormously expensive and will produce unprecedented increases in public spending and debt levels. This impact will be even worse in countries with large populations, precarious economies and weak health care systems, which means that nations such as India, Nigeria, Pakistan, Brazil, South Africa, Bangladesh and Mexico can expect to be particularly hard hit.

This is why a pandemic that requires action at the local level — such as "stay home" orders and "social distancing" — also calls for urgent international coordination. Countries must coordinate their financial, monetary and trade policies. They should also eliminate barriers to the transfer of medicines, medical materials, and hospital equipment, among others.

In other words, the world must strive to act locally at the smallest possible scale and multilaterally at the most global level possible.

We know we can do it because the world has done it before. In the midst of the Great Recession from 2007 to 2009, the Group of Twenty (G20) took a leading role. Founded in 1999, it had had little relevance until then. Its rotating leader at the time, British Prime Minister Gordon Brown, and other members decided to make the G20 the coordinating power of the global recovery. And even though mistakes were certainly made in their response to the financial crisis, G20 coordination made the damage much less severe.

In our current crisis, individual isolation saves lives. But, between countries, isolation will make the costs — both human and economic — much higher.

We should remember that in this unprecedented pandemic there are still some historical precedents that we can follow.

March 31, 2020

We Are All Neighbors

Earthquakes destroy much, but they also reveal valuable information about the deepest layers of the earth. Similarly, pandemics cause immense pain and suffering but also teach us a great deal. And not just about biology, epidemiology and medicine. They also reveal who we are, as individuals and as a society. For example, are we, as people, more altruistic or selfish? Is it better to have a country that is open to the world or one that has closed borders? Do we trust our politicians or the experts? And what should guide our behavior: emotions or data?

Those who advocate integration between countries clash with supporters of nationalism and protectionism. "We reject globalism and embrace the doctrine of patriotism," President Trump told the United Nations in 2018. He also made clear his disdain of multilateralism, that is, initiatives based on agreements among many countries. Multilateralism led to the creation of agencies such as the United Nations and the World Bank, for example. It also encourages agreements in which participating countries commit to making joint efforts to deal with problems that no country can effectively tackle alone, regardless of how big, rich or powerful it may be. Climate change, immigration and terrorism are some examples. President Trump does not like these multilateral agreements. "The U.S. will always choose independence and cooperation over global governance, control and domination," the president said. As we know, Trump is not the only critic of globalization. Countless political leaders, as well as leading intellectuals, regularly denounce globalization.

It is in this context that Covid-19 has made its revolutionary appearance. If globalization is based on the international movement of products, ideas, people and technology, then this virus is a powerful example of the globalization of biological connectivity. It also confirms how shortsighted it is to think of globalization only as a commercial, financial or media phenomenon.

It turns out that some biological exports, for example, travel faster, farther, have more immediate effects, and have a greater impact than the other exchanges that characterize globalization. But the reaction to the coronavirus also reveals how tempting isolationism remains. An increasing number of governments are trying to seal their borders and isolate the most affected cities and regions, blocking the free movement of people. We're experiencing a real time clash between globalism and isolationism. But at the same time that some governments are closing their borders, they are also discovering how much they need the support of other countries and the help of multilateral entities such as the World Health Organization or the World Bank.

The coronavirus is also placing scientists and other experts back in the limelight and giving them a leading role. One of the unfortunate surprises of the early 21st century has been a loss of credibility for experts and the corresponding rise of credibility for con artists and demagogues. This new trend had an iconic moment in 2016 when Michael Gove, then the UK's Secretary of State for Justice, reacted to a study in which renowned experts criticized Brexit, a project he promoted. The secretary stated bluntly: "The people in this country have had enough of experts." Another politician who despises experts is Donald Trump. He has said that climate change is a Chinese hoax, that he knows more about war than his generals, and that he understands "this stuff" — the coronavirus — better than scientists. "Maybe I have a natural ability," he said. "Maybe I should have done [medicine] instead of running for president."

Well, no. It turns out that when dealing with "this stuff" the scientists must be — and fortunately are — the main protagonists. Moreover, many of them are public-sector employees, another category of professionals that is often scorned by populist leaders who have gained power by fanning the frustrations and anxieties of the people they claim to represent. Populists don't coexist harmoniously with experts and with data that contradict their public claims and interests. They detest public institutions that house experts and produce irrefutable data. But the coronavirus crisis has shown that these public bureaucracies, whose budgets and capabilities are often eroded by leaders who despise them, are our main line of defense against phenomena like this unprecedented and threatening pandemic.

The pandemic not only obliges experts and multilateral organizations to play a central role, but it also gives new urgency to the old debate between altruism and individualism. The altruist is willing to help others — including strangers — even at the expense of his own interests. In contrast, the individualist tends to act without regard to the effects that their actions have on the well-being of others.

In the coming weeks and months, we will discover which people — and which countries — are willing to act with others in mind, and which will only think of themselves. This will be easy for us to see because the coronavirus has made it clear that we are all neighbors. Even with those on the other side of the world.

March 16, 2020

You Want a Coronavirus Vaccine?

Recently, U.S. televangelist Jim Bakker interviewed Sherrill Sellman, a "naturopathic doctor," who explained the extraordinary properties of the "Silver Solution," a product that Bakker sells on his show's website.

"This influenza, that is now circling the globe, you're saying that Silver Solution would be effective?" Bakker asked his guest while showing a bottle of the precious liquid. "Well, let's say [Silver Solution] hasn't been tested against this strain of the coronavirus," Sellman replied, "but it's been tested on other strains of the coronavirus and has been able to eliminate it within 12 hours. Totally eliminate it. Kills it, deactivates it. And then it boosts your immune system."

If you think that sounds good, you can order a package of two bottles of the magical potion, and, as a special bonus, you'll get two Silver Solution gel tubes. But that's not all! Bakker also reminds us that this stuff cures all (all!) venereal diseases. "It's a miracle in a tube," he says enthusiastically. "It's like God created it in Heaven to help us." And can you believe it can be yours for a "donation" of a mere $100 (€90)?

Bakker has had a long and lucrative career betting on the unsuspecting, the naive and the desperate. In the 1980s, he became one of the most popular televangelists in the United States, and millions of followers donated hundreds of millions of dollars to his church. But that phase of the con man's career ended in both a sex scandal and a financial scandal, earning him a long prison term.

179

In announcing the sentence, Judge Robert Potter said: "Those of us who do have a religion are sick of being saps for money-grubbing preachers and priests." But Judge Potter was mistaken. Bakker's followers apparently weren't sick of it at all. As soon as Bakker got out of jail, he launched another church and continued to preach God's message and sell miracle cures.

Con artists always surprise us with the audacity of their lies. But even more surprising is that they manage to find believers who trust them. That leads us to expect that most of their victims are naive and uninformed. But that's not the case.

You cannot call the former U.S. secretaries of state Henry Kissinger and George Schultz, or former secretaries of defense Bill Perry and General Jim Mattis, or the business mogul Rupert Murdoch naive or uninformed.

These are just some of the prestigious groups of backers who were taken in by Elizabeth Holmes, a 19-year-old woman, who founded and led a company called Theranos. According to her, the company would revolutionize blood testing and health care, and fill its shareholders' pockets along the way.

While Jim Bakker relies on alleged divine influence to persuade his followers, Elizabeth Holmes bet on the greed that clouds the judgment of even savvy, seasoned leaders. When a journalist asked General Mattis what words came to mind when he thought of Holmes, the military leader replied: "integrity" and "competence ... She is really a revolutionary in the truest sense." Holmes raised $700 million (€630 million) from an initial group of investors. Holmes continued to fundraise and a decade later the company's value reached $10 billion (€9 billion).

It was all a lie. Holmes didn't have the technology she claimed to have. She kept Theranos afloat by lying to investors, clients, employees, government agencies and journalists. When the real, fraudulent situation became known, Holmes lost everything and now faces several lawsuits that could land her in jail.

The other iconic example of a con man that used his clients' greed to swindle them is Bernie Madoff, who offered juicy returns to those who gave him their money to invest. Upon discovery, Madoff was fined more than $17 billion (€15 billion) and is now serving a 150-year prison term.

However, it's not religious con men or financial fraudsters that are the most dangerous. The greatest threat comes from the political con artists who come to power by cheating their voters with promises they can't fulfill, false claims, and policies that end up hurting everyone. Unfortunately, we are living in a golden age for scammers who, aided by the internet, are feeding a confused and anxious society the hope people desperately want to hear. Rapid change — in climate, technology, the workplace, the economy, politics, our values and security — creates a plethora of opportunities for demagogues.

Con artists offer their followers a safer and more predictable world in which they will be protected from foreigners and from those who look or think differently. The followers who empower the political charlatans harm us all more than the charlatans themselves.

March 3, 2020

P+P+P = C

This is the equation that captures a big chunk of the forces driving the decline of liberal democracy: populism plus polarization plus post-truth lead to continuism. And what is continuism? It's one of those words from Spanish that English lacks — but increasingly needs. *Continuismo* is what happens when leaders manipulate institutions, the law and even the constitution in order to grab and retain power.

Populism is nothing new. In theory, it is the defense of the noble masses (the populous) from the abuses of the elite. In practice, it is used to describe policies, people and situations that can be radically different — Donald Trump and Hugo Chávez, for example. By itself, populism is highly problematic and it rarely ends well. But when it's coupled with polarization and post-truth, its destructive power multiplies.

Few leaders define themselves as populists. Rather, the term is typically used as a derisive description used against political adversaries. A common mistake is to assume that populism is an ideology. But there are populists who defend economic and cultural openness to the world and others who are isolationists. There are some who trust the market and others who prefer government-centered approaches. "Green" populists prioritize environmental protection while industrialists favor economic growth, even if it pollutes the environment. In short, populism comes in many flavors and what history shows is that it is not an ideology but a strategy to take power and do whatever possible to hold on to it.

The latter is the most dangerous. A country can recover from a populist government whose policies damage the economy, stimulate corruption, and weaken democracy. But the longer that bad government hangs on, the more damage it does, the harder it is to replace it, and the longer and more expensive it is to recover.

Venezuela, for example, may have survived a single term of Hugo Chávez. What devastated that country, and is making its recovery so difficult, are the two decades of the same inept, corrupt and autocratic regime that was initiated by Chávez and is being prolonged by Maduro.

Continuism is an enemy that we must defeat. We have seen its effects in Fujimori's Peru, in Kirchner's Argentina, Lula and Rousseff's Brazil, in Evo Morales' Bolivia and Ortega's Nicaragua. Of course, clinging to power in violation of the constitution, or changing it to extend presidential terms, is not just a Latin American phenomenon. There is also Xi Jinping's China, Putin's Russia, Erdogan's Turkey and Orbán's Hungary, not to mention the list of longevous African dictators.

Populism and polarization make for comfortable bedfellows. It is normal for a democracy to have antagonistic groups that compete for power. In fact, it's healthy. But in recent times and in many countries, we have seen how that healthy competition has mutated into an extreme polarization that threatens democracy. Radical polarization makes it impossible for rival political groups to reach the agreements that are necessary to govern in a democracy. The political rivals become irreconcilable enemies who do not recognize the legitimacy of the "other" and do not accept their right to participate in any policy-making process or, much less, to rule.

Increasingly, the cleavages that have always divided societies (inequality, immigration, religion, regionalism, race, values or the economy) are no longer the primary source of polarization. Instead, group identity is the determining factor. In addition, this group identity is usually defined in opposition to the identity of the "other," the rival group. From this perspective, everything becomes simpler because there are no grey areas. Everything is black and white. Either you are "one of my own" or you are from the group whose political existence I don't tolerate.

This is how encouraging polarization by deepening existing disagreements and creating new social conflict becomes a powerful tool for continuism. The "we" against "them" mentality mobilizes and energizes the polarizing leader's followers who are motivated to defeat the "other side." They, in turn, become an important support base for that leader, legitimizing their need to cling to power and perpetuating a cycle of division.

But a new vice has joined populism and polarization: post-truth. Misinforming, confusing, alarming, distorting and lying has always been part of politics and governing. Now, however, its impact has been greatly amplified by the digital revolution and, specifically, by social media. Paradoxically, at a time when information is more abundant and accessible, we are more confused about what and who to believe. One answer has been that nowadays people believe less and less in institutions and more and more in their friends or those who share their prejudices, preferences and political views. In today's democracies the truth is what "friends" on Facebook, Instagram or Twitter believe is true. Even if it's a lie.

Destructive populists have come and gone, as have leaders who thrive on polarization. Societies suffer them and then overcome them. How? By holding on to the truth. Today that old defense is faltering. Post-truth threatens the antibodies that democracies use to fight off populism and repel continuism. Today these are shifting from recoverable illnesses to chronic conditions where mendacity and deception are the norm. When the line between truth and lie is blurred, the primary weapon we have always had for countering the populist's aspirations to stay in power indefinitely is lost.

February 20, 2020

Venezuela's Problem Is Not Socialism

In the last three years, tragic scenes of poverty and mayhem have dominated the coverage of Venezuela, a nation that used to be one of the wealthiest and most democratic countries in South America. Venezuela has become both a byword for failure and, curiously, something of an ideological hot potato, a rhetorical device dropped into political conversations around the world.

In election campaigns from Brazil to Mexico, from Italy to the United States, politicians invoke Venezuela as a cautionary tale of the dangers of socialism. Left-wing candidates from Jeremy Corbyn, in the United Kingdom, to Pablo Iglesias, in Spain, find themselves accused of sympathizing with socialist Chavismo — and suffer real political damage from the association with Venezuela's rulers. The charge, endlessly repeated, is that Venezuela's failure is the failure of an ideology; socialism is to blame, and if you make the wrong choice at the ballot box, the chaos of Venezuela could come to your doorstep, too.

Like all good propaganda, this line is effective because it contains an element of truth. The socialist policies of former President Hugo Chávez have devastated the country. Wide-ranging and chaotic expropriations, disastrous price and currency controls, stifling regulations, and unbridled hostility toward the private sector and foreign investment have all helped produce the economic catastrophe that now engulfs Venezuela. Few wars have destroyed as much of a nation's wealth as have the policies of Chávez and his handpicked successor, Nicolás Maduro.

185

But also like all good propaganda, the charge obscures more than it reveals. The deeper driver of Venezuela's implosion isn't Maduro's doctrinaire adherence to socialism but, rather, the country's slide into kleptocracy. To focus on Venezuela as a failure of socialism is to miss the real story: the collapse of the Venezuelan state and the takeover of its resources by a confederation of ruthless criminals from both inside and outside the country.

This dynamic is commonly ignored in much of the commentary about Venezuela, which continues to treat Maduro's standoff with his opponents as some variant of a recognizable left-right political confrontation. Such commentary tends to describe Venezuela as if it were like other fractious democracies where the battles of rival parties are fierce and occasionally violent. But thinking of Venezuela as a democracy gone wild or just as an example of the failure of socialism fails to fully capture the causes and consequences of the country's predicament.

In truth, Venezuela's democracy collapsed years ago. Polls consistently show that four out of five Venezuelans want to see Maduro step down immediately, but no democratic mechanism will fulfill their demand. With elections crudely rigged, the remaining options are all problematic: a foreign military intervention against Maduro remains a remote prospect, as do military and palace coups. Foreign experts and do-gooders, from the Vatican to the Norwegian Foreign Ministry, counsel negotiations and put themselves forward as intermediaries. But attempts to facilitate talks elide the major problem: the opposition in Venezuela isn't like a faction that sits across the aisle of a normal parliamentary democracy. Members of the opposition are more like hostages — and, in the case of the many political prisoners, are quite literally hostages — of a criminal clique ruthlessly exploiting the country's mineral wealth for its own benefit.

DEN OF THIEVES

Maduro continues to peddle the rhetoric of socialism, but his authoritarian government has constructed not a worker's paradise but a den of thieves. The classic twentieth-century Latin American dictatorship —

what political scientists called a "bureaucratic authoritarian regime" — was a highly institutionalized affair. An oppressive but efficient state machine, propped up by a large, permanent bureaucracy, worked hard to maintain power and squeeze out dissent. Contemporary Venezuela is nothing like that.

Rather than a professionalized bureaucracy, the Maduro regime amounts to a loose confederation of foreign and domestic criminal enterprises with the president in the role of mafia boss. The glue that holds the government together is neither ideology nor the quest for rigid order, it's the scramble for the spoils that flow from a dizzying array of illegal sources.

Today, Venezuela is a hub for traffickers in every kind of contraband: from price-controlled consumer staples to cocaine bound to the United States and Europe, as well as diamonds, gold, coltan, weapons and sex workers. The proliferation of bodegones — semi-legal retailers that flout price controls in hawking contraband consumer goods — has increasingly reshaped the domestic market for what remains of the middle class. These middlemen then funnel the proceeds straight to the friends, family and accomplices of the governing elite.

But government cronies and the military are not the only ones controlling large-scale criminal enterprises. Sprawling prison-based criminal gangs are the effective civil authority over vast territories, as are rebel fighters from neighboring Colombia's guerrilla movements. They extort payments from thousands of small businesses, farmers and ranchers. Some run illegal mines, relieving local authorities of the savage business of keeping order in the mining settlements, and providing the government its last reliable source of foreign currency in the wake of oil sector sanctions. Back in their air-conditioned offices in Caracas, regime bigwigs sit atop a mountain of loot. Jorge Giordani, one of Chávez's economic policy chiefs and now an opponent of the regime, calculated that officials had skimmed $300 billion off the top during the oil boom from 2003 to 2014. The precise figure can be disputed, but the macroeconomic scale of Chavista kleptocracy cannot.

Caracas has become one of the world's capitals for money laundering. Having stolen unfathomable sums, Venezuelan officials and their cronies have forged high-powered friendships around the world. The Washington Post recently revealed that one of Venezuela's most notorious crony capitalists has retained the legal services of Rudy Giuliani, while Erik Prince, the owner of the military contractor Blackwater, jets to and from Caracas to drum up business. When U.S. and European law enforcement officials look at Venezuela, they see a sprawling racketeering network clumsily hidden behind the façade of a government.

Libya on the Caribbean

To diplomats charged with managing the fallout of Venezuela's collapse, the country looks like a failed state. Much of its vast territory is ungoverned and remote from the squabbling politicians in the capital. Since the beginning of 2019, when Guaidó became, in the eyes of many inside and outside Venezuela, the constitutionally sanctioned interim president, Venezuela has been mired in an unresolved dispute over the legitimacy of its regime. The country risks becoming Libya on the Caribbean: a nation with two governments jockeying for power, each with the support of a separate coalition of foreign nations.

Most major democracies — and more than 50 countries — recognize Guaidó's claim to the presidency. But within the country's borders, the men with guns remain loyal to Maduro. He has gone to great lengths to sustain his monopoly on violence, even as he has lost international recognition. In early January of this year, Maduro made one more push to sideline his challenger, installing an erstwhile ally of Guaidó's as speaker of the National Assembly. Undeterred, Guaidó ignored Maduro's travel ban and toured the world in January, meeting with Latin American leaders and U.S. Secretary of State Mike Pompeo, as well as with Emmanuel Macron, Angela Merkel, Boris Johnson and Justin Trudeau, and taking a coveted spot on the plenary speaker roster at the World Economic Forum meeting in Davos. The world's democracies stand with Guaidó. Yet when in Venezuela, the threat of political prison hangs constantly over his head.

Like Libyans, Venezuelans are learning that having two presidents is a lot like having no president. Bankrupted by corruption, misman-agement and sanctions that have crippled the oil sector — the main source of foreign currency — the de facto state is broke and living off of the comparatively meager proceeds of illegal mining and illicit oil exports facilitated by Russian companies. The exodus of refugees from Venezuela since 2017 is another unmistakable sign of state failure. Approximately 10% of the population has left the country in the last few years. Venezuelans are fleeing not only destitution but also the collapse of law and order and of the most basic services: electricity, running water, telecommunications, usable roads, a workable cur-rency, and basic health and education. Refugees aren't fleeing "social-ism," they're escaping from a hellishly broken country.

THE CAVALRY AREN'T COMING

Venezuela's collapse threatens the stability of the wider region. Neighboring Colombia is the country most exposed, but the failure of the Venezuelan state reverberates across the hemisphere, from Brazil, whose northernmost state is straining under the weight of hun-gry and sick Venezuelan refugees; to Trinidad and Tobago, where flotillas of Venezuelans arrive to a hostile welcome; and to Aruba, a transit point for trafficked people and narcotics.

Venezuela's leaders have tried to export instability as well. Since the Chávez years and with Cuban direction, the Venezuelan regime has lent enthusiastic support to far-left fringe groups throughout Latin America. Maduro often speaks publicly of his desire to undermine opponents around the region. To the extent that a stable, democratic Latin America is a long-standing U.S. national security priority, the implosion of Venezuela is a problem not only for the security of neighboring countries but for that of the United States.

As Maduro destabilizes the region, the prospect of military intervention to depose him never entirely fades out of view. For more than a year, the Trump administration has made a show of keeping "all options on the table." This diplomatic formulation — a sly wink at a military intervention — seems aimed more at

Venezuelan exiles registered to vote in Florida than at military planners in the Pentagon. Desperate for a quick, magical solution to a problem that has upended their lives, exiles have rallied to Trump's cause. Unsurprisingly, many Venezuelans clamor for the removal of Maduro and his henchmen.

But foreign governments have little desire to invade Venezuela and risk blood and treasure to force regime change. Latin American countries and the European Union have stridently rejected the suggestion of military intervention. In truth, the United States has no appetite to carry out a major military operation in Venezuela. An invasion — which, to be clear, nobody is seriously contemplating — would risk becoming a tropical quagmire given the presence of armed groups scattered throughout the country. Maduro's government cooperates closely with Russia on defense, making Venezuela a tricky military theater. And in addition to Russia, China, Cuba and Turkey would surely oppose any U.S.-led intervention. Many Venezuelan exiles may be convinced that nothing short of outside force will dislodge Maduro, but no foreign government is willing to answer their call.

THEORIES OF CHANGE

Over the last three years, various "theories of change" seemed to offer possible ways out of Venezuela's current calamity. These theories have so far failed, in many cases because they continue, wrongly, to see Venezuela's crisis in ideological terms.

Throughout 2017, hopes centered on the ballot box. Activists petitioned for a recall referendum to cut short Maduro's term in office. Such a measure is enshrined in the country's constitution, and it seemed the last, best hope for securing an orderly transition. Maduro's handpicked Supreme Court snuffed it out. Then Maduro won a presidential vote in 2018 widely viewed as fraudulent: top opposition figures were disqualified from running, Maduro's allies engaged in widespread voter intimidation, no foreign election monitors were allowed to scrutinize the polls, and the media was tightly controlled. In retrospect, the hope that the ballot box could displace a thuggish kleptocracy now looks hopelessly naive.

Having given up on the ballot box, some Venezuelans came to wish for a military coup. Facing economic catastrophe and daily street protests, this line of argument went, Venezuela's military might decide to oust Maduro before things got entirely out of hand. But a cycle of protests in late 2017 left thousands jailed and dozens killed, and the military remained loyal to the government.

As 2017 turned into 2018, the economic implosion of the country raised the prospect of an uprising of impoverished Venezuelans pushed to the brink by food shortages. Opponents of the regime hoped that the same soldiers who had shown little compunction in attacking middle-class protestors the year before might be less willing to attack hungry people in the slums. After all, Venezuela's authorities presided over an ostensibly socialist revolution. Once more, an ideological frame distorted the reality on the ground: the military moved against the working-class food rioters just as ruthlessly as they had against the middle-class protesters in 2014 and 2017.

The rise of Guaidó as a lightning rod of protest in 2019 inspired further visions of sweeping change. Democratic countries from Chile to Croatia no longer recognized the Maduro regime, and oil income collapsed; surely now the government's days were numbered. But Maduro responded by doubling down on efforts to fund his security forces through the internationally laundered proceeds of gold mined by desperate, hungry Venezuelans working in slavery-like conditions under the control of armed gangs.

Throughout this period, dovish voices continued to press for a negotiated solution. They hoped that a neutral player in the international community (perhaps Norway or Uruguay) might broker a power-sharing deal that could pave the way to a managed regime change. But Maduro has a strong grip over his criminal enterprise; he felt no compulsion to entertain significant concessions during the various talks that have taken place in the last few years. Instead, he has used negotiations to pit his opponents — both domestic and foreign — against one another.

A BETTER TRANSITION

Any conceivable end game to the Venezuelan crisis will hinge on an internationally backed deal between Maduro and his opponents. But such a negotiation can only succeed once Maduro is convinced it is his last resort. Until such conditions come true, talks will simply play into his cynical strategy of stringing along his opponents.

Only when the regime feels it has run out of money, friends and options will a negotiated settlement become inevitable. But to ease an odious regime out of power bloodlessly entails difficult compromises. In Spain in 1978, in Chile in 1988 and in South Africa in 1991, hated figures from the old autocratic regimes kept substantial shares of power through successful transitions to full democracy.

Venezuelans today are far from prepared to countenance this kind of resolution — the government is not ready to consider it because it doesn't feel its hold on power is truly under threat, nor will the opposition because the regime's crimes remain too raw. People will recoil at a settlement that, for instance, guarantees seats in the legislature to figures in the regime, thereby shielding them from prosecution, or allows those potentates to keep their stolen loot.

Confoundingly, the history of successful late-twentieth-century transitions to democracy undermines their viability today. The arrest and eventual prosecution of Chile's former leader Augusto Pinochet in 1998 (a decade after he had ceded power) created a precedent that obliges the international community to treat gross human rights abuses as subject to universal jurisdiction. Maduro and his henchmen have not merely stolen huge sums, they have imprisoned, tortured and murdered hundreds of opponents. With Pinochet's arrest in mind, they have very good reason to doubt the reliability of any amnesty offered to them. The arrest of an erstwhile right-wing dictator dramatically narrows the options for Venezuela's supposedly socialist revolutionaries, underlining, once more, how tangential ideology is to understanding the crisis.

Even if Maduro's henchmen could be persuaded to accept a negotiated outcome, Venezuela's problems will be very far from over.

The end of the Maduro regime, when it does come, will reveal a hollowed-out husk of a state. The competent public administrators fled years ago. Rapidly rebuilding critical physical infrastructure may be possible, but rebuilding the institutional infrastructure will take much longer. The fall of the regime will just be the necessary start to a tumultuous decade of Venezuela's rebirth.

January 27, 2020

How is Corruption Like Snow?

In countries where snow abounds, words abound to describe it. And the same goes for corruption. Where there's a lot of corruption, it goes by many names.

In the Sami language, spoken in Norway, Sweden and Finland, there are more than 300 words for snow. In Latin America, and in countries such as Italy, Greece, Nigeria and India, there are hundreds of words for corruption. *Coima, mordida, moches, ñeme-ñeme, guiso, mermelada* and *cohecho* are some of the words for corruption used in Spanish-speaking countries. But just as interesting as the concepts we have too many words for, are those we have none for.

In Spanish, for example, there is no word for "whistleblower" — no one-word description of a person who nobly reports illegal activity or unethical behavior.

One notorious whistleblower was Jeffrey Wigand. He was a senior tobacco company executive who famously announced on national television that his company was lacing tobacco with ammonia to make nicotine more addictive. Naturally, the disclosure had an immense impact that, among other effects, forced the government to crack down on the tobacco industry. Not surprisingly, after Wigand filed his complaint, he was threatened.

It is for this reason that many countries now have laws that protect those who expose the illegal or improper behavior of the government and private companies. What's more, there are awards and accolades for those who publicize nefarious behavior. In the United States there

194

is even the National Whistleblowers Center, an NGO that provides legal assistance, protection and support for those who reveal corruption in government or the private sector.

But in Spanish the word "whistleblower" doesn't exist. It is revealing that the closest equivalents all have negative connotations, sounding more like snitch, sneak, toad or rat. Another word that doesn't appear in Spanish but is widely used in English is "accountability" — taking responsibility for one's public actions.

The closest thing in Spanish is *rendición de cuentas*, or "rendering accounts," and it refers to the information that the government and corporations are required to disclose. But it's not the same thing. In Latin America and Spain, public bodies account for their actions in a bureaucratic and accounting sense, but seldom truly accept the political or moral responsibility for what they have done. What's more, there are plenty of situations where governments do not feel obliged to "render accounts" to their citizens. On the contrary, opacity, obstruction, disinformation and lies are the norm.

In principle, regimes with leaders who are transparent and responsible are expected to have better "governability." That's another word that Spanish speakers have missed out on. In fact, it was only added to the Dictionary of the Royal Spanish Academy in the 1990s. According to its definition, *gobernabilidad* is the "quality of being governable," and the word *gobernanza* (governance) refers to the "art, or a way, of governing."

Bad government and weak governability are a plague on many countries. Frequently, this is due to the *continuismo* of those who hold power. According to the Dictionary of the Royal Spanish Academy, *continuismo* is a "situation in which the power of a politician, a regime, a system, etc., continues without signs of change or renewal."

The word *continuismo* is often used in the Ibero-American political debate to denounce the way leaders try to hang on to power by changing rules and laws and even rewriting the constitution. How do you say *continuismo* in English? You can't. There is no corresponding word. Interesting, isn't it?

More than ever nations need a culture of accountability, where we honor the whistleblowers whose grievances contribute to improving our governability while short-circuiting *continuismo*.

The problem is that Ibero-America can't even have this discussion without using multiple awkward anglicisms. It's time to start expanding Spanish with words that pay homage to decency and honesty.

February 11, 2020

Expensive Murders

Each year, about half-a-million people are murdered worldwide. Naturally, these deaths have devastating effects on the victims' families and loved ones. But there are also killings that reach far beyond friends and family and change the world. These transcendental murders can turn out to be very expensive. The iconic case is the 1914 assassination of the Austrian Archduke Franz Ferdinand in Sarajevo. His death set off a chain of events that led to the outbreak of World War I and the deaths of 40 million people.

Recently, there have been other costly murders such as that of Saudi journalist Jamal Khashoggi in October 2018 and that of Iranian General Qassim Suleimani on January 3, 2020. Although the victims could not be more different, they have something important in common: both were killed by a government that ordered their execution. The Saudi journalist was killed by his own government while the killing of the Iranian general was ordered by the president of the United States.

While Donald Trump is celebrating his decision to eliminate the murderous Iranian military leader, the crown prince of Saudi Arabia, Mohammed bin Salman, denies any involvement in Khashoggi's killing, a murder that occurred at the Saudi consulate in Istanbul. The prince blames rogue members of his secret service, some of whom have already been accused, tried and sentenced to death. However, investigators from both the Turkish government and The New York Times have concluded that the abduction, murder and dismemberment of the journalist were carried out by agents close to Mohammed bin Salman. The agents traveled to Istanbul for that very purpose. The 34-year-old prince clearly underestimated the consequences that the killing would have on his global reputation, and that of his country. Jamal Khashoggi has already become a symbol of the extreme dangers faced by journalists who challenge authoritarian regimes willing to kill their critics.

While it is too early to know the full extent of the fallout from General Suleimani's assassination, there is no doubt that it will be significant. So far Tehran's reaction has been moderate, and both the Iranian supreme leader, Ayatollah Ali Khamenei, and President Trump have shown signs that they want to avoid a military escalation. But it is risky to assume that the Iranian response will remain limited to the launching of 11 missiles at two bases in Iraq. That attack caused neither casualties nor major material damage.

Tehran does not usually respond immediately to the aggressions of its adversaries but rather waits to attack them where and when it is least expected. For example, in 2012 an important Iranian scientist whose work has significant military uses was assassinated. The Iranian government accused Israel. Some time later, Israeli diplomats were attacked in Georgia, India and Thailand, countries that had nothing to do with the murder of the Iranian scientist. In 1992, Israel killed a Hezbollah leader. Two months later, an Iranian-sponsored suicide bomber drove a truck loaded with explosives into Israel's embassy in Buenos Aires, causing 29 deaths.

The repercussions of the decision to assassinate Suleimani will be many and varied, but two are already quite clear. The first is that the U.S. military's presence in the Middle East will expand, at least in the near term. "Bringing soldiers home" was an electoral promise and is still a common slogan used by President Trump. This promise, which was already proving difficult to fulfill, now looks out of reach. The second effect of the murder of Suleimani is that Iran's nuclear agreement, in which the Islamic Republic promised to curtail its nuclear program, is dead. In fact, Iran has already announced that it will begin enriching uranium beyond the agreed limits, which it had not done since signing the 2015 agreement.

The assassination of the Iranian general also reinforces an important — albeit unintended — lesson to America's enemies: that they must have nuclear weapons in order to defend themselves. They know that Trump would never try what he did in Iran in North Korea, for example. Kim Jong-un, the North Korean leader, has the ability to respond with a nuclear strike. This is just an example of how the murder of Suleimani could spur nuclear proliferation, something that endangers us all.

History shows that, more often than not, great powers' reactions to attacks have more lasting consequences than the attacks themselves. For example, the September 11, 2001 terrorist attacks on the U.S. cost Al Qaeda an estimated $500,000 and caused around 3,000 deaths. Washington's reaction to these terrorist attacks triggered the wars in Iraq and Afghanistan — the longest in U.S. history — resulting in hundreds of thousands of civilian and military deaths in different countries and causing untold economic costs.

Eliminating Suleimani, undoubtedly a dangerous terrorist, will surely bring some benefits to the United States and its allies. But it will also have significant costs, many of them unexpected and, for now, invisible. Suleimani's murder has the potential of becoming very expensive.

January 14, 2020

2019

Revolting Alliances

Here are a few of last week's headlines:
"Sweden's dominant centrist party reverses its position and announces willingness to work with right-wing nationalists."
"To retain power, [Canadian Prime Minister] Trudeau must learn to work with rivals."
"Israel faces third election in less than a year."
"Iraq prime minister says he will resign amid protests."
"Finnish Prime Minister Antti Rinne resigns after coalition collapses."
"Pelosi asks committee chairs to proceed with articles of impeachment."

In some countries, opposing political groups figure out how to reach agreements, govern and share power. In others, long-standing hatreds make it impossible for them to move forward. Opponents are not seen as political rivals but as illegitimate enemies with toxic agendas and unforgivable past behaviors. The mere possibility of any deal with people or groups that promote unacceptable platforms — or worse, that have been accused of crimes and abuses — becomes morally and psychologically intolerable. A compromise with them often means political suicide for those who dare to propose it. But sometimes it's the solution. Hard to swallow, certainly, and easy to denounce by appealing to morality and justice, yet a solution nonetheless. Other times, however, the inability of political opponents to reach an agreement dooms a country to political paralysis. Between 2010 and 2011, for example,

Belgium spent 589 days without a working government because opposing factions could not reach an agreement.

While polarization has always existed, it is now becoming the norm in most of the world's democracies. That's a problem. Naturally, the divisions in any democracy are reflected in each election, but more and more often nations are finding themselves in political gridlock because no single group receives enough votes to form a government or is able to form a durable coalition.

This was not always the case. Decades ago, South Africa and Chile managed to avoid political violence and, as a result, experienced prolonged periods of stability and progress thanks to alliances between historical enemies.

Nelson Mandela achieved what no one believed possible: a peaceful transition from white minority rule and apartheid to a democracy in which the black majority reached power. In Chile, the process took a lot longer, but eventually succeeded. To transition away from the military dictatorship of General Augusto Pinochet, the democratic movement had to negotiate an agreement with the dictator that many Chileans found unacceptable. Not only was he allowed to remain a senator-for-life but he also remained the untouchable commander of the Armed Forces, who was able to prevent elected presidents from removing military officers from their posts. The Chilean Constitution also protected the military's right to name a certain number of senators and automatically allocated 10% of the nation's copper export revenue, one of the country's main sources of income, to the Armed Forces. Obviously, for those who had suffered the persecutions and torture of the military junta, this compromise was revolting. Yet this distasteful compromise between the military and the forces of democracy paved the way for a peaceful transition from dictatorship to democracy.

As we know, neither Chile nor South Africa have been able to save themselves from the recent political convulsions that are causing massive protests and unrest. But both societies benefited from a long period when political enemies managed to live together.

After the abolition of apartheid in South Africa the economy expanded, inflation fell and social programs proliferated, many of which benefited the needy black majority for the first time. In Chile, the various political factions — including those who supported Pinochet and those who suffered under him — managed to agree on economic reforms. The result was one of the world's most successful economies. According to the World Bank, in 2000, more than a third of Chileans lived in poverty. By 2017, the proportion had dropped to 6.4%.

Yet, these successes were not enough. In South Africa, unemployment, rampant corruption and an inept government fueled widespread frustration. In Chile, vast sectors of society were neglected. In both countries, economic inequality is now among the highest in the world.

It remains to be seen whether these two countries can create coalitions that can move their nations forward. But the challenge facing Chile and South Africa is the same that most of the world's democracies are facing today: how to create consensus between groups that hate each other.

It is quite possible that the world will soon be divided into democracies that are mired in irreconcilable conflicts that cause them to stagnate indefinitely and others that — because they can still broker compromises between political enemies — manage to form working governments. In the 21st century, compromise between people who hate each other may become a requirement for the survival of democracy.

December 10, 2019

Junk TV Is More Toxic Than We Thought

Some TV enriches our lives, some TV debases us. Some television opens minds, makes us think, takes us to places we would never get to visit and brings us face to face with life's great dilemmas. There is also television that deliberately degrades, deceives and confuses. And of course, there is TV that simply aims to distract us. Frequently, television that seeks to educate us is unbearably boring, while the shows that try to manipulate us end up polarizing and deceiving us. In contrast, TV that only aims to entertain is politically irrelevant. Or so we thought.

Recent research has found that bland, superficial, mindless television can have dire consequences. This type of television — Junk TV — is not politically neutral, even if its programs never talk about politics. This conclusion comes from an unexpected source: The American Economic Review, perhaps the world's most respected academic economics journal. A recent edition included an article by Professors Rubén Durante, Paolo Pinotti and Andrea Tesei titled "The Political Legacy of Entertainment TV." The authors took advantage of the data generated in the early 1980s by the Italian TV station Mediaset — Silvio Berlusconi's network — as it entered different regions of the country, in order to assess its political impact.

The researchers combined data on the locations Mediaset TV reached in the different regions with information about the audience and its exact geographical distribution. They also obtained opinion polls, psychological test results, information about the nature of each program, and other data. The researchers then analyzed it all using sophisticated statistical models that allowed them to identify the characteristics of those who grew up watching Mediaset — almost solely Junk TV — and those who did not.

The results are surprising.

Those who grew up watching Mediaset ended up being less cognitively sophisticated and civic-minded than their peers who did not have access to the same programming. In another example, psychological tests administered to a contingent of young soldiers revealed that those who came from regions where Berlusconi's stations were available performed between 8 and 25% worse than their peers who did not watch those programs in their formative years. They found similar results in math and reading tests. As adults, the children and adolescents who had watched Mediaset scored significantly lower than those who had not.

Everyone knows television influences our behaviors and opinions. That's nothing new or surprising. Similarly, the use of political propaganda campaigns to influence the masses is both ancient and universal. That the powerful — or those who want to become powerful — use television to achieve their goals is not a novel revelation. It is therefore tempting to disregard this study. It is also easy to assume that Silvio Berlusconi's propaganda efforts with Mediaset wer   " "   '
his political ambitions.

But it's not as simple as that. At least it wasn't the case when Berlusconi's companies were first entering the Italian TV market. Italian television had been dominated by a state monopoly: RAI, a network that, since its founding in 1944, had a clear educational and cultural mission. In the late 1970s, however, this monopoly was cracking as private broadcasters began to enter the regional markets. Berlusconi was one of the most acquisitive media moguls. He quickly consolidated those disparate regional stations into a single network, Mediaset.

But at that time Berlusconi had no intention of entering politics, which were then tightly controlled by a few parties and their entrenched leaders. Nor did his stations broadcast political or ideological content. Instead, Mediaset had a commercial strategy focused tightly on low-brow programming: variety shows, sports, movies and game shows.

It was only in the 1990s, when the corruption crisis known as Mani Pulite (Clean Hands) decimated Italy's political system and opened the doors for Berlusconi's political ambitions. The system changed, the traditional parties collapsed, and new political actors were able to compete for votes. No one took advantage of this opportunity better than Silvio Berlusconi, who quickly and effectively put his television companies at the service of his political ambitions. By 1990, half of Italians already had access to Mediaset. And in 1994, Berlusconi was elected prime minister of Italy.

The political impact of all this was also analyzed by the authors of the study on Junk TV. Those who watched Mediaset programming as children and teenagers grew up to show a greater propensity than their peers to support populist ideas and politicians. The consequences of all this have been immense. And Italy and Mediaset are not isolated examples.

November 28, 2019

Why Are the Streets On Fire?

It is down to inequality. And low wages, compounded by limited social mobility and a bleak outlook for young people. The issue extends to subpar public services, the ramifications of globalization and the displacement of jobs due to immigration, Chinese imports, or automation. Contributing factors include politicians who have become disconnected from the public, prioritizing their own interests and those of the elite. Social media, manipulated by clandestine agents, further amplifies discord, fosters resentment and fuels distrust, actively dividing the population and instigating new conflicts.

The breakdown of the family weakens society's core. Dignity, community, and the traditions that shape identity and foster a sense of belonging are eroding. Racial discrimination and tensions among ethnic, religious or regional groups worsen the situation. In some cases, the pushback against oppressive political regimes or the resistance against unjust laws adds to the complex web of challenges.

These represent just a sampling of the myriad explanations circulating for the global wave of street protests. It's a complex mix, encompassing both debunked myths and verifiable truths. Each explanation is delved into in numerous essays, articles and books, all attempting to uncover the underlying causes of street riots triggered by specific events.

Whether it's the surge in onion prices in India, the cost of wheat in Egypt, fuel prices in Ecuador and France, the tax on WhatsApp usage in Lebanon, the introduction of an extradition law in Hong

Kong, electoral manipulation by the Bolivian and Russian govern-ments, the sentencing of pro-independence leaders in Catalonia, or the subway fare increase in Santiago de Chile, these diverse incidents propel people to the streets. At times, they lead to the toppling of governments or force significant alterations to their plans. It's a testa-ment to the multifaceted nature of the issues driving these protests.

Many of the deeper reasons for street protests are also used to explain political surprises such as Brexit, Donald Trump, or the rise of populist regimes. The idea is that these surprises are manifestations of deeper discontents. Of course, they are. But many of those discontents are long-standing and abound in countries where these types of pro-tests have not occurred. The commonly used explanations do not serve to predict when or where protests will erupt that will be ampli-fied by chronic grievances.

A common factor of the protests is that they take governments by surprise. Neither Emmanuel Macron, nor Sebastián Piñera nor Xi Jinping were prepared to anticipate and respond to the escalation of protests and violence that have paralyzed Paris, Santiago de Chile and Hong Kong.

The success of the protests surely also comes as a surprise to those who take part in them. The young Chileans whose rampage forced the government to bring the military into the streets and implement a curfew did not expect that their protests would force the president to apologize on television. Or, more to the point, that the government would swiftly adopt a package of economic measures aimed at correct-ing some of the disparities affecting Chileans. The same goes for the young people of Hong Kong, who succeeded in getting the govern-ment to desist from imposing the extradition law that originally brought them to the streets.

The big question these days is whether we are in the presence of a great conspiracy or a great contagion. The conspiracy theory holds that, in Latin America, Cuba provides the intelligence, the Maduro regime provides the money and Russia provides the digital technology that helps sow chaos and promote protests. The contagion theory, on the other hand, emphasizes that the so-called "demonstration effect" now spreads faster and more widely than ever. Protesters in Chile saw their peers on the streets of Hong Kong and they have surely seen what is happening on the streets of Paris or Barcelona. Contagion is easy, even inevitable.

Which of the two explanations do you believe in? Both. As we have seen, the triggers for protests are always local and those that take place elsewhere surely serve as inspiration and example. Once protests gain momentum, those who oppose the government they target will do their best to directly or indirectly support the protesters.

Street protests are like forest fires that have increased in frequency and intensity. Experts warn that these huge fires will continue and we will have to learn to live in fire-prone ecosystems.

Societies and their leaders will have to learn to live with frequent street protests that, in some cases, will be only irritating and transitory events and, in others, the beginning of a process of revolutionary changes.

October 27, 2019

The World's Most Dangerous Place

International security experts often draw up lists of the most dangerous places on earth. These are not places that are just dangerous to their population, but rather places that irradiate conflict and instability to neighboring nations or even to other continents.

Kashmir just about always makes the list. The heavily disputed border between India, Pakistan and China has long been a flashpoint for armed conflicts. It doesn't help that both India and Pakistan have nuclear weapons, which increases the possibility that a skirmish could escalate into a serious threat to world peace. Syria, another country that often ranks high on the list, illustrates how these localized conflicts can end up destabilizing an entire region, if not the globe. Now Turkey is taking advantage of international circumstances to conquer new territory, alter borders and subdue the Kurds. And there are many other places where local or cross-border clashes have the potential to explode into larger international conflicts, including in the Arabian Peninsula, the Persian Gulf, the countries of the North Caucasus and the Korean Peninsula, to name a few.

But our list of world trouble spots needs an update. Today, the most serious threats to global stability are radiating from one point: Washington, D.C. Or, more precisely, the White House.

The president who portrayed himself as a master negotiator and a perpetual winner has not only proved to be a loser but also someone easily manipulated by the most infamous dictators of our time. Let's take a look at the scorecard: Trump's new friend, the sadistic dictator of North Korea, convinced him that he was willing to dismantle his country's nuclear arsenal if Washington lifted sanctions. But of course, the Korean tyrant has continued testing his warheads and the long-range missiles that could carry them. The autocratic president of Turkey, Recep Tayyip Erdogan, persuaded Trump to withdraw U.S. troops from Syria and let Turkish forces invade the north in order to "neutralize" Kurdish militias. Trump ignored the decisive role the Kurds played in the fierce fight against the Islamic State. Trump's concession to his Turkish friend is costing him big inside and outside of the United States. In fact, allowing Erdogan's bellicose adventure achieved what had hitherto been impossible: uniting Republicans and Democrats in Congress against the president's decision.

It is also evident that President Trump feels more comfortable with his other best friend, Vladimir Putin, than with his own country's Congress. Exhibit A: Trump's decision to veto a resolution proposed by the European Union condemning Turkey's invasion of Syria. Which other country vetoed the resolution? Russia.

Trump keeps piling on the losses: a destructive trade war with China, withdrawing the U.S. from the Iran nuclear deal, his handling of the crisis between Saudi Arabia and its neighbors, his negotiations with the Taliban, his weakening of America's relationship with its European allies, and, of course, his attempts to put U.S. foreign policy at the service of his personal interests, whether that be winning the next election or making money. America's loss of power and influence during Trump's watch will likely be remembered as one of the most devastating instances of geopolitical self-sabotage in history. Yet despite Trump's amazing ability to destabilize the world, the greatest danger emanating from the White House today is not international. It's domestic.

The president is increasingly testing the Constitution and the rules on which American democracy depends. Trump has challenged Congress by denying lawmakers their constitutional right to obtain documents as well as their right to subpoena public officials or citizens who have relevant information. The president's vitriolic attacks on his political opponents, on former allies and co-workers who have since renounced him, and on journalists and the media, are constant and growing. This is not simply the verbal excess of a histrionic politician, it is dangerously antidemocratic behavior.

The threats facing democracies were memorably noted by a young American politician in 1838. Abraham Lincoln, then 28, explained that, to counteract those threats, his country had to cultivate a "political religion" that emphasized reverence for the rule of law and a dependence on "reason, cold, calculating, unimpassioned reason." It is obvious that Donald Trump does not feel beholden to the laws or the truth, which means that the United States must depend on its institutions and its other leaders to preserve its democracy. Much is at stake.

A strong American democracy not only benefits the U.S., but also the rest of the world. That is why the recent attempts to undermine democracy in Washington make it the most dangerous place on Earth.

October 25, 2019

The War On Truth

What's been happening to information is very strange. It is both more cherished and more disdained than ever.

Propelled by the digital revolution, information will surely be the most important engine of change in economics, politics and science in the 21st century. But, as we've seen, it will also be a dangerous fount of confusion, social fragmentation,and conflict.

Large amounts of data that previously meant nothing can now be converted into information that can help better manage governments and businesses, cure diseases, create new weapons, or determine who wins an election, among many other things. It is the new oil: after processing and refining, it acquires great economic value. And if in the last century several wars were fought over control of oil, then in this century it is likely that cyberwars will be fought over who controls data and information.

But, while some information saves lives and is used for good, there is another type that's toxic and kills. We are being bombarded by new problems caused by misinformation, fraud and manipulation that are hitting just as fast as the information can be extracted from these massive, digitized databases. Some of those who control these technologies know how to convince us to buy certain products. Others know how to get us excited about certain ideas, groups or leaders... as well as how to get us to detest their rivals.

The great irony is that, at the same time that we have more information today than ever before, the veracity of that information is often in doubt. Alan Rusbridger, former editor of The Guardian, has said that "a society that cannot agree on a factual basis for discussion or decision-making cannot progress. There can be no laws, no votes, no government, no science, no democracy without a shared understanding of what's true and what isn't."

The debate about what is true and what is false is as old as humanity. Discussions on this matter between philosophers, scientists, politicians, journalists, or simply between people with different ideas, are frequent and fierce. Often, instead of focusing on the facts, these debates focus on discrediting those who voice them. Scientists and journalists are frequently the targets of those who, due to interests or beliefs, defend ideas or practices based on lies.

For example, scientists who publish incontrovertible data on global warming or those who warn of the imperative need to vaccinate children are already used to being slandered over their motivations and interests.

Journalists have it even worse. We know that powerful people will attack the media when they feel threatened, but the hostility of the current president of the United States is unprecedented. Donald Trump has said, "You know, these animals in the press. They're animals. Some of the worst human beings you'll ever meet... just terrible dishonest people." He has championed the idea that journalists are the "enemy of the people" who spread fake news. Trump has mentioned "fake news" on Twitter more than 600 times and mentions it in all his speeches. The worst part is that Trump has not only undermined the confidence of Americans in their media, but his accusation has been readily adopted by the worlds autocrats. According to A. G. Sulzberger, the publisher of The New York Times, "In the past few years, more than 50 prime ministers, presidents and other government leaders across five continents have used the term 'fake news' to justify varying levels of anti-press activity." Sulzberger acknowledges that, "The media aren't perfect. We make mistakes. We have blind spots." However, he is steadfast in affirming that the mission of The New York Times is to seek the truth. In today's confusing world, where everything seems relative and nebulous, it is good to know that there are still those who believe that the truth is out there and can be found. Perhaps more importantly, defending the truth is a prime antidote against leaders with authoritarian inclinations.

In 1951, Hannah Arendt wrote that "the ideal subject of a totalitarian state is not the convinced Nazi or Communist, but people for whom the distinction between fact and fiction and the distinction between true and false no longer exist."

More than six decades later, this description has acquired renewed relevance. It is imperative that we defeat those who have declared war on truth.

October 16, 2019

This Is Not Normal

What do Spain, Italy, Israel and the United Kingdom have in common? They can't seem to form stable governments able to rule. And it's not just these four countries where, after all, the division of powers and limits on executive power still hold. As we know, plenty of other countries are much more dysfunctional.

Around the world, governing is becoming more difficult and, in many cases, impossible. Elections no longer serve as an anchor that stabilizes the political landscape and helps establish effective government. Rather, elections and referendums now reveal the deep polarization of the electorate, promote gridlock and render decision-making impossible. These days, election results formalize and quantify the deep fissure within society and, in many cases, this tension makes civilized coexistence between contending factions difficult. And how do politicians try to solve this impasse? By holding more elections.

This is not normal.

And it's not only democracies that are finding it harder to govern. It also doesn't seem quite normal that Xi Jinping and Vladimir Putin — two of the most powerful men in the world — are worried about spontaneous street protests led mainly by unarmed youths. Xi and Putin exercise tight control over their respective countries and those who protest in the streets of Hong Kong and Moscow are not a threat to the survival of these regimes. But what's surprising is that Xi and Putin so far have refrained from crushing the protests with a massive use of force. That would be normal. Perhaps the relative tolerance these two autocrats have shown is a symptom of their strong grip on power, how safe they feel and, also, of the irrelevance of the protests. Another possibility, however, is that they don't know how to quell them.

These protests have no obvious leaders, no clear hierarchies, and they are organized, coordinated and mobilized via social media. In Hong Kong, pro-Beijing government leaders complain that, although they want to seek arrangements with those on the streets, they don't know who to negotiate with. Obviously Xi and Putin could end the protests through the normal ways of dictators: brutal, wholesale repression. But the disproportionate use of force could backfire and, instead of ending the protests, spark a more serious political crisis.

That's what happened in Syria when marches in the city of Daraa over the imprisonment and torture of 15 students for painting graffiti against the government escalated into a civil war that has now raged for eight years and left half a million dead.

But if what's happening in world politics is not normal, what is happening to the environment is even less so. The scientific data is clear. Indeed, every day we are seeing images from all over the planet of disasters caused by gigantic fires, torrential rains, prolonged droughts and fierce hurricanes. The scientific evidence is overwhelming, yet our inaction to address this threat is equally sobering. In fact, the greatest danger facing our civilization is undoubtedly our ongoing paralysis in effectively combating climate change.

The inability of governments to cope with the climate emergency is deepened by economic interests. ExxonMobil and the brothers Charles and David Koch are just two examples of companies and wealthy individuals who for decades funded "research centers" and "scientists" dedicated to sowing doubts about the seriousness of the climate problem, confusing the ill-informed and stopping governments from adopting needed policies.

That large companies are influencing the government to prevent it from making decisions that would hit their profits is nothing new. In fact, it is normal.

What is not normal is that leaders of some of the world's largest companies would publicly repudiate the idea that their primary objective should be to maximize profits. Yet that was what happened a few weeks ago when the heads of 181 of the largest American companies signed a statement that maintains exactly that. These senior executives affirmed that private companies must reconcile the interests of their shareholders with those of their customers, employees and suppliers, as well as those of the communities in which they operate.

Obviously, these titans of capitalism are late to the conversation. For many it's already obvious that it is untenable for any company to ignore the interests and needs of the group on which it depends, beyond its shareholders. The debate is about how to do it and, above all, how to ensure that companies do what they promise. There are some important business leaders who have ideas about this. Brad Smith, the president of Microsoft, for example, has published an article in The Atlantic magazine entitled "Tech Firms Need More Regulation."

This is not normal. No doubt it is surprising that the president of one of the world's largest companies would urge governments to regulate his industry. But this, like the other anomalies we have discussed here, just confirms once again how fiendishly difficult it is to decipher the world in which we live.

September 26, 2019

What Has a Bigger Impact,
Elections or Street Protests?

What do North Korea and Cuba have in common? The obvious answer is that both are dictatorships. Less obvious is that both recently held elections. On March 12, the North Koreans reported that 99.99% of their citizens had gone to the polls and that 100% of the votes were for the 687 candidates put forward by the regime. There were no others. Weeks earlier, Cubans voted in a referendum in which they were asked if they approved of a new constitution. Ninety-one percent of them said yes.

This propensity for dictatorships to carry out fraudulent elections is odd. It is based on the assumption that an election, even if it is only theater, can somehow compensate for the illegitimacy of an autocratic government.

Holding elections and referendums has become more frequent in both democracies and dictatorships. There are now more elections than ever before. This year, for example, 33 countries will have presidential elections and 76 nations will hold parliamentary votes.

But another form of political expression is becoming much more frequent than elections: street protests. In addition to marches and rallies, blocking traffic has also become a common form of political expression.

Only last week there were massive popular protests in several countries. In Moscow, for example, police arrested more than 400 demonstrators who were protesting the arrest of Ivan Golunov, a journalist who investigates corruption in the Kremlin. The police accused him of drug possession and trafficking, charges that other journalists and politicians denounced as spurious. At the same time, in Hong Kong, more than a million people took to the streets to protest an extradition law that would have facilitated Beijing's repression of one of its most important territories. Thanks to the protests, Golunov has been released, and in Hong Kong the passing of the extradition law was postponed. While this was happening, tens of thousands of Swiss women took to the streets of Zurich and other cities in protest against gender discrimination.

In Sudan there were also protests. The government brutally suppressed them and more than a hundred protesters lost their lives. The Khartoum government also blocked cellphones and internet access throughout the country. Since December, the Sudanese have been demanding an end to autocratic rule, fair elections and democratic freedoms. Which is exactly what the Venezuelans — led by Juan Guaidó — are asking for on the other side of the world.

This is nothing new. Politics and street protests have always gone hand in hand. But in their current 21st-century form, they have several peculiarities.

The first is their frequency. Thomas Carothers and Richard Youngs, two of the world's leading experts on political protests, have thoroughly investigated this and concluded that they have increased in both frequency and size. As we know, the use of mobile phones and social medias facilitates the organizing of political gatherings and other forms of public protest. It also helps that, in many countries, a new, more numerous, connected and energized middle class has awoken politically.

The reasons for this wave of protests are many: some of them have broad objectives, such as ending corruption or economic inequality. Others, such as those in Hong Kong, are specific: to prevent the approval of the extradition law. Still others start with specific claims but quickly evolve into more wide-ranging demands. In France, the increase in fuel taxes triggered the protests of the "yellow vests," but soon enough their list of demands included an increase in the minimum wage, the dissolution of the National Assembly and the resignation of President Emmanuel Macron. There are also protests focused on removing the president, as in the case of Egypt's Hosni Mubarak, Guatemala's Otto Pérez Molina and Brazil's Dilma Rousseff.

The big question is whether protests work. This is not so clear. Most protests achieve minor concessions or fail completely. But some have caused substantial political changes. What characterizes those that succeed? Clearly, the combination of new communication technologies with old methods of political organization is indispensable. Social medias, by themselves, are not enough. To be successful, protests must involve a large part of society and not only through the internet. In some cases, international pressure and the involvement of the armed forces have been decisive. But, as always, the most important thing is leadership. Success requires leaders who take charge. The illusion of a political movement based on collective decisions and without clearly identifiable leaders usually ends up being just that: an illusion.

June 19, 2019

Economic Inequality: What's New?

"I'm a capitalist, and even I think capitalism is broken," said Ray Dalio, the founder of Bridgewater, one of the largest private investment funds in the world. According to Forbes, Dalio ranks 60th on the list of richest people on the planet. "I believe that all good things taken to an extreme become self-destructive and that everything must evolve or die," he said. "This is now true for capitalism."

Jamie Dimon, the head of JPMorgan Chase, is also concerned about the health of capitalism. Dimon, whose salary last year was $30 million, says: "[Capitalism] has helped lift billions of people out of poverty... This is not to say that capitalism does not have flaws, that it isn't leaving people behind and that it shouldn't be improved."

This is something new. Bashing capitalism and the inequality it generates and perpetuates is as old as Karl Marx. What's new is that the titans of industry, whose interests are intricately tied to capitalism, are criticizing it as fiercely as the most aggrieved left-wing activists. The businessmen want to repair it, while radical critics want it replaced.

Big business leaders are not the only ones newly critical. According to a recent Gallup poll, the share of Americans between 18 and 29 who have a favorable view of capitalism has fallen from 68% in 2010 to 45%. Today, 51% of them have a positive opinion of socialism. This is also new.

In the academic world there are the same concerns. Paul Collier, for example, is a renowned economist and professor at the University of Oxford who published *The Future of Capitalism* last year. In his book he warns that modern capitalism has the potential to lift us all to an unprecedented level of prosperity, but nowadays it is morally bankrupt and is heading toward a tragedy.

Criticisms of capitalism are many and varied and, most of them, very old. The most common is that capitalism condemns the masses to poverty and concentrates income and wealth in a small elite. This criticism was temporarily tempered by the success of countries such as China, India and others in reducing poverty. This was due, to a large extent, to the adoption of liberalizing reforms that stimulated growth, employment, and increased incomes, creating the largest middle class in history, another novelty.

But the financial crash of 2008 brought back concerns about inequality and revived people's skepticism against capitalism. For countries like Brazil and South Africa, economic inequality had been the norm, but for others it meant the return of a painful reality that many thought had been overcome. Several European countries as well as the United States joined the group of nations that saw inequality grow.

With the recent eruptions of populism and political instability, a widespread sense of urgency over the need to reduce inequality became a fixture of national conversations in many countries. But the agreement on the need to intervene has not been matched by agreement on how to do it. The lack of consensus has a lot to do with differing opinions about the root causes of inequality. For Donald Trump there is no doubt: China's imports and illegal immigrants are the reasons for the economic suffering of those "left behind" and also the explanation of why so many Americans can't reach the American Dream.

But that's not true. Studies show that the main drivers of inequality are the new technologies that destroy jobs and keep salaries low for blue-collar jobs. A variant of this theory is that a growing number of sectors are dominated by a small number of very successful, large companies whose business strategies inhibit wage increases, inflation and economic growth. In the United States, the financial and health sectors — with their disproportionate economic weight and political influence

— are often cited as examples. For economists such as Thomas Piketty, Emmanuel Sáenz and others, economic inequality is mainly caused by the unequal ownership of capital, both private and public.

But these generalizations are deceptive. The causes of the increase in inequality in India are different from those of the United States, and the culprits in Russia are different from those in Chile or China. In some countries, the main cause of inequality is corruption, in others it is not.

Most likely we are simply re-fighting the ideological wars of the last century and these new challenges will require new ideas. The impact of artificial intelligence on inequality, for example, is still uncertain, but there's good reason to believe it will be large. And this one innovation can make all our received ideas about the causes of inequality and its consequences obsolete. This and other changes of the 21st century will create new and powerful sources of inequality that will require new and equally unprecedented policies to close the gap between rich and poor.

June 12, 2019

Politician-eating Beasts

Most animals do not eat human flesh. But some do. It's said that once a tiger, a lion or a leopard incorporates homo sapiens into its diet, it becomes a man-eater. Some say that once they develop a taste for it, they can't stop.

Something similar is happening in politics. Once the political system in some countries learns how to toss out a head of state, it seems to develop a taste for it, and starts doing it again and again. The act becomes a sort of ritual sacrifice that takes place within the courts, the legislature and the media, as well as in the streets. The proliferation of these "politician-eating" beasts appears to be a worldwide phenomenon. But why?

Many nations across the globe are dealing with a volatile mixture of social unrest, polarization and retaliatory politics in addition to a widespread backlash against politics (and politicians) in general. This has created the perfect breeding ground for the types of sudden uprisings we are seeing against many rulers, which culminate in impeachment, incarceration, and, in some cases, death. As we know, the politician-eating beast uses social media as a powerful weapon to corner its prey. We also know that voter frustration is neither artificial nor capricious: economic uncertainty, inequality, corruption and poor government performance have whetted the appetite of the politician-eating beast.

Sometimes it can be salutary to get rid of bad presidents before the end of their term. This should be applauded, not condemned. Brazil, for example, owes a lot to the judges who fought some of the country's most powerful politicians and businessmen and managed to send them to prison. And we shouldn't forget the hundreds of thousands of Brazilians — outraged by widespread corruption — who took to the streets and created the atmosphere that led to President Dilma Rousseff's impeachment. Perhaps most intriguing, the same Brazilian politician-eating beast that inadvertently opened the way for President Jair Bolsonaro could devour him, too.

In Central America, the natural habitat of nearly half of all former presidents appears to be prison. According to the Mexican newspaper El Universal, of the 42 presidents who governed Guatemala, El Salvador, Honduras, Nicaragua, Costa Rica and Panama between 1990 and 2018, 19 have been, or remain, in jail.

In South America, Peru makes a fascinating case study. President Pedro Pablo Kuczysnki was forced to resign in 2018 and was recently sentenced to three years of house arrest. Former President Ollanta Humala was also imprisoned, as was his wife Nadine Heredia. Alejandro Toledo is a fugitive from the Peruvian justice system. Since 2017 the authorities have been requesting his extradition from the U.S. government. His wife, Eliane Karp, is wanted on an arrest warrant and is staying abroad. Keiko Fujimori, the leader of the opposition, has been sentenced to three years of house arrest, while her father, former President Alberto Fujimori, continues to serve a 25-year sentence. Prison would have likely been the fate of twice president Alan García, had he not, just a few weeks ago, turned a gun on himself when the police arrived at his house to arrest him.

Unfortunately, this is not just a Latin American phenomenon, it is a global trend. The politician-eating beast is also haunting Europe. And Asia, too. Park Geun-hye, 67, accused of corruption, was forced to resign as president of South Korea and is serving a 24-year sentence, which in her case amounts to life imprisonment. Lee Myung-bak, one of her predecessors, was tried for corruption and sentenced to 15 years, while another former president, Roh Moo-hyun, also implicated in a corruption scandal, committed suicide. In Thailand, Malaysia and Indonesia there are similar stories.

One of the surprises of all these coups is the absence of the military. In the past, generals were central players. Not anymore. Now it's the people in the streets and the judges in the courts. The problem is that, sometimes, the pressure from the streets overflows into the courts, and the judges, instead of seeking justice, simply aid and abet the beast.

What can we make of all this? First, that impunity is not as rampant as most believe. Many corrupt politicians end up in prison. Second, it doesn't seem to be making a dent in the levels of corruption. Nothing seems to indicate that it has diminished. Third, in these judicial crusades against corrupt officials, often fueled by the indignation of the people on the street, surely injustices are being committed. Fourth, accusations of corruption are part of the arsenal used by politicians against their adversaries.

What to do? We must not limit judicial activism against the corrupt, but rather depoliticize it. The most powerful weapons against corruption are public policies that inhibit it. Public policies should increase the transparency of officials' decisions and reduce their ability to operate with impunity. Lastly we should promote the scrutiny of public officials by watchdog groups, the media and non-governmental organizations.

Alas, this isn't nearly as entertaining as watching the politician-eating beast devouring its next victim. But it's much healthier.

May 1, 2019

Six Toxins That Weaken Democracy

Sometimes elections and referendums change the course of history.

For example, in June 2016, Britain decided to leave the European Union in the famous Brexit referendum. Also in 2016, Donald Trump won the U.S. election and found himself in the White House. And in December 1998, Venezuelans elected Hugo Chávez president.

Today Brexit has plunged the English political system into a deep crisis, Trump has transformed American politics and perhaps the world, and Chávez is responsible for a national catastrophe that is now becoming a crisis for much of Latin America.

These three cases are, of course, very different. But they also have similarities that reveal some important toxins that are undermining modern democracies.

1. Antipolitics. All three of these examples are manifestations of the troubling rejection of the established political system and the presumption that traditional politicians use politics for their personal benefit and not for the common good. Those who voted for Brexit, Trump and Chávez felt that just evicting those who had governed in the past would improve their personal situation or, at least, serve as lesson to the powerful. "Throw them all out!" and "Nothing could be worse than what we have now!" are the common slogans that energize antipolitics everywhere.

2. Weak political parties. In these three examples, the unexpected election results were made possible in significant measure thanks to a weakening of the established political parties. The two traditional

British parties — the Labour Party and the Conservative Party — were split internally, which prevented them from effectively confronting Brexit's promoters. The same thing happened to the Republican Party in the U.S., whose fragmentation made it possible for an outsider such as Trump to become its presidential candidate. This was also the case in Venezuela, where the two historical parties had collapsed, leaving the door open for a dark horse like Hugo Chávez.

3. The normalization of lying. Almost immediately after the Brexit vote, it became clear that its promoters had lied, exaggerating the benefits for the UK if it left the European Union and minimizing the costs and difficulties. In his first year as president, Donald Trump — on average — lied or made misleading statements around six times every day according to a running count kept by The Washington Post. In his second year in office his average rose to more than 16 a day and, so far in 2019, he has been lying 22 times a day. The U.S. president has normalized the lie. Hugo Chávez did the same. A quick Google search will reveal a huge collection of videos of the Venezuelan president blatantly lying.

4. Digital manipulation. Donald Trump's Twitter account is undoubtedly one of his most powerful political weapons. Chris Wylie, the repentant former research director of the company Cambridge Analytica, told the British parliament that the company and others used social medias to influence the outcome of the Brexit referendum. *Aló Presidente*, the weekly Venezuelan talk show starring Hugo Chávez, became a major instrument of government propaganda and political mobilization as well as a tool for manipulating public opinion. All politicians, everywhere and always, have used the media to obtain and retain power. But few have done it with the skill, brazenness and technological sophistication with which Trump, Chávez and the Brexit advocates have done so.

5. Foreign interference. U.S. intelligence agencies and special prosecutor Robert S. Mueller concluded that the Russian government clandestinely influenced the 2016 U.S. election. Before the Brexit referendum, more than 150,000 Twitter accounts in Russian sent tens of thousands of messages in English urging the British to leave the

European Union. Cuba's influence on Venezuela had been kept secret, but today it is a widely acknowledged fact. Invasions are now cheaper, clandestine, and are carried out with computers and the weapons of the digital age.

6. Nationalism. The promises of self-determination as well as revenge against the (real or imagined) mistreatment by other countries were key to the electoral successes of Chávez, Trump and Brexit. In all three cases, denouncing globalization, international trade and "countries that take advantage of us" yielded political dividends. Chávez blamed the U.S., while Trump and Brexit's promoters railed against immigrants.

These six factors illustrate the type of toxins that are infecting the political body of many countries. In some of them, antibodies have arisen that resist the toxins. Yet it is too early to say how sick each patient will get or even if they will survive. All we know is that the clash between these toxins and their political antibodies is sure to shape our changing world.

April 4, 2019

Islam By Numbers

"Why do they hate us?" That was the question posed on the cover of Newsweek magazine after the terrorist attacks of September 11, 2001. The headline nodded to the fact that all the perpetrators were Muslims with a deep hatred of the U.S. and the West. The attacks provoked a massive military response from the U.S. and its allies, as well as an intense debate about the causes of this hatred and how to confront it. The debate popularized the theory of a "clash of civilizations," suggesting that, in the new century, religion and culture — not ideologies like communism and capitalism — would be the primary sources of international conflict. This attack pitting Islam and the West was seen as evidence of this new world view.

But now we know that this theory was wrong. Instead of a clash between civilizations, what we really have is a bloody clash within a civilization. And that civilization is Islam. The vast majority of the victims of terrorism worldwide are innocent Muslims murdered or wounded by radicalized Muslims. The attacks of Islamist terrorists against Europeans and Americans have been serious and remain a real threat. And the recent attack on the mosque in New Zealand is part of a new criminal activism by white supremacists. But the number of victims of Islamic terrorism in the U.S. and Europe is significantly lower than the deaths caused by these terrorists in Muslim countries.

In order to successfully confront this terrorism, we need to better understand Islam and its current circumstances, practices and demographic outlook. This is not just important for fighting terrorism. In

233

this century Islam will mold many of humanity's most critical issues, from the fight against poverty to mass migration, and from the future of Africa and the Middle East to how to prepare hundreds of millions of young new workers for a workplace defined by the digital revolution. Sadly, it is also possible that new tragedies like those that have already occurred in Syria and Yemen and with the Rohingya people of Myanmar may occur.

Today there are 1.8 billion Muslims and they are the world's fastest growing religious group. By the end of this century there will be more Muslims than Christians in the world, and by 2050, 10% of Europeans will be Muslims.

Until the late 1990s, analysis of the role of Islam in economic performance had been mostly left to theologians, sociologists and political scientists. Today, however, more and more economists are applying the latest theories and methods to help us understand Islam's impact. Timur Kuran, a professor at Duke University, has just published a comprehensive review of the relationship between Islam and the economy. The scope of this work is vast and impossible to summarize but the full text is in The Journal of Economic Literature.

One of the most critical questions is whether Islam retards economic development since countries with a predominantly Muslim population are, on average, poorer than the rest of the world. In 2017, the average income per person of the 57 member nations of the Organization of Islamic Cooperation (OIC) was $11,073, while that average for the rest of the world was $18,796. Moreover, in countries with Muslim majorities, life expectancies are lower and illiteracy higher. In countries such as India, where there are many different religions, Muslims tend to be the poorest group. The relative poverty of Muslims occurs both in countries where they are a minority and in those where they constitute the largest religious group. Nonetheless, professor Kuran warns that although these data are suggestive, "On the whole, cross-country research on whether Islam harms growth is inconclusive." After all, he correctly notes, the economies of the poor countries of South Asia and Latin America also suffer from a chronically mediocre economic performance.

This review of scientific articles published since 1997 reveals other interesting results. For example, those who make the annual pilgrimage to Mecca bring home attitudes that favor economic growth and greater tolerance toward non-Muslims. Individuals whose mothers fasted while pregnant with them during Ramadan have shorter lives, poorer health, less mental acuity, lower educational attainment and poorer work performance. Islamic charities tend to favor the middle class over the poor. The rules that govern the so-called "Islamic finance" have little effect on the financial behavior of Muslims. And the rulers of Muslim countries have contributed to the persistence of authoritarianism "by treating Islam as an instrument of governance."

The study includes the explanations and data that support these conclusions as well as many other surprising findings. We need more and better studies of this kind. Now more than ever we need to fully understand Islam, its problems and its promise.

March 28, 2019

Who Do You Trust?

One interesting modern phenomenon is the collapse in trust. According to the polls, people don't trust the government, politicians, journalists and scientists, let alone bankers and business executives. Not even the Vatican has escaped this crisis of confidence.

In the United States, for example, public confidence in the government is at its lowest point since opinion polls first included questions related to trust. Today, 82% of Americans do not trust their government to do the right thing. This has become a global trend: distrust and skepticism are the norm.

There is a great paradox at work here. At the same time that our confidence in the government has fallen abysmally low, our faith in messages that reach us through the internet is at a new high. This is the paradox of trust. We do not believe in the government or the experts, but we trust anonymous messages on Facebook, Twitter and WhatsApp.

Who hasn't gotten an email forward or a post from family or friends that later turned out to be false? All it takes to trick us is to reinforce our ideals and beliefs. When a message does that, we automatically drop the skepticism that we use to shield ourselves from the lies and manipulations so common on the internet. If the message is aligned with our prejudices, we forward it to our "digital tribe" — the people we know who think like us — without a second thought.

There is a connection between the broad decline of trust and the growing faith in internet messages that confirm our biases. With regard to governments, we want them to be subject to scrutiny and criticism and we should celebrate the fact that the internet facilitates this. All governments have flaws and are deserving of criticism. But we must be careful when the criticism of government is based on falsehoods, because this weakens democracy, polarizes society and nourishes anti-politics, specifically the feeling that nothing works anyway, so why not engage in reckless political experiments such as giving power to demagogues and populists?

A telling example of the paradox of trust is the anti-vaccine movement. Its adherents maintain that vaccines against measles, mumps and rubella, for example, are dangerous and may be associated with autism, so they refuse to vaccinate their children.

However, the scientific evidence on this subject is overwhelming: there is no link between vaccines and autism. And not vaccinating children is dangerous for them, and for the children and adults with whom they interact. Unfortunately, scientific research can't make a dent in the beliefs of those who are convinced that vaccines are harmful. For them, the recommendations of specialized public institutions are not credible, while the lies about vaccines circulating on the internet are treated as immutable truths. Worse, anti-vaccine advocates have powerful allies. Both Donald Trump and the current Italian government have questioned the need to vaccinate children.

Heaping scorn on and demonizing the experts is part of the populists' playbook. After all, the experts are, by definition, an elite and therefore not "the people" that populists claim to champion. Their questioning of scientific knowledge often has the support of "skeptics" who always seem to crawl out of the woodwork at just the right time. They are the kinds of scientists who, for decades, placed the link between tobacco and cancer in doubt, or those who doubt that global warming and climate change are real. Or the "experts" who question the theory of evolution. Or those who believe that vaccines produce autism. Skeptics are almost always a small minority who take pride in questioning the "group-think" shared by the vast majority of scientists. Inevitably, some skeptics turn out just to be frauds paid to sow doubt.

The paradox of trust exists everywhere, but in no arena does it have consequences as far reaching as in politics. Political propaganda has always existed and the use of advertising in elections is a long-es-tablished practice. But the paradox of trust has supercharged both forms of manipulation to new levels. It is clear, for example, that the strategy of the Russian government is not to invade other countries with tanks and airplanes, but with stealthy attacks and seductive lies that sow fear, uncertainty and doubt.

What to do? Surely technologies will appear that will facilitate the detection of these digital poisons, as well as laws and regulations that reduce the impunity of the cyber attackers and the companies that give them the platforms from which they launch their attacks. But the most powerful antidote is to have engaged and well-informed citizens who refuse to allow themselves be blinded by political passions.

February 28, 2019

The Globalization of Polarization

The government of the world's superpower is at a standstill, while the government of a former superpower — the United Kingdom — sits paralyzed after suffering a barrage of self-inflicted wounds. Angela Merkel, who was until recently the most influential European leader, is heading toward retirement. Her French colleague faces a surprising social uprising by the now famous "yellow vests." Italy, the country with the seventh-largest economy in the world, is now governed by a fragile coalition whose leaders are so diametrically opposed and whose declarations are so perplexing that we are left not knowing whether to laugh or to cry. It appears that the Italians have decided to see what it's like when government mismanagement is pushed to its most extreme limits. Meanwhile, the Spanish prime minister wasn't even elected to office thanks to his party enjoying a parliamentary majority, but instead arrived there with the help of a tortuous legislative process. In Israel, the only democracy in the Middle East, the prime minister faces indictment for corruption, fraud and other charges. In the coming months Benjamin Netanyahu could either be re-elected or sent to jail.

All these countries seem to be suffering from a type of "political autoimmune disease" — as part of each society wages war on the rest of the social body. The root cause of the disease is the polarization of society and, by extension, its politics. What's also clear is that the disease is spreading and is very contagious. This does not mean that polarization didn't exist before, only that it is becoming much more acute and could prove deadly, as evidenced by all these extreme examples of governmental dysfunction. The closing of important parts of the U.S. government is only the latest and most-revealing consequence of the spreading disease. Indeed, in all likelihood this type of government paralysis and chaos could soon become the norm.

Before, democratic governments managed to reach agreements with their opponents or could organize coalitions that allowed them to make decisions and effectively govern. Now, political rivals often mutate into irreconcilable enemies, which makes agreements, compromises or coalitions impossible. Polarization is a pandemic that has gone global and is now manifesting itself in most of the world's democracies.

To what do we owe this fragmentation of so many societies into diverse groups who are completely intolerant of one another? The increase in economic inequality, growing economic uncertainty and a sense of social injustice are undoubtedly some of the causes of political polarization. The popularity of social medias and the crisis of journalism and the traditional media also help to encourage it. Social medias such as Twitter and Instagram only allow short messages. Such brevity privileges extremism, since the shorter the message, the more radical it must be for it to "go viral." On social medias there is no space, nor time or patience for grays, ambivalence, nuances, or the possibility for conflicting viewpoints to find common ground. Everything is either very white or very black. And, of course, this favors sectarianism and makes it more difficult to reach agreements.

But there is more. Polarization is not only caused by belligerent tweets and resentment over inequality. The rise of anti-politics — or the total repudiation of politics and traditional politicians — is another important catalyst for polarization. Political parties now face a plethora of new competitors ("movements," "collectives," "tides," "factions," NGOs) whose agenda is based on the repudiation of the past and who peddle in the rhetoric of intransigence. Ironically, to retain followers and be electorally competitive, traditional political parties must also adopt positions shaped by anti-politics. In addition, many of these new players entice followers who are attracted to the idea of belonging to political organizations made up of people with whom they share a certain identity. This identity can be religious, ethnic, regional, linguistic, sexual, generational, rural, urban, etc. The assumption is that the identity that unites adherents to a political group generates similar interests and preferences. As identity tends to be more permanent and less fluid than "normal" political positions, this type of political group finds it more difficult to make concessions on issues that concern the identity of its members. This naturally makes them inflexible and, as we know, rigidity and polarization tend to go together.

Political polarization will not be alleviated very soon. Many of its causes are powerful and unstoppable. And now it has been globalized.

The hope is that in the same way that polarization generates paralysis in governments or a toxic political environment, it can also produce changes and ruptures in countries with corrupt, mediocre and ineffective political systems. Like cholesterol, which can be good and bad, there are cases in which political polarization can have positive effects.

I hope there are many.

January 23, 2019

Venezuela's Suicide: Lessons From a Failed State

Consider two Latin American countries. The first is one of the region's oldest and strongest democracies. It boasts a stronger social safety net than any of its neighbors and is making progress on its promise to deliver free health care and higher education to all its citizens. It is a model of social mobility and a magnet for immigrants from across Latin America and Europe. The press is free, and the political system is open; opposing parties compete fiercely in elections and regularly alternate power peacefully. It sidestepped the wave of military juntas that mired some Latin American countries in dictatorship. Thanks to a long political alliance and deep trade and investment ties with the United States, it serves as the Latin American headquarters for a slew of multinational corporations. It has the best infrastructure in South America. It is still unmistakably a developing country, with its share of corruption, injustice and dysfunction, but it is well ahead of other poor countries by almost any measure. The second country is one of Latin America's most impoverished nations and its newest dictatorship. Its schools lie half deserted. The health system has been devastated by decades of underinvestment, corruption and neglect; long-vanquished diseases, such as malaria and measles, have returned. Only a tiny elite can afford enough to eat. An epidemic of violence has made it one of the most murderous countries in the world. It is the source of Latin America's largest refugee migration in a generation, with millions of citizens fleeing in the last few years alone. Hardly anyone (aside from other autocratic governments) recognizes its sham

242

elections, and the small portion of the media not under direct state control still follows the official line for fear of reprisals. By the end of 2018, its economy will have shrunk by about half in the last five years. It is a major cocaine-trafficking hub, and key power brokers in its political elite have been indicted in the United States on drug charges. Prices double every 25 days. The main airport is largely deserted, used by just a handful of holdout airlines bringing few passengers to and from the outside world.

These two countries are in fact the same country, Venezuela, at two different times: the early 1970s and today. The transformation Venezuela has undergone is so radical, so complete and so total that it is hard to believe it took place without a war. What happened to Venezuela? How did things go so wrong?

The short answer is Chavismo. Under the leadership of Hugo Chávez and his successor, Nicolás Maduro, the country has experienced a toxic mix of wantonly destructive policy, escalating authoritarianism, and kleptocracy, all under a level of Cuban influence that often resembles an occupation. Any one of these features would have created huge problems on its own. All of them together hatched a catastrophe. Today, Venezuela is a poor country and a failed and criminalized state run by an autocrat beholden to a foreign power. The remaining options for reversing this situation are slim; the risk now is that hopelessness will push Venezuelans to consider supporting dangerous measures, such as a U.S.-led military invasion, that could make a bad situation worse.

CHAVISMO RISING

To many observers, the explanation for Venezuela's predicament is simple: under Chávez, the country caught a strong case of socialism, and all its subsequent disasters stem from that original sin. But Argentina, Brazil, Chile, Ecuador, Nicaragua and Uruguay have also elected socialist governments in the last 20 years. Although each has struggled politically and economically, none — aside from Nicaragua — has imploded. Instead, several have prospered. If socialism cannot be blamed for Venezuela's demise, perhaps oil is the culprit. The most calamitous stage of Venezuela's crisis has coincided neatly with the sharp fall in international oil prices that started in 2014. But this explanation is also insufficient. Venezuela's decline began four decades ago, not four years ago. By 2003, Venezuela's GDP per worker had already declined by a disastrous 37% from its 1978 peak — precisely the decline that first propelled Chávez into office. Moreover, all of the world's petrostates suffered a serious income shock in 2014 as a result of plummeting oil prices. Only Venezuela could not withstand the pressure. The drivers of Venezuela's failure run deeper. Decades of gradual economic decline opened the way for Chávez, a charismatic demagogue wedded to an outdated ideology, to take power and establish a corrupt autocracy modeled on and beholden to Cuba's dictatorship. Although the crisis preceded Chávez's rise to power, his legacy and Cuba's influence must be at the center of any attempt to explain it. Chávez was born in 1954 into a lower-middle-class family in a rural town. He became a career military officer on a baseball scholarship and was soon secretly recruited into a small leftist movement that spent over a decade plotting to overthrow the democratic regime. He exploded into Venezuela's national consciousness on February 4, 1992, when he led an unsuccessful coup attempt. This misadventure landed him in jail but turned him into an improbable folk hero who embodied growing frustration with a decade of economic stagnation. After receiving a pardon, he launched an outsider bid for the presidency in anchored Venezuelan democracy for 40 years.

What drove the explosion of populist anger that brought Chávez to power? In a word, disappointment. The stellar economic performance Venezuela had experienced for five decades leading up to the 1970s had run out of steam, and the path to the middle class had begun to narrow. As the economists Ricardo Hausmann and Francisco Rodríguez noted, "By 1970 Venezuela had become the richest country in Latin America and one of the 20 richest countries in the world, with a per capita GDP higher than Spain, Greece and Israel and only 13% lower than that of the United Kingdom." But by the early 1980s, a weakened oil market had brought the era of fast growth to an end.

Lower oil revenue meant cuts in public spending, scaled-down social programs, currency devaluation, runaway inflation, a banking crisis, and mounting unemployment and hardship for the poor. Even so, Venezuela's head start was such that when Chávez was elected, it had a per capita income in the region that was second only to Argentina's.

Another common explanation for Chávez's rise holds that it was driven by voters' reaction against economic inequality, which was driven in turn by pervasive corruption. But when Chávez came to power, income was more evenly distributed in Venezuela than in any neighboring country. If inequality determined electoral outcomes, then a Chávez-like candidate would have been more probable in Brazil, Chile or Colombia, where the gap between the well-off and everyone else was larger.

Venezuela may not have been collapsing in 1998, but it had been stagnating and, in some respects, backsliding, as oil prices slumped to just $11 per barrel, leading to a new round of austerity. Chávez was brilliant at mining the resulting discontent. His eloquent denunciations of inequality, exclusion, poverty, corruption and the entrenched political elite struck a chord with struggling voters, who felt nostalgic for an earlier, more prosperous period. The inept and complacent traditional political and business elite who opposed Chávez never came close to matching his popular touch.

Venezuelans gambled on Chávez. What they got was not just an outsider bent on upending the status quo but also a Latin American leftist icon who soon had followers all around the world. Chávez became both a spoiler and the star attraction at global summits, as well as a brilliant leader of the burgeoning global wave of anti-American sentiment sparked by U.S. President George W. Bush's invasion of Iraq. At home, shaped by his career in the military, Chávez had a penchant for centralizing power and a profound intolerance of dissent. He set out to neuter not just opposition politicians but also political allies who dared question his policies. His collaborators quickly saw which way the wind was blowing: policy debates disappeared, and the government pursued a radical agenda with little forethought and no real scrutiny. A 2001 presidential decree on land reform, which Chávez handed down with no consultation or debate, was a taste of things to come. It broke up large commercial farms and turned them over to peasant cooperatives that lacked the technical know-how, management skills or access to capital to produce at scale. Food production collapsed. And in sector after sector, the Chávez government enacted similarly self-defeating policies. It expropriated foreign-owned oil ventures without compensation and gave them to political appointees who lacked the technical expertise to run them. It nationalized utilities and the main telecommunications operator, leaving Venezuela with chronic water and electricity shortages and some of the slowest internet connection speeds in the world. It seized steel companies, causing production to fall from 480,000 metric tons per month before nationalization, in 2008, to effectively nothing today. Similar results followed the seizure of aluminum companies, mining firms, hotels and airlines.

In one expropriated company after another, state administrators stripped assets and loaded payrolls with Chávez cronies. When they inevitably ran into financial problems, they appealed to the government, which was able to bail them out. By 2004, oil prices had spiked again, filling government coffers with petrodollars, which Chávez spent without constraints, controls or accountability. On top of that were the easy loans from China, which was happy to extend credit to Venezuela in exchange for a guaranteed supply of crude oil. By importing whatever the hollowed-out Venezuelan economy failed to produce and borrowing to finance a consumption boom, Chávez was able to temporarily shield the public from the impact of his disastrous policies and to retain substantial popularity.

The relationship between Cuba and Venezuela became more than an alliance.

But not everyone was convinced. Oil industry workers were among the first to sound the alarm about Chávez's authoritarian tendencies. They went on strike in 2002 and 2003, demanding a new presidential election. In response to the protests, Chávez fired almost half of the work force in the state-run oil company and imposed an arcane currency-exchange-control regime. The system morphed into a cesspool of corruption, as regime cronies realized that arbitraging between the state-authorized exchange rate and the black market could yield fortunes overnight. This arbitrage racket created an extraordinarily wealthy elite of government-connected kleptocrats. As this budding kleptocracy perfected the art of siphoning off oil proceeds into its own pockets, Venezuelan store shelves grew bare. It was all painfully predictable — and widely predicted. But the louder local and international experts sounded the alarm, the more the government clung to its agenda. To Chávez, dire warnings from technocrats were a sign that the revolution was on the right track.

Passing the torch

In 2011, Chávez was diagnosed with cancer. Top oncologists in Brazil and the United States offered to treat him. But he opted instead to search for a cure in Cuba, the country he trusted not only to treat him but also to be discreet about his condition. As his illness progressed, his dependence on Havana deepened, and the mystery about the real state of his health grew. On December 8, 2012, an ailing Chávez made one final television appearance to ask Venezuelans to make Maduro, then vice president, his successor. For the next three months, Venezuela was governed spectrally and by remote control: decrees emanated from Havana bearing Chávez's signature, but no one saw him, and speculation was rife that he had already died. When Chávez's death was finally announced, on March 5, 2013, the only thing that was clear amid the atmosphere of secrecy and concealment was that Venezuela's next leader would carry on the tradition of Cuban influence. Chávez had long looked to Cuba as a blueprint for revolution, and he turned to Cuban President Fidel Castro for advice at critical junctures.

In return, Venezuela sent oil: energy aid to Cuba (in the form of 115,000 barrels a day sold at a deep discount) was worth nearly $1 billion a year to Havana. The relationship between Cuba and Venezuela became more than an alliance. It has been, as Chávez himself once put it, "a merger of two revolutions." (Unusually, the senior partner in the alliance is poorer and smaller than the junior partner but so much more competent that it dominates the relationship.) Cuba is careful to keep its footprint light: it conducts most of its consultations in Havana rather than Caracas. It did not escape anyone's attention that the leader Chávez anointed to succeed him had devoted his life to the cause of Cuban communism. As a teenager, Maduro joined a fringe pro-Cuban Marxist party in Caracas. In his 20s, instead of going to university, he sought training in Havana's school for international cadres to become a professional revolutionary. As Chávez's foreign minister from 2006 to 2013, he had seldom called attention to himself: only his unfailing loyalty to Chávez, and to Cuba, propelled his ascent to the top. Under his leadership, Cuba's influence in Venezuela has become pervasive. He has stacked key government posts with activists trained in Cuban organizations, and Cubans have come to occupy sensitive roles within the Venezuelan regime. The daily intelligence briefs Maduro consumes, for instance, are produced not by Venezuelans but by Cuban intelligence officers. With Cuban guidance, Maduro has deeply curtailed economic freedoms and erased all remaining traces of liberalism from the country's politics and institutions. He has continued and expanded Chávez's practice of jailing, exiling, or banning from political life opposition leaders who became too popular or hard to co-opt. Julio Borges, a key opposition leader, fled into exile to avoid being jailed, and Leopoldo López, the opposition's most charismatic leader, has been moved back and forth between a military prison and house arrest. Over 100 political prisoners linger in jails, and reports of torture are common. Periodic elections have become farcical, and the government has stripped the opposition-controlled National Assembly of all powers. Maduro has deepened Venezuela's alliances with a number of anti-American and anti-Western regimes, turning to Russia for weapons, cybersecurity, and expertise in oil production; to China for financing and infrastructure; to Belarus for homebuilding; and to Iran for car production. As Maduro broke the last remaining links in Venezuela's traditional alliances with Washington and other Latin American democracies, he lost access to sound economic advice. He dismissed the consensus of economists from across the political spectrum: although they warned about inflation, Maduro chose to rely on the advice of Cuba and fringe Marxist policy advisers who assured him that there would be no consequences to making up budget with freshly minted money. Inevitably, a devastating bout of hyperinflation ensued.

A toxic combination of Cuban influence, runaway corruption, the dismantling of democratic checks and balances, and sheer incompetence has kept Venezuela locked into catastrophic economic policies. As monthly inflation rates top three digits, the government improvises policy responses that are bound to make the situation even worse.

ANATOMY OF A COLLAPSE

Nearly all oil-producing liberal democracies, such as Norway, the United Kingdom and the United States, were democracies before they became oil producers. Autocracies that have found oil, such as Angola, Brunei, Iran and Russia, have been unable to make the leap to liberal democracy. For four decades, Venezuela seemed to have miraculously beaten these odds — it democratized and liberalized in 1958, decades after finding oil.

But the roots of Venezuelan liberal democracy turned out to be shallow. Two decades of bad economics decimated the popularity of the traditional political parties, and a charismatic demagogue, riding the wave of an oil boom, stepped into the breach. Under these unusual conditions, he was able to sweep away the whole structure of democratic checks and balances in just a few years.

When the decade-long oil price boom ended in 2014, Venezuela lost not just the oil revenue on which Chávez's popularity and international influence had depended but also access to foreign credit markets. This left the country with a massive debt overhang: the loans taken out during the oil boom still had to be serviced, although from a much-reduced income stream. Venezuela ended up with politics that are typical of autocracies that discover oil: a predatory, extractive oligarchy that ignores regular people as long they stay quiet and that violently suppresses them when they protest.

The resulting crisis is morphing into the worst humanitarian disaster in memory in the Western Hemisphere. Exact figures for Venezuela's GDP collapse are notoriously difficult to come by, but economists estimate that it is comparable to the 40 percent contraction of Syria's GDP since 2012, following the outbreak of its devastating civil war. Hyperinflation has reached one million percent per year, pushing 61 percent of Venezuelans to live in extreme poverty, with 89 percent of those surveyed saying they do not have the money to buy food for their families and 64 percent reporting they have lost an average of 11 kilograms (about 24 pounds) in body weight due to hunger. About ten percent of the population — 2.6 million Venezuelans — have fled to neighboring countries.

The Venezuelan state has mostly given up on providing public services such as health care, education and even policing. Heavy-handed, repressive violence is the only thing left that Venezuelans can expect consistently from the government. In the face of mass protests in 2014 and 2017, the government responded with thousands of arrests, brutal beatings and torture, and the killing of over 130 protesters. Meanwhile, criminal business is increasingly conducted not in defiance of the state, or even simply in cahoots with the state, but directly through it. Drug trafficking has emerged alongside oil production and currency arbitrage as a key source of profits to those close to the ruling elite, with high-ranking officials and members of the president's family facing narcotics charges in the United States. A small connected elite has also stolen national assets to a unprecedented degree. In August, a series of regime-connected businessmen were indicted in U.S. federal courts for attempting to launder over $1.2 billion in illegally obtained funds — just one of a dizzying array of illegal scams that are part of the looting of Venezuela. The entire southeastern quadrant of the country has become an exploitative illegal mining camp, where desperate people displaced from cities by hunger try their luck in unsafe mines run by criminal gangs under military protection. All over the country, prison gangs, working in partnership with government security forces, run lucrative extortion rackets that make them the de facto civil authority. The offices of the Treasury, the central bank and the national oil company have become laboratories where complicated financial crimes are hatched. As Venezuela's economy has collapsed, the lines separating the state from criminal enterprises have all but disappeared.

THE VENEZUELAN DILEMMA

Whenever U.S. President Donald Trump meets with a Latin American leader, he insists that the region do something about the Venezuelan crisis. Trump has prodded his own national security team for "strong" alternatives, at one point stating that there are "many options" for Venezuela and that he is "not going to rule out the military option." Republican Senator Marco Rubio of Florida has similarly flirted with a military response. Secretary of Defense James Mattis, however, echoed a common sentiment of the U.S. security apparatus by publicly stating, "The Venezuelan crisis is not a military matter." All of Venezuela's neighboring countries have also voiced their opposition to an armed attack on Venezuela.

And rightly so. Trump's fantasies of military invasion are deeply misguided and extremely dangerous. Although a U.S.-led military assault would likely have no problem overthrowing Maduro in short order, what comes next could be far worse, as the Iraqis and the Libyans know only too well: when outside powers overthrow autocrats sitting atop failing states, open-ended chaos is much more likely to follow than stability — let alone democracy.

Nonetheless, the United States will continue to face pressure to find some way of arresting Venezuela's collapse. Each initiative undertaken so far has served only to highlight that there is, in reality, little the United States can do. During the Obama administration, U.S. diplomats attempted to engage the regime directly. But negotiations proved futile. Maduro used internationally mediated talks to neutralize massive street protests: protest leaders would call off demonstrations during the talks, but Chavista negotiators would only stonewall, parceling out minor concessions designed to divide their opponents while they themselves prepared for the next wave of repression. The United States and Venezuela's neighbors seem to have finally grasped that, as things stand, negotiations only play into Maduro's hands.

Some have suggested using harsh economic sanctions to pressure Maduro to step down. The United States has tried this. It passed several rounds of sanctions, under both the Obama and Trump administrations, to prevent the regime from issuing new debt and to hamper the financial operation of the state-owned oil company. Together with Canada and the EU, Washington has also put in place sanctions against specific regime officials, freezing their assets abroad and imposing travel restrictions. But such measures are redundant: if the task is to destroy the Venezuelan economy, no set of sanctions will be as effective as the regime itself. The same is true for an oil blockade: oil production is already in a free fall.

The other Latin American countries are finally grasping that Venezuela's instability will inevitably spill across their borders.

Washington can sharpen its policy on the margins. For one thing, it needs to put more emphasis on a Cuban track: little can be achieved without Havana's help, meaning that Venezuela needs to be front and center in every contact Washington and its allies have with Havana.

The United States can cast a wider net in countering corruption, preventing not just crooked officials but also their front men and families from enjoying the fruits of corruption, drug trafficking and embezzlement. It could also work to turn the existing U.S. arms embargo into a global one. The Maduro regime must be constrained in its authoritarian intent with policies that communicate clearly to its cronies that continuing to aid the regime will leave them isolated in Venezuela and that turning on the regime is, therefore, the only way out. Yet the prospects of such a strategy succeeding are dim.

After a long period of dithering, the other Latin American countries are finally grasping that Venezuela's instability will inevitably spill across their borders. As the center-left "pink wave" of the early years of this century recedes, a new cohort of more conservative leaders in Argentina, Brazil, Chile, Colombia and Peru has tipped the regional balance against Venezuela's dictatorship, but the lack of actionable options bedevils them, as well. Traditional diplomacy hasn't worked and has even backfired. But so has pressure. For example, in 2017,

Latin American countries threatened to suspend Venezuela's membership in the Organization of American States. The regime responded by withdrawing from the organization unilaterally, displaying just how little it cares about traditional diplomatic pressure.

Venezuela's exasperated neighbors are increasingly seeing the crisis through the prism of the refugee problem it has created; they are anxious to stem the flow of malnourished people fleeing Venezuela and placing new strains on their social programs. As a populist backlash builds against the influx of Venezuelan refugees, some Latin American countries appear tempted to slam the door shut — a temptation they must resist, as it would be a historic mistake that would only worsen the crisis. The reality is that Latin American countries have no idea what to do about Venezuela. There may be nothing they can do, save accepting refugees, which will at least help alleviate the suffering of the Venezuelan people.

POWER TO THE PEOPLE

Today, the regime is so solidly entrenched that a change of faces is much more likely than a change of system. Perhaps Maduro will be pushed out by a slightly less incompetent leader who is able to render Cuban hegemony in Venezuela more sustainable. Such an outcome would merely mean a more stable foreign-dominated petro-kleptocracy, not a return to democracy. And even if opposition forces — or a U.S.-led armed attack — somehow managed to replace Maduro with an entirely new government, the agenda would be daunting. A successor regime would need to reduce the enormous role the military plays in all areas of the public sector. It would have to start from scratch in restoring basic services in health care, education and law enforcement. It would have to rebuild the oil industry and stimulate growth in other economic sectors. It would need to get rid of the drug dealers, prison racketeers, predatory miners, wealthy criminal financiers and extortionists who have latched on to every part of the state. And it would have to make all these changes in the context of a toxic, anarchic political environment and a grave economic crisis.

Given the scale of these obstacles, Venezuela is likely to remain unstable for a long time to come. The immediate challenge for its citizens and their leaders, as well as for the international community, is to contain the impact of the nation's decline. For all the misery they have experienced, the Venezuelan people have never stopped struggling against misrule. As of this summer, Venezuelans were still staging hundreds of protests each month. Most of them are local, grass-roots affairs with little political leadership, but they show a people with the will to fight for themselves.

Is that enough to nudge the country away from its current grim path? Probably not. Hopelessness is driving more and more Venezuelans to fantasize about a Trump-led military intervention, which would offer a fervently desired *deus ex machina* for a long-suffering people.

But this amounts to an ill-advised revenge fantasy, not a serious strategy. Rather than a military invasion, Venezuelans' best hope is to ensure that the flickering embers of protest and social dissent are not extinguished and that resistance to dictatorship is sustained. Desperate though the prospect may seem, this tradition of protest could one day lay the foundations for the recovery of civic institutions and democratic practices. It won't be simple, and it won't be quick. Bringing a state back from the brink of failure never is.

January 4, 2019

2018

A Booming Market for Charlatans

Sixty years ago, CBS had a hit western called *Trackdown*. In one prophetic episode titled "The End of the World," a huckster arrives in a quintessential western town and summons the townspeople to come hear his urgent news.

A "cosmic explosion" is about to take place that will end the world, he says. But he can save them. Him and only him. To survive they must build a wall around their homes and use special umbrellas that deflect the fireballs that will rain down from the sky — and which he will sell them. The name of the quack that stars in this episode? Trump. Walter Trump.

In the episode — which is available on YouTube — Hoby Gilman, a Texas Ranger who represents common sense, tries to persuade his neighbors to stop listening to Trump. "How long are you going to let this conman walk around town? He's a fraud!" he tells them. Just like his real-life namesake half a century later, the Trump from the TV western deploys lawyers to neutralize his critics and rivals: Walter Trump threatens to sue Texas Ranger Gilman.

Charlatans and conmen have always existed. They are scoundrels who, leveraging their skills for persuasion, manage to sell some type of product, remedy, elixir, business or ideology to unsuspecting people who believe that the charlatan will — without much effort — redeem their sorrows, alleviate their pains or make them wealthy.

Lately, the market for quackery — especially in politics — has reached new heights. The demand for (and supply of) simple solutions to complex problems has skyrocketed. Demand is being driven by one crisis after another, while social medias are boosting the quacks' ability to supply simplistic solutions to large audiences.

The current plethora of global crises is the result of powerful forces: technology, globalization, crime, corruption, bad governments, racism, xenophobia, economic instability,and inequality, among others. The result is the proliferation of societies where many people feel rightly aggrieved, frustrated and fearful of the future. They make up an irresistible market for charlatans who offer simple, instant and painless solutions.

In the 1958 television series, an anonymous narrator tells us what happened: "The people were ready to believe. Like sheep they ran to the slaughterhouse. And waiting for them was the high priest of fraud."

Half a century later, these phrases are ever more relevant. There are more and more societies willing to vote for the candidate who makes the simplest promise and who, in addition, says he will break from the past and take power away from the "establishment."

The tricksters of today are, in essence, similar to those who have always existed, only now they have access to technology that gives them heretofore unimaginable opportunities. They are digital charlatans.

The clandestine intervention of one country in the elections of another nation is a good example of old practices that have been "super-powered." Today's digital charlatans operate through online bots. Bots use software algorithms to disseminate targeted information through social media to millions of users based on certain characteristics such as age, sex, race, location, education, religion, social class, political preferences, habits of consumption, etc.

Like all good charlatans, bot administrators know how to identify people prone to believe them. Before, hucksters used their intuition to identify their victims; now they use sophisticated algorithms and micro-targeting. Once their victims are identified, the creators of the bots send messages that confirm and reinforce their victims' beliefs, fears, hopes and prejudices. Digital charlatans know how to stimulate certain behaviors in their target audience (vote for a candidate and defame their rival, support a certain group and attack another, disseminate false information, join a group, protest, make donations, etc.).

These new digital technologies have another interesting characteristic: they can be simultaneously global and individualized. Their makers can concurrently contact millions of people and make each one of them feel that they are interacting in a direct, personal and almost intimate way with someone who shares their values, goals and way of thinking.

This is exactly what happened in the U.S. elections that took Donald Trump to the White House. The consensus of the U.S. intelligence community (as well as those of other countries) is that this was a brilliantly designed and executed operation financed — at very low cost — by the Russian government, under Vladimir Putin's direct supervision.

But it would be a mistake to assume that digital charlatans are only meddling with elections in the United States. Some 27 countries have likely been victims of political interference orchestrated by the Kremlin. Both in the crisis of Spain's Catalonia region and with Brexit, intense bot activity and other forms of digital manipulation were detected, and the evidence shows they were controlled or influenced by the Russian government. The Kremlin has set out to sow chaos and confusion and to sharpen social conflicts in pursuit of a broader goal: to weaken its Western rivals.

In fact, one of the most revealing facts about the impact of the modern charlatans was the Google searches after Brexit. That is, after the United Kingdom decided — by a margin of only 4% — to get a divorce from the rest of Europe. "What is Brexit?" was one of the most frequently searched-for questions after the referendum was decided. Keep in mind that many of the claims and data used by the pro-Brexit campaign were known to be false. It didn't matter: just like the townsfolk in the 1950s television series, "the people were ready to believe."

The same goes for Donald Trump's mendacity. According to The Washington Post, Trump made a staggering 7,645 false or misleading claims in 710 days as president, about 11 a day. Last October, speaking at a rally in Johnson City, Tennessee, the president made a whopping

84 false statements. This fact-checking by what he calls the mainstream media doesn't seem to bother the president, as he knows that, like his old television namesake, "the people are ready to believe him."

All this points to a regrettable reality: the people who get taken in by charlatans are just as guilty or even more guilty than the charlatans themselves when they allow their society to support bad ideas, choose bad rulers or believe their lies. Often the followers are irresponsibly uninformed, lackadaisical and willing to believe in any proposition that seduces them, however preposterous.

This has to change. As we leave 2018 behind, we must face the fact that we have made life too easy for charlatans and we have been too accommodating of their followers. We must rebuild the capacity of society to differentiate between truth and lies, between facts confirmed by incontrovertible evidence and propositions that merely make us feel good, but offer solutions that are not really solutions at all or, worse, aggravate the problem.

We need more education about the uses and abuses of information technology and we have to accept that democracy requires more effort than just casting a vote every few years. We have to be better informed, keep an open mind to ideas that are at odds with ours, and develop the critical sense that alerts us when we are being manipulated. The need for governments to take action and create rules and institutions that shield consumers from the predatory behaviors of social media companies is becoming increasingly apparent.

Above all, we must develop the ability to differentiate between well-meaning, decent leaders and the charlatans who are out to con us.

December 30, 2018

What FIFA and the Vatican Have in Common

Few human activities arouse as much passion as religion and sports. Within Christianity — the world's largest religion — the Catholic Church has the greatest number of adherents, while soccer has the most fans of any sport. The Vatican rules the Catholic Church, and FIFA — the International Federation of Association Football — leads global soccer. Both are important institutions even though Pope John Paul II once famously clarified that "out of all the unimportant things, football is the most important."

The origins, histories and *raison d'être* of these two institutions could not be more different. The Vatican is a sovereign state that has been around for centuries while FIFA was founded in Switzerland a mere 114 years ago. Nevertheless, despite their profound differences, they also have interesting similarities.

For example, they share an odd paradox in that both are essentially European institutions, but most of their followers live in less-developed countries. And neither of them has any women in their leadership. And the global standard-bearers of Catholicism and soccer are Argentines: Pope Francis and Lionel Messi.

Both organizations control vast financial resources. Although the Holy See has an immense artistic and real-estate heritage, its main sources of income come from investments, rents from its property holdings, and donations from individuals, dioceses and other institutions. Its finances are opaque, but an investigation by The Economist concluded that in 2010 the budget of the Catholic

Church in the United States was $170 billion, most of it channeled to charitable organizations.

FIFA's income is derived from broadcast rights, product merchandising, ticket sales and investments. Between 2015 and 2018 these revenues totaled more than $5.5 billion.

In recent years both the Vatican and FIFA have found themselves in legal hot water. In May 2015, more than a dozen plainclothes policemen stormed the Baur au Lac, a luxury hotel in Zurich, where the annual meeting of FIFA officials was taking place. Seven of them were arrested. A few months later, the scene was repeated. At 6 a.m. on December 3, 2015, the Swiss police arrived at the Baur au Lac again and arrested more members of the FIFA leadership. While the police who conducted the raids were Swiss, they were acting at the request of U.S. authorities. The FBI had been investigating corruption in FIFA for three years. The U.S. Department of Justice accused FIFA of "unbridled, systemic and entrenched corruption." FIFA executives were receiving illegal payments in exchange for voting in favor of a particular country that aspired to host the World Cup, or wanted broadcast rights or special marketing privileges.

On the initiatives of a U.S. attorney in New York, the FBI and other U.S. government agencies, several FIFA leaders were extradited, tried and sentenced to prison. The leadership of the organization was replaced. The corruption scandal led several other countries to launch their own investigations. It is interesting to note that the revelations of corruption in FIFA did not surprise those familiar with its inner workings. It was an open secret that many of its decisions were for sale.

What was a surprise is that those who ended up confronting FIFA's culture of corruption were the prosecutors, judges and law enforcement agencies of the United States — a country where soccer does not yet have the weight in society that it enjoys almost everywhere else.

The legal problems of the Vatican are well known and have interesting similarities with those of FIFA, even though its corruption was financial while the Catholic Church was mired in sexual abuse scandals.

In both there is a long history of unacceptable behavior on the part of some of its members, and an equally long history of denial of the problem, concealment, tolerance, obstruction and impunity. Again, and despite the fact that Catholicism is not the leading religious denomination in the United States, it was the authorities of that country that most aggressively confronted sexual abuse in the Church.

A recent article in The Washington Post notes that "the swift and sweeping response by civil authorities contrasts sharply with the Vatican's comparatively glacial pace." The Illinois Attorney General has said that "the Catholic Church has proven that it cannot police itself. And civil authorities can't let the Church hide child sexual-abuse allegations as personnel matters. They're crimes. We need a full accounting of the Church." In the United States, 15 states have initiated extensive criminal investigations into sexual abuse. In contrast, according to statistics, in European countries where Catholics are the majority of the population, silence and impunity remain the norm. But this is about to change.

Not only because civil society is more activated and empowered, information is more accessible and crimes are more difficult to hide. But also because, in soccer as in the Catholic Church, the followers are much better than their leaders.

December 5, 2018

It Wasn't the Caravan or the Economy,
It Was the Women

Donald Trump bet on the caravan and lost the House of Representatives. While the president was busy using every campaign stop to frighten his supporters about an imminent invasion by a caravan of Central American refugees, American women were getting out to vote for women candidates.

In the wake of the mid-term elections, two things have become clear. The first is that nobody talks that much about the caravan anymore, not even Trump. The second is that, as a result of their recent electoral victories, there are now more women in positions of power in the United States than ever before.

This milestone was made possible by President Trump himself. His policies, his behavior, and even his style, have mobilized millions of women against him. As soon as he was sworn in, they began to organize massive women's marches. Then they organized themselves so that their grievances would be heard. Next, thousands of them decided to run for elected office — they ran for Congress, for governor, for attorney general and for seats in the state legislatures. Then, finally, they voted *en masse*. And they won.

So far, this wave of women's politicization has primarily benefited the Democratic Party. Why? There are two reasons. First, for decades the Republican Party has been suffering from the so-called "gender gap," that is, a chronic inability to attract women to their ranks. Second, as the polls and election results indicate, Donald

Trump's "seizure" of the Republican Party has widened the gender gap even further.

Another surprise was that women's issues had more weight in the election than the economy. And an even bigger surprise was that Trump devoted much more time and attention to the caravan than to the country's buoyant economic situation. Right now the U.S. economy is expanding, unemployment is at its lowest level in decades, and wages are increasing at a rate not seen since 2009. Trump, of course, always touted the economy in his campaign speeches, but what always got the most enthusiastic applause from his followers were his vitriolic criticisms of immigrants, journalists ("the enemy of the people") and the other divisive issues that the president so skillfully exploits.

In 1992, James Carville, an advisor to then-presidential candidate Bill Clinton, coined the phrase, "It's the economy, stupid," to remind his communication team to always emphasize the weak state of the economy at the time. The phrase ended up being the campaign slogan and it has been adopted as a kind of electoral mantra: Don't get distracted by other issues. The economic situation is the key to winning (or losing) an election.

We will never know what would have happened if Trump had respected this golden rule of electoral lore and concentrated his attention on celebrating the country's economic prosperity instead of placing his emphasis on the issues that divide American society. There is no doubt that his agenda and his polarizing discourse served to motivate his base and helped the Republican Party increase its majority in the Senate. But there is also no doubt that his policies and messages also inflamed and mobilized his opposition. Despite all the president's efforts, Republicans lost the House of Representatives by a significant margin.

Finally, a revealing surprise of the mid-term elections was the disappearance of any meaningful debate about one pressing national issue: gun control.

In February, a 19-year-old boy entered a high school in Parkland, Florida, and killed 17 people and wounded 17 others, most of them students. Some of the survivors turned out to be intelligent, organized and very effective communicators. In the days and weeks following the tragedy, this group of young people managed to create a broad and intense national discussion about the need to regulate the purchase and possession of firearms. The intensity of the debate seemed to foretell that the issue would certainly linger and end up being a crucial factor in the midterm elections. But it was not to be so. While it is true that several Democratic candidates who dared to openly confront the NRA, the powerful gun lobby, were elected, the discussion about the need to reform the nation's gun laws was conspicuous in its absence.

The leadership of the Democratic Party decided to center the campaign on Trump and, especially, on the need to protect the Affordable Care Act from the Republicans' intention to dismantle some of its most sensitive provisions, such as the guaranteed coverage of pre-existing conditions, for example. Clearly this strategy worked. But the national conversation about gun control that can lead to stronger legislation is still pending.

While a broad debate on the ease with which firearms can be obtained may be on hold, this very unique American tragedy continues unabated. The day after the elections, an armed man entered a bar in California and, without saying a word, killed a dozen people and then committed suicide. So far this year there have been 307 similar attacks in the United States.

Will the newly elected contingent of women abandon the peaceful coexistence with the gun lobby that the majority of American politicians have had until now?

November 14, 2018

Forgiving Trump

On Tuesday, millions of Americans will cast their votes for Donald Trump. Technically, of course, they won't be voting directly for the sitting president, but rather for the senators, representatives, governors and state legislators that he supports. Yet this election will undoubtedly be a referendum on Donald Trump.

Although the polls predict that the president will not do as well as in the last election, the polls also find that he has the support of close to 40% of voters.

It's a shocking number. It means that 40% of Americans forgive Trump for behavior that should be considered unforgivable in any decent world: from the constant, unabashed lying to the inhuman cruelty of some of his decisions. To be sure, many Trump supporters feel that there is nothing to forgive. They accept, and even celebrate, the president's behavior, even when he says that being a celebrity entitles men to grope any woman they want.

Any number of theories has been put forward to explain why some people are so strongly attracted to charismatic politicians and why they so often support them unconditionally. They run the gamut from the psychological (a search for identity or dignity) to the economic (a response to increasing inequality) to the international (a backlash to globalization) to the sociological (racism).

Whichever of these you prefer, it is also true that many support Trump because they like his policies and are willing to overlook actions they would criticize in other circumstances in order to see them enacted. Take the tax cut, for instance. The rich, who hate paying taxes, were delighted with the cuts and are showing their gratitude to Trump by keeping mum about behavior they should abhor.

Another example is deregulation. For many business leaders, the huge benefits they have received because of Trump's elimination of regulations that were curbing their autonomy or increasing their costs are seen as a fair trade for having him in the White House. They are willing to forgive any trespass, as long as their businesses get deregulated. Many are happy that the lobbyists who were previously paid to influence the government have now become the government. Trump has put a good many of them in charge of the agencies responsible for regulating the very companies for which they previously worked. And to which they will surely return at the end of their "public service."

But support for Trump is not just motivated by financial interests. Evangelical groups whose pastors regularly denounce the same behaviors that Trump habitually exhibits (infidelity, mendacity, greed, materialism, cruelty, egomania, etc.) are an enthusiastic part of his base. Seeing babies separated from their mothers on the border and then lost in the black hole of an insensitive U.S. bureaucracy made no dent in the evangelical leaders' support for Trump. Ignoring the president's vices and sins is a price they are willing to pay as long as he promotes initiatives that make abortion and same-sex marriage difficult or minimize the presence of Charles Darwin's ideas in America's classrooms.

That citizens vote for candidates who represent their particular interests or reflect their values is nothing new. That's democracy. The big surprise is that Donald Trump has kept the support of voters who stand to lose out from his policies. His popular tax cut, for instance, is deeply regressive. It disproportionately benefits a very wealthy minority and penalizes the middle and working classes, groups that make up the vast majority of Trump's followers. Many of the regulations Trump has eliminated were designed to protect low-income consumers from the abusive practices of big companies. The same goes for the health care reform put forth by Barack Obama and now under withering attack from Trump, who has made every effort to dismantle and sabotage it. Again, the great paradox is that those who will lose the most from a gutted health care system are the Trump followers who need it the most.

The list of Trump's actions that require his supporters' forgiveness is long and growing. The list of his associates in business, politics and government who are being tried or have already been convicted of crimes has revealed a vast criminal ecosystem revolving around the president. But all that, too, might be forgiven by his followers, thus affirming Donald Trump's own appalling statement from January 2016: "I could stand in the middle of Fifth Avenue and shoot somebody and I wouldn't lose voters."

This Tuesday, we'll see if that is really true.

November 5, 2018

Mexico's AMLO and Brazil's Bolsonaro:
Very Different... and Very Similar

One has already been elected, the other looks certain to be. The first is president-elect of Mexico, Andrés Manuel López Obrador (known by his acronym AMLO), and the second is Jair Bolsonaro (often referred to as Bolso), the front runner in Brazil's upcoming second-round election. Their success says a lot about how the world is changing.

The differences between them are profound, certainly, but it's their similarities that are most revealing. Their roots, political careers, ideologies, styles and platforms are poles apart. López Obrador is a man of the left, Bolsonaro of the right. AMLO has antagonized big business, Bolso promises to liberalize the economy. The Brazilian has declared a no-holds-barred war on crime, while the Mexican talks about amnesty. Bolsonaro liked the military while López Obrador likes the labor unions. The media tend to paint Bolsonaro as homophobic, misogynist, sexist and racist. Naturally, he is against abortion and same-sex marriage. AMLO, on the other hand, avoids these issues altogether, saying that on decisions on these matters he will "consult the people." Jair Bolsonaro admires Donald Trump while Andrés Manuel López Obrador is cautious with his words about Trump despite the fact that the American president often refers to the Mexicans with disdain and derision.

On Venezuela, the Mexican president-elect has taken great care to avoid expressing sympathy for Hugo Chávez and his Bolivarian revolution, something that many in his party — historically known for their solidarity with the Venezuelan regime — have not been shy about. Many in AMLO's court defend Caracas' current rulers. In one of his first statements after the election, Marcelo Ebrard, López Obrador's incoming secretary of foreign affairs, announced that his government will treat the Venezuelan crisis as an internal affair and therefore will not intervene in its domestic politics. In sharp contrast, General Hamilton Mourão, Bolsonaro's running mate, said that they support a regime change in Venezuela and will not recognize Nicolás Maduro's government.

Yet, the similarities between AMLO and Bolsonaro are more interesting than their differences. Both owe their success at the polls to global trends that favor disruptive candidates who know how to persuade voters that they have nothing to do with the traditional politics and politicians of their country. Both have crafted a persona as outsiders, as radical voices largely excluded by the ruling political elites and, until now, victimized by those AMLO calls "the power mafia."

Their campaigns are based on ruthless attacks on a political system that they promise to uproot. That, of course, is not true. Both are long-standing professional politicians. AMLO was a long-time member of Mexico's hegemonic Institutional Revolutionary Party (PRI). For five years he ruled the sprawling, populous capital, Mexico City, and has been a presidential candidate in each of the last three elections. Bolsonaro, for his part, has been a congressman for almost three decades and three of his sons are already successful politicians who have won congressional seats.

The fact that AMLO and Bolso present themselves as "anti-establishment" candidates is not surprising. That is exactly what you have to do to win elections these days. It's a global trend. Anti-politics reigns: the broad-brush rejection of all leaders and parties that have been close to power. It's not surprising either that politicians are passing themselves off as newcomers to the scene. They want to put as much distance as possible between themselves and the incumbent politicians who have so enraged voters. The new mantra, which is now almost universal, is "kick all the rascals out!"

From this perspective, AMLO and Bolso are normal candidates.

Unfortunately, these days it has also become normal for the winning candidate to have a deep disdain for the rules and institutions that limit the power of the president. In country after country, we are seeing efforts to undermine the independence of congress, stack the judiciary with "friendly" judges, attack the media while creating alternative media channels under their control, as well as spread frequent and abundant lies that deepen existing social divisions, create new ones and polarize voters. They are, sadly, part of the political milieu that has become popular everywhere: from Hungary and Thailand, to the United States and Turkey.

Bolso and AMLO have done and said things that reveal that, in this way too, they are normal politicians.

This worldwide onslaught on the checks and balances that limit executive power benefits greatly from the deep disappointment that voters have with democracy. More than half of Brazilians say they would accept an undemocratic government if it "solves problems." The same sentiments have become common in Mexico.

Brazil and Mexico have fallen in love with a very dangerous political narrative. It's the story of the proverbial strong man: a fresh and uncompromised figure willing to fight corruption, defend "the people" and give hope to an entire society traumatized by terrible levels of graft and violence. Promises of salvation garner more votes than talk of institutions that keep presidential power in check and protect citizens. It's a lesson Bolso and AMLO have learned all too well.

October 22, 2018

What if Money Disappears?

What's going to happen to money? Until recently the idea of doing without bills and coins seemed like science fiction. But today, it's a reality. In many countries, money — as we know it — is becoming obsolete. Wallets are being replaced by our ubiquitous smartphones, while banknotes and metal coins are being replaced by digital ones and zeros.

In Sweden, for example, 93% of transactions are made through direct transfers using a mobile phone app called Swish. It allows even small amounts to be transferred between individuals instantly and at very low cost. But it's not only the prosperous and technologically savvy Swedes who make do more and more without old-fashioned money. China, Kenya, Tanzania, Bangladesh and India have also made huge strides in the use of electronic payments through mobile phones. Increasingly, the use of cash is becoming an anachronism: relying on bits of colored paper as a means of payment doesn't feel very 21st century.

For governments, the advantages of the widespread use of technologies such as Swish are obvious: every transaction is registered and can be tracked by, among others, the authorities. For those who launder money, evade taxes, traffic drugs or finance terrorists, the digital trail left by digital money transactions is a problem. In contrast, for hackers who know how to break into an account and transfer funds to another owner, these new technologies open up immense opportunities.

The rise of cryptocurrencies, for example, brings unprecedented challenges. These virtual currencies (or digital assets) are complex encrypted algorithms that can be used as a verifiable and guaranteed method of payment. The most common is the ubiquitous Bitcoin, although there are other cryptocurrencies — 2,000 others, in fact, and growing.

The most transformative feature of these currencies is that — save for a few fraudulent exceptions — governments and central banks have nothing to do with them. Another important feature is that cryptocurrency transactions can be done anonymously. Digital technologies and the internet facilitate the possibility of acting anonymously in many areas (in business, romance, crime, terrorism, etc.). At the same time that some new technologies hinder anonymity, others are deliberately designed to ensure it.

One example is ZCash, a cryptocurrency that promises to do everything cash does, only virtually... and anonymously. Using extremely complex cryptographic mechanisms, ZCash offers absolute privacy over the chain of transactions in which its "coins" are involved. When you receive a $100 bill there is no way to know who had it before the person who gave it to you, or who will have it after the person you give it to. ZCash promises to do the same thing: anonymity across the entire chain of users.

Naturally, governments don't like ZCash. The feeling is mutual. Like many cryptocurrencies, ZCash was developed by a community of libertarian programmers hostile to government control. Governments are right to be alarmed, simply because the destabilizing potential of platforms like ZCash is unlimited. For a drug trafficker, transporting $10 million in bills through customs at an airport is as logistically dicey as it is legally risky. But with ZCash anyone can transfer any sum, at any time, and to any destination instantly, without cumbersome briefcases full of paper money. And without risking the identity of the participants.

Governments are quickly learning the unprecedented challenges posed by new technologies like ZCash. The great advantage that the authorities still have is that they control the so-called "off ramp" from the crypto-highway. Since the number of businesses that accept payments in cryptocurrencies is still relatively small, it is often necessary to trade them for one of the traditional currencies still issued by governments. This gives the authority the possibility of controlling that exit ramp and this is, of course, a critical lever that governments have.

But there's no reason to think that advantage will remain indefinitely. Today, there are already more than 100,000 virtual businesses that accept cryptocurrencies as a form of payment and this number will continue to grow rapidly. It is perfectly conceivable that, in a few years, you will be able to buy a car, a trip or a house with ZCash.

We still cannot tell if the future belongs to transparent technologies such as Swish or opaque ones like ZCash. Most likely, they will coexist, depending on the country and the sector of the economy. But there is no doubt that, as the 21st century marches on, it will become more common to find bills and coins in museums rather than in our pockets.

October 11, 2018

Are You Going to Lose Your Job?

I recently took part in an exercise aimed at assessing the ability of large organizations to anticipate the external shocks that might impact them the most. To do this, their previous strategic plans and annual budgets were compared with what actually happened. The exercise revealed many things, but three are especially noteworthy. The first is that none of the organizations studied saw major events such as the 2008 financial crisis, Brexit or the election of Donald Trump coming. The second is that even those that correctly identified the trends that would affect them were wrong in their estimates of how long it would take to feel their consequences. Everything happened faster. The third is that one of the trends whose speed was most underestimated was the digital revolution. (The other was climate change.)

The impact of new digital technologies has been amplified by the rapid spread of artificial intelligence, robotization, the blockchain, big data and other innovations in this area. These new technologies will bring about enormous changes, and very soon.

But the consensus that exists about the changes and their speed disappears when talk turns to likely consequences. For some, the digital revolution opens up unprecedented possibilities for humanity. For others, these technologies constitute one of the main threats of these times.

The concern is that the digital revolution will destroy an enormous number of jobs and that, in the coming decades, it will create what historian Yuval Harari has called "the useless class," a permanently unemployed social group that the rest of society will have to support.

This is not a new concern. The fear that automation produces unemployment appeared with the industrial revolution and has not abated. President John F. Kennedy warned that one of the major challenges of the 1960s would be to maintain the level of employment at the same time that "machines are replacing men." These anxieties proved unfounded as new technologies not only "replaced men" but also created jobs in new industries, more than compensating for the jobs lost.

Will the digital revolution create more jobs than it will destroy? Joseph Schumpeter called this process "creative destruction."

There are those who argue that this time it is different and that this technological shock will be broader and faster. If so, if a tsunami of joblessness is indeed coming our way, what to do? So far there are only four ideas.

The first is digital protectionism. This consists of making the use of robots and digital technologies that reduce employment more expensive through taxes, tariffs and other mechanisms. This is a very bad idea. Economies that discourage the adoption of new technologies lose competitiveness and suffer significant lags and economic distortions.

The second idea is to retrain those who have lost their jobs. This is a laudable objective and most countries already have programs in place to give the unemployed new skills. Unfortunately, the results have been limited. There is no successful experience of large-scale retraining. Such initiatives must be further refined and efforts must be made to equip workers with skills more in line with those demanded by the labor market.

The third idea is not new: public employment. Whenever a society experiences a drastic increase in its unemployment rate, the government tries to alleviate the situation by creating jobs that, while not necessary, serve to give an income to those who have lost it. This may work as a temporary emergency measure, but its adoption as a permanent policy is costly, counterproductive and unsustainable in the long run.

The fourth proposal is to guarantee a universal basic income. This means that all adults will have a guaranteed and permanent minimum income, regardless of whether they work or not. This idea is very costly and may discourage work. But if it is used to replace inefficient subsidies its costs can be reduced. Moreover, people not only work to earn an income, but also have other non-monetary motivations.

The good news is that none of this may be needed. So far there are no signs that Schumpeter's creative destruction has become inoperative. It is perfectly possible that these new technologies will produce more and better jobs than they will destroy.

But if this time is different and the new jobs do not appear in time, we will be facing one of the greatest challenges of this century. That is why it is urgent to start thinking about what to do if that happens.

September 30, 2018

It Started with Porn

At the end of last year a series of pornographic videos began showing up on the internet. This is nothing new, but these were different because they starred some of the world's top actresses and singers. Naturally, they went viral: millions of people around the world saw them. Very quickly it became clear that Scarlett Johansson, Taylor Swift, Katy Perry and other artists were not the real protagonists of the sex videos, but rather the victims of a new technology that — using artificial intelligence and other advanced digital tools — allows their creators to insert anyone's face into a very credible video.

And this was just the beginning. It wasn't long before Angela Merkel, Donald Trump and Mauricio Macri were also victims of what is known as "deepfake." Barack Obama was used, without his consent, to exemplify the possible nefarious uses of the new technology. We can watch Obama saying what the forger wants him to but has never said before. But it is, nevertheless, a very realistic video.

Image manipulation is nothing new. Authoritarian governments have a long history of "disappearing" disgraced leaders from official photographs. And since 1990, Photoshop has allowed users to alter digital photographs, a practice that has become so common it is considered a verb by Merriam-Webster.

But deepfake is different. And much more dangerous. In just the year since the fake celebrity porn videos appeared, the technology has improved dramatically. Everything about these videos is hyper realistic, and the person's voice and gestures are so exactly rendered that it becomes impossible to know it is a forgery without using sophisticated verification programs. And perhaps the biggest danger of deepfake is that the technology is available to anyone.

A distraught ex could create (and anonymously distribute) a video that perfectly imitates the voice, gestures and face of the woman who left him and in which she appears to be doing and saying the most shameful and degrading things. A video of the police brutally beating an elderly woman who is participating in a street march could provoke violent clashes between protesters and the police. The respected leader of a racial or religious group could incite his followers to attack members of another race or religion. Some students could produce a compromising video of a teacher they despise. Or digital extortionists could threaten a company with disclosing a damaging video if the company does not pay a hefty ransom.

The possible uses of deepfake in politics, economics or international relations are as varied as they are sinister. The release of a video showing a presidential candidate saying or doing reprehensible things shortly before the elections will certainly become a more commonly used election trick. Even if the candidate's opponent doesn't approve the hoax, his most radical followers can produce and distribute the video without asking for anyone's permission.

The counterfeit videos' potential to cloud relations between countries and exacerbate international conflicts is also enormous.

And this is not hypothetical. It has already happened. Last year, the Emir of Qatar, Tamim bin Hamad al-Thani, appeared in a video praising and supporting Hamas, Hezbollah, the Muslim Brotherhood, and Iran. This provoked a furious reaction from Saudi Arabia, the United Arab Emirates, Bahrain and Egypt, countries that already had strained ties with Qatar. They denounced the emir's speech as supporting terrorism, broke diplomatic relations, closed the borders, and imposed a blockade by air, sea and land. The reality, however, is that the Emir of Qatar never gave that speech. While the video that escalated the conflict was not produced with deepfake technologies it was sufficient to provoke a dangerous escalation of the conflict that was already simmering. The video was still a fake but the boycott that resulted is very real, and remains in force.

The threat that deepfake represents to social harmony, democracy and international security is obvious. The antidotes to this threat are much less clear, although there are some proposals. All organizations that produce or distribute photographs or videos should be forced to use technology blocks that make their visual and audio material unalterable. People must also have access to technologies that protect them from being victims of deepfakes. Laws must be adapted so that those who defame or cause harm to others through the use of these technologies can be brought to justice. The ease with which it is now possible to operate anonymously on the web should not be tolerated. All this is necessary, but insufficient. We will need to do much more.

We have entered an era in which the ability to differentiate the truth from lies, facts from fiction, is being eroded. And with it, trust in institutions and in democracy. Deepfake is another new and powerful weapon in the arsenal that the merchants of lies have at their disposal.

We have to fight them.

September 27, 2018

Interesting Times Ahead

"May you live in interesting times." This expression, which seems a blessing, is really laced with stinging irony: interesting times are often fraught with conflict, instability and danger.

Who can deny that we are living in interesting times? And what could be more interesting than the Helsinki press conference in which President Donald Trump stated before the whole world that he trusted Vladimir Putin more than his own intelligence services? The spy agencies insist that they have definitive proof that the Russian government interfered in the 2016 presidential election. But Putin told Trump that he didn't, and the American president believed him... at least for a few hours.

The backlash against Trump's conduct was so intense and widespread that he had no choice but to retract his comments, in typical Trump fashion. According to the President, his error was grammatical, not geopolitical. He meant to say "wouldn't" not "would". The next day he invited Putin to Washington for a second meeting.

Meanwhile, two pieces of news were quietly published that will have enormous consequences for Russia, the United States and the relationship between them.

The first was a prediction by the respected energy analysis company Wood Mackenzie that world oil demand will peak in just 18 years, much earlier than previously expected. The report cites "tectonic changes" in the transport sector — especially the use of more efficient electric and autonomous vehicles — to argue that peak crude oil demand may come as early as 2036. From that point on the world's appetite for oil will wane. Of course, hydrocarbons will not disappear as an energy source, but their importance will decline more rapidly than experts had anticipated previously.

What does all this have to do with the Helsinki meeting? Well, Russia is a petrostate, a country whose economy is critically dependent on oil and gas exports. Putin has failed to diversify the Russian economy and reduce its dependence on oil and gas. As a result, a drop in the world's demand for its main export product will reduce the nation's revenues and have a major negative impact on the lives of ordinary Russians. And history shows that dictatorships are not immune to the adverse and unpredictable political consequences of a deteriorating economy.

The second piece of news is an alert from the Institute of International Finance (IIF), a private organization based in Washington, DC, that collects and analyzes information on the health of the world economy. According to the IIF, the world suffers from a serious addiction to indebtedness. Global debt has grown at an alarming rate and has reached levels never before seen. Back in 2003, total global stock of debt amounted to 248% of the world economy. Today it is 318%.

Debt is not a problem for a person, a company or a country if they have the income to service it. Or if they can find someone willing to lend them the funds. But if one's income is not enough to cover the interest due, or if the lenders lose confidence in the borrower's ability to pay, then they will stop lending. When this starts to happen, the lenders also try to recover what is still owed to them as quickly as possible. This is how financial crises are hatched.

Does this mean that we are on the verge of an economic crash like the one that shook the world in 2008? Not necessarily. The global financial system is stronger today and is relatively better regulated. High indebtedness can be sustained without giving way to a crisis as long as the world's economy grows and generates the income necessary to service the debt. The concern is that global economic growth, which had been recovering, will be hamstrung by the trade wars unleashed by Donald Trump.

Laurence Fink, the CEO of BlackRock, the largest investment management company in the world, has just warned that the White House's continued increase in import tariffs, as well as the tit-for-tat reprisals that the affected countries have taken, could hinder economic growth and cause the stock market to fall. Jerome Powell, Chairman of the Federal Reserve, issued the same warning.

The main lesson of the 2008 financial crisis is that the economic diseases of one country infect others very quickly. What happens to the American economy will shake the rest of the world and, of course, Russia, too. Naturally, this will affect the relations between the two countries. Another lesson is that economic crises distract us from our political problems, while political instability distracts us from our economic problems. This is precisely what is happening now.

Alas, it's safe to say that our times will remain enormously interesting.

July 27, 2018

Lopez Obrador's Dangerous Temptation

Mexico is not Venezuela and Andrés Manuel López Obrador is not Hugo Chávez. The differences are many and have already been fleshed out by others.

But that does not mean that Venezuela's experience over the last 20 years has nothing to add to our understanding of the ways Mexico could change under López Obrador.

Perhaps the most important lesson from Venezuela is that prolonged mandates are a much more dangerous threat than populism. What sunk Venezuela was not so much Hugo Chávez and Nicolás Maduro's populist policies, but how long they have stayed in place. Venezuela today — a failed state unable to feed or provide health care to its people, protect them from crime, or cut the highest inflation rate in the world — is what happens when a regime does the same thing over and over again for 20 years. Five or six years of bad policies will, of course, hurt any country. But decades of bad government from the same authoritarian clique will destroy it.

What does this have to do with Mexico? Hopefully nothing. Article 83 of the Mexican Constitution, in place since 1933, bans the president's reelection. So far, no president has managed to change this rule. Not because they haven't tried, but because that same Constitution imposes highly demanding requirements for amendments. Namely, a two-thirds majority in both the Chamber of Deputies and the Senate, as well as a simple majority in the state legislatures and the government of Mexico City. It has been decades since any Mexican government has had that level of political control. Until now.

López Obrador's landslide victory was so huge that his coalition would only need to "flip" a few deputies and senators to have enough votes to change the Constitution. They already have control of most of the state legislatures.

It is, therefore, likely that if President López Obrador so chooses, he can change Article 83. If he did, he would not be an exception, but rather one more in a long list of presidents who have changed the rules to extend their stay in power. Russia, Bolivia, Turkey, China and South Africa are recent examples of what, unfortunately, is a global trend.

The rulers who propose a constitutional amendment usually justify it as an indispensable requirement to combat the country's ills. Corruption, poverty and inequality are more effectively confronted with a new constitution, the people are told. In reality, these justifications often are just a trick to distract the public's attention from the true motivation to change the Constitution: allow for the president's re-election. Hugo Chávez, for example, justified the elimination of term limits, and the adoption of other reforms that further concentrated power in his hands, by repeating *ad nauseam* that he could only eliminate social injustice if the Constitution was amended as he wished. As we now know, it did not turn out that way. In fact, it was this change that created the conditions that are currently decimating the same poor people whose interests Chávez claimed to champion.

It is possible that Mexico will not follow the same path as Venezuela and that President López Obrador will content himself with his six-year term. Perhaps he has no intention of taking more power than he already has. After all, as president he will be the head of state, the head of the government and the head of the Armed Forces. He is also the leader of his party and the leader of the coalition that brought him to power, which will have an absolute majority in Congress. This guarantees the legislative approval of the new president's initiatives. In addition, López Obrador will be able to appoint trusted allies in all key positions throughout the judiciary, including the Supreme Court.

The danger, of course, is that he will be tempted to stay for six more years. Paradoxically, international experience shows that the worse things get for a president, the more he tries to hang on to power. Another important lesson to keep in mind is that populist governments usually start well and end badly. After a few years, populist economic policies tend to be difficult to sustain, while the political costs of abandoning them becomes prohibitively high. Inevitably, the government's need to stay the course only aggravates the disastrous consequences of populism.

None of this has to happen to Mexico. In fact, the conciliatory tone that López Obrador has adopted since winning the election has given great hope to the millions of Mexicans who did not vote for him. But the same thing happened in Venezuela after Chávez won his first election. He promised everything to everyone. Yet he never hesitated to do the exact opposite of what he had promised.

Hopefully this is not another lesson that Mexicans will have to learn.

July 7, 2018

An Opaque World

Crimea was not invaded by the Russian Army, but rather by armed civilian militias. In February 2014, they rose up against the Ukrainian government in order to "free the region" and annex it to the Russian motherland. That, anyway, is the official version of events according to the Kremlin-controlled media. Never mind that there is irrefutable proof that the "patriots" who took Crimea by force were, in fact, Russian troops who were ordered to remove any identifying badges and insignia from their uniforms, tanks and equipment just before the invasion.

Something similar is happening in the world of finance. Forty percent of the world's foreign direct investment is essentially fictitious. When a company or person invests in tangible assets (machines, buildings, etc.) in another country, they are making a foreign direct investment. But it turns out that 40% of all these investments are, like Crimea's "civilian patriots," a deception. Economists Jannick Damgaard and Thomas Elkjaer have just published the results of their research on "phantom investments." They discovered that "a stunning $12 trillion... is completely artificial: it consists of financial investment passing through empty corporate shells with no real activity." This movement of funds is used to hide fortunes, launder assets or avoid taxes. Despite regulators' best efforts, the international financial system remains opaque. With the emergence of cryptocurrencies such as Bitcoin, Ethereum and others, carrying out financial transactions anonymously has become easier than ever.

The proliferation of entities that claim to be one thing, but which in reality are another, also occurs in non-governmental organizations (NGOs) that presumably have philanthropic purposes and purport to help others. Often, they do nothing of the sort. They are vehicles used to surreptitiously defend particular interests and non-benevolent causes. Some governments also use them to act without being seen. These types of organizations are called GONGOs: government-organized non-governmental organizations. An example of this is a non-profit called World Without Nazism. It is based in Moscow, run by a politician linked to Vladimir Putin, and its mission is to spread anti-fascist ideology in former Soviet republics. In fact, it's a propaganda tool to back the Kremlin's international line.

Vladimir Putin's government is an enthusiastic and effective user of the many new options offered by our increasingly opaque world. "Pope Francis surprises the world and endorses Donald Trump for the U.S. presidency." This was one of the "news" headlines that went viral on social media just before the 2016 election. It was false, of course. But it was only one of the millions of messages aimed at voters that, according to U.S. intelligence agencies, were part of a deliberate attack by Moscow. In January 2017, these same agencies announced that they were certain that the Kremlin favored Donald Trump to win the elections and that President Vladimir Putin personally ordered an "influence campaign" aimed at weakening Hillary Clinton and intended "to undermine public faith in the U.S. democratic process." In November 2017 Spain accused Russia of intervening in the Catalan crisis by surreptitiously disseminating false information. The British government also denounced Russian interference in its recent elections. All of these operations were done covertly.

Naturally, the best antidote to an opaque world is an independent media that operates without the interference of governments, political parties, private companies or criminal cartels. We depend on them to find out what lies hidden behind the innocent-looking fronts used by organizations and individuals who are really out to harm society. That's why the most worrisome aspect of the rise in opacity is the wholesale destruction of the editorial independence of the very media outlets that warn us of the plots and misdeeds of the bad guys. In Russia, Hungary, Turkey, Venezuela and many other autocracies that try to pass themselves off as democracies, the furtive takeover of a newspaper, magazine, radio or television station by "private investors" who are in fact government allies and fund their investment with public funds is now the rule.

The danger is that this trick is also becoming common in countries that still have functioning democracies.

Preventing the proliferation of this and similar practices that make the world more opaque is one of the most important and defining struggles of our time.

June 25, 2018

Kleptocracy and Kakistocracy

Scoundrels have always been in the halls of power, along with amateurs, the inept and the deranged. But these days the criminality of some political leaders has reached levels worthy of the tyrants of antiquity. And the ineptitude of those in power now has much graver consequences due to globalization, technology, the complexity of society, as well as the speed with which things happen.

We are no longer talking just about "normal" corruption, such as when a government official gets a kickback for a weapons procurement deal or for awarding a lucrative construction contract to a friend. Nor is it an isolated case in which the class dunce arrives, to the surprise of his former colleagues, to the highest office in the land.

No, in a kleptocracy criminal behavior is not individual, opportunistic or sporadic, but rather collective, systematic, strategic and permanent. It is a system in which all the high-level government officials are complicit, where they deliberately work to enrich themselves, and then use their accumulated wealth to perpetuate themselves in power. For the kleptocrats the common good and people's needs are secondary and only looked at when they are at the service of their primary goal: to fatten their fortunes and make sure they stay in power.

The case of the inept in power is something different. Kakistocracies (literally, governments by the worst) proliferate in weak and disorganized political systems that repel the talented and attract the inept and most debased. Obviously, sometimes they come together producing a government that is both criminal and incompetent. When the two coincide, the kleptocracy and the kakistocracy feed back on each other.

An example that illustrates the outrageous conduct of kleptocratic governments was recently revealed by the respected Brazilian journalist Leonardo Coutinho. Coutinho gathered the testimony of a Bolivia Air Force pilot named Marco Antonio Rocha who was involved in the trafficking of large volumes of cocaine from Bolivia to Venezuela and Cuba. Rocha says that every week he flew an Air Force plane from La Paz, Bolivia, to Caracas, Venezuela, and Havana, Cuba, carrying sealed "diplomatic pouches" that were delivered to the plane by the Venezuelan embassy's military attachés in La Paz. In this case, however, they were not diplomatic pouches but rather enormous bundles containing 500 kilos of cocaine. Obviously, an operation of this magnitude, regularity and impunity requires the complicity of high-level officials in at least three countries. Which makes this not just the story of another drug-trafficking operation, but rather a glimpse into the activities of an alliance of kleptocratic governments.

Other instances of the kleptocrats' audacity abound. The newly deposed prime minister of Malaysia, Najib Razak, has been accused of organizing a financial scam that allowed him to transfer $42 billion from a government fund to private accounts controlled by his relatives and accomplices. In Brazil, the scandal known as "Operation Car Wash" revealed a vast, sophisticated and permanent network of corruption that went on for years and involved hundreds of powerful politicians, governors and businessmen not only in Brazil, but throughout Latin America.

A common mistake is to assume that kleptocracies only occur in the poorest and most underdeveloped corners of the globe. Yet Russia, a rather advanced country, shows all the marks of a kleptocracy. One of the fundamental pillars of the Russian regime is a small but powerful coterie of oligarchs: former secret agents of the KGB who run huge companies that work hand in hand with the Kremlin. In his testimony before the United States Senate in 2017, Bill Browder, a businessman with vast experience in Russia and a staunch critic of its government, asserted that Putin has become the richest man in the world. "I estimate that he has accumulated $200 billion in ill-gotten gains," Browder said.

It is also a mistake to think that it is only in countries with weak institutions and immature political systems that thieves and goons can reach the most important positions. What we are seeing today in the United States and in many European countries that have long democratic traditions simply shows that no nation is immune to the rise of a kakistocracy. Internet searches for this word, derived from ancient Greek, have seen a huge boom since Donald Trump got to the White House.

Like all good illusionists, the kleptocrats know how to distract us from looking at their misdeeds and the kakistocrats know how to distract us from their ineptitude. They do it by talking to us about ideology and attacking those of their rivals. While we watch and play our part in these ideological circuses, they steal. Or tinker with government policies they don't really understand.

And we pay the price.

June 18, 2018

Two Paradoxes

Times of great change breed contradictions, uncertainties and perplexities. Indeed, the world seems to grow ever more paradoxical. Among the many paradoxes that baffle us, two in particular have caught my attention.

First, why do dictators seem to have fallen in love with democracy? In its latest annual report, the NGO Freedom House concluded: "Democracy faced its most serious crisis in decades in 2017 as its basic tenets — including guarantees of free and fair elections, the rights of minorities, freedom of the press and the rule of law — came under attack around the world. Seventy-one countries suffered net declines in political rights and civil liberties, with only 35 registering gains. This marked the 12th consecutive year of decline in global freedom. Over the period since the 12-year global slide began in 2006, 113 countries have seen a net decline, and only 62 have experienced a net improvement." All opinion polls reveal that people's doubts about the democratic process are increasing, especially among the young, and that this is a global trend.

The paradox is that, among dictators, some democratic practices — namely, presidential elections — are very popular. It doesn't seem to bother them that everyone knows that these elections are a sham. In mid-March there were presidential elections in Russia and Egypt and, in May, in Venezuela. Vladimir Putin won with 75% of the votes, Abdel Fattah el-Sisi with 97% and Nicolás Maduro with 68%. Certainly a good performance, but nothing compared to Saddam

Hussein, who in 2002 garnered 100% of the vote in Iraq. Why do they bother put on this show? Why don't they simply declare themselves presidents for life and openly exercise their dictatorial power instead of putting on this ridiculous democratic charade? The answer is that democracy gives them something repression can't: a modicum of legitimacy that — despite the fact that they aren't fooling anyone — simplifies their lives before certain audiences. The elections, though rigged, allow them to present a democratic facade to their people and to certain key audiences around the world, something that they hope will distract the world a little from the fact that those who oppose them are tortured in prison and murdered in the streets.

Second, why have hackers and whistleblowers been more successful in the fight against money laundering than governments?

After the attacks of September 11, 2001, many governments decided that "follow the money" was one of the best strategies for identifying and neutralizing terrorist networks. Many nations adopted more restrictive laws and regulations in order to make it more difficult for the wealthy to hide their identity or move money around the world.

The result was that although governments had some success in making the financial system more transparent, their efforts were hampered by the difficulties that nations typically face when they are trying to coordinate efforts as well as the obstacles that were quickly created by the lawyers, accountants, and financial and computer experts who were hired by wealthy clients to help them keep their money hidden from tax authorities, law enforcement agencies or simply litigious former spouses, business partners or disgruntled employees.

At least until the whistleblowers and hackers turned up.

John Doe is the pseudonym of someone who made 11 million files from the Panamanian law firm Mossack Fonseca public. Each file had detailed information of assets in different banks, the identities of their owners and all the movements of the money in the accounts between 1970 and 2015. The disclosure of this information, known as the Panama Papers, had repercussions throughout the world. It included data on the accounts of 12 heads or former heads of state, some of them with inexplicable fortunes; more than 60 relatives and partners of well-known politicians, including Vladimir Putin; eight members of the elite that governs China; and several companies linked to Donald Trump. But perhaps the main contribution of the Panama Papers was that they revealed how the international financial system — a system that hides behind front men and companies with unidentified owners — actually works, as well as the sophisticated legal and financial instruments used to launder money or simply hide and move it around surreptitiously.

The Panama Papers were not the only leak of bank secrets. There were others before and more will surely come. These leaks — which are always the outcome of unauthorized access to private information — create important ethical dilemmas. But they also open the world's eyes. It is paradoxical that it has been the hackers and whistleblowers, acting illegally, who have pulled back the curtain on the international financial system.

The money launderers, the tax evaders and the corrupt who hide their money in these institutions can no longer sleep easy at night. Not so much because of the threat from governments, but from other citizens who have taken on the task of obtaining and revealing the world's banking secrets.

Nor can the dictators of our day sleep in peace, even if they disguise themselves as democrats.

June 5, 2018

Why Nicolas Maduro Clings to Power

It's difficult to describe the state of Venezuela today without coming across as a little hysterical. Phrases like "zombie movie set" and "post-apocalyptic hellscape" keep turning up in the accounts of recent visitors, who are staggered to see a society reach the levels of decay normally associated with wartime, but without a war.

In an engrossing recent account, The Wall Street Journal's Anatoly Kurmanaev — who reported out of Caracas from 2013 until a few weeks ago — compared the nation's state unfavorably with the Siberia of his youth in the 1990s:

"Venezuela's collapse has been far worse than the chaos that I experienced in the post-Soviet meltdown. As a young person, I was still able to get a good education in a public school with subsidized meals and decent free hospital treatment. By contrast, as the recession took hold in Venezuela, the so-called socialist government made no attempt to shield health care and education, the two supposed pillars of its program."

The statistics of Venezuela's implosion are at once mind-blowing and somehow not quite up to the task of expressing the full horror of what's happening there. In a country that had been Latin America's beacon of peace, stability, democracy and development throughout the second half of the 20th century, about two-thirds now report involuntary weight loss due to hunger. Out of those who reported losing weight, the average loss was approximately 20 pounds last year.

That, amid all this, the sitting president was recently returned to office with 68% of the vote stands as its own sick joke. The election, it nearly goes without saying, was rigged. The opposition boycotted it, and virtually every large democracy and the organizations that represent them slammed it as grossly undemocratic and refused to recognize it: the EU, the U.S., Canada, the G7, every large country in Latin America. The measure of Venezuela's democratic implosion is the list of countries that did recognize it: Cuba, Russia, Nicaragua, Bolivia and Iran. Even Syria's Bashar al-Assad took a break from his war to send Maduro a congratulatory message.

The surprise, in a way, is less that Nicolás Maduro won "reelection" (the scare quotes are sadly mandatory here) than that he wanted another term in the first place. A former bus driver and Cuban-trained hard-line Marxist operative, Maduro has been painfully out of his depth ever since he took over the presidency following Hugo Chávez's death in March 2013. Five years later, he has no achievements of any kind to show for his time in office, except for managing the considerable feat of hanging on to power through a crisis that would've seen off any leader even slightly interested in his people's well-being.

Maduro plainly has no clue how to reverse any of the multiple crises he has set off, and is reduced to recycling the same promises he has been making and failing to keep for years now. His "campaign" this year centered on the claim that another term is all he needs to defeat the shadowy economic conspiracy he incongruously blames for hyperinflation and economic collapse. And how does he propose to do this? By doubling down on the rigid price controls and uncontrolled money printing that, economists of all stripes agree, are the actual cause of hyperinflation and economic collapse.

The total absence of credible new policies with an adamant refusal to acknowledge the scale of suffering his policies continue to cause are now the regime's defining characteristics.

So why does he want to keep a job that's so plainly beyond him?

The reality is that for Nicolás Maduro and the clique around him, the goal of staying in power is just to be in power. Nothing more. Because at this point he's dug himself into a hole so deep, the alternative to a presidential palace is very likely a jail cell. Or worse.

The ghost of Manuel Noriega, the former Panamanian dictator, hangs heavily over any discussion of Maduro's future. Like Noriega, Maduro runs a regime knee-deep in the drug trade, and one that has been the subject of intensive DEA surveillance for years. Two of the first lady's nephews were convicted in the United States last year of offering undercover DEA agents 800 kilograms of cocaine for sale during a sting operation in Haiti some years back. Maduro's vice president, Tareck El Aissami, is designated a drug kingpin (technically a "Specially Designated Narcotics Trafficker") by the United States Treasury Department. Whatever role Maduro himself played in this trade, it's very likely U.S. investigators have the evidence on it. That Noriega died last year while still in custody after three decades in a variety of jails on three different continents is not a fact that will have escaped Maduro.

And drugs are just the beginning. Maduro and members of his inner circle are now under international sanctions for a dizzying variety of misdeeds. Over the years, regime members have been accused of gross human-rights abuses, big-time money laundering, Olympic-level bribery and embezzlement, aiding Hezbollah, sanctions busting in Iran, large-scale environmental crimes, allegations of false imprisonment, torture — the list goes on and on. In February this year, the prosecutor at the International Criminal Court announced that her office had launched a preliminary examination into human-rights abuses in Venezuela committed since 2017. Before it's all said and done, Maduro could conceivably find himself on the dock in The Hague, Milosevic-style.

All of which goes a long way toward explaining why a man who visibly has no idea of what he's doing is so determined to hang on to power. He's scared. He has good reason to be scared.

A generation ago, it would've gone differently. A long tradition guaranteed a soft landing to washed-up autocrats suddenly needing to spend more time with their families. Uganda's notorious Idi Amin ended his days quietly in a compound in Saudi Arabia, far from power but living in relative luxury. The Filipino dictator Ferdinand Marcos spent his golden years sipping cocktails in Hawaii and Guam; Zaire's

Mobutu Sese Seko wound up in Morocco and Haiti's "Baby Doc" Duvalier on the French Riviera. Time was when even the worst of the worst could be entreated to leave power with the promise of a nice villa and a bulging bank account. That's over.

Conversations about Maduro's fate usually include some speculation about Cuba as a place of exile. It's easy to see why: Cuba's been by far the regime's most important ally. In fact, "ally" doesn't quite do justice to the deep bond between the two governments: The Venezuelan revolution sometimes feels like a wholly owned subsidiary of the Castro regime, with tens of thousands of Cuban trainers, advisers and spies embedded into the very core of the Venezuelan state, and no decision of any import made without consulting Havana first. Earlier this month, for instance, the Reuters reporter Marianna Párraga revealed that even as its economy and oil industry collapse, and even though the government lacks the hard currency to import critical medicines, Venezuela has been buying oil on international markets to ship to Cuba on concessional credit terms: a hugely valuable source of revenue for the Cuban regime.

And this points to the problem with the Cuban luxury-exile scenario: Keeping Nicolás Maduro in power is far too valuable to the Cubans for them to aid his exit. Saudi Arabia's grand strategy never depended on keeping Idi Amin in power in Kampala in the way that Cuba's strategy demands keeping Maduro in place. But Venezuelan oil and diplomatic support are a key survival strategy for the Cuban regime. If there's a scenario in which the Cubans would permit his exit, Maduro would swiftly transform from asset into bargaining chip in the Cubans' eyes. Who's to say they wouldn't trade him away to the United States in return for relaxing aspects of the trade embargo, for instance?

A quiet retirement at home is out of the question for a leader who has done so much damage to so many people: The specter of prosecution would always loom. Even if he could handpick a trustworthy successor willing to extend elaborate guarantees, he'll be hard-pressed to forget that Chile's General Augusto Pinochet spent the last years of his life battling prosecutions at home and abroad.

300

In fact, it's difficult to conceive of a credible exit plan that Maduro — relatively young at 55 — would trust to safeguard him two or three decades into the future. Much better to trust the protection of Venezuela's grandiloquently named National Bolivarian Armed Forces — increasingly just a Praetorian Guard with all the arms and intelligence capabilities of a nation-state.

Nicolás Maduro clings to power because he's trapped there. Every alternative arrangement sounds like prison to him. That being the case, he's not so much governing Venezuela anymore as using the state as a protective cocoon: His one last alternative to a life behind bars.

May 30, 2018

The Secret Memo to Raúl Castro

To: President Raúl Castro
From: XXXXXX in Caracas
Subject: A Proposal for Venezuela

It is almost time for you to hand over the Cuban presidency to your successor. This coincides with the end of my time as head of our clandestine operations in Venezuela. But I'm not writing to bid farewell and celebrate our achievements. The time for that will come.

I am writing because I am worried. The situation here is no longer tenable and calls for drastic change. The purpose of this memo is to make a proposal to ensure the continuity of our relationship with Venezuela.

The stability of Cuba depends on keeping a friendly, generous government in Caracas. To that end we have devoted — for almost two decades now — our best talents, institutions and resources. And we've done well.

We kept control over the nation with the largest oil reserves on the planet without firing a single shot and without openly involving our armed forces. And, thus far, we've done it without the world realizing that the most important decisions dealing with Venezuela's economy, politics, internal security and foreign affairs are ones we shape — or even make. The same goes for key appointments in the armed forces, the judiciary and in the intelligence and security services. In all the areas that matter to us, we've been in the driver's seat.

The benefits to Cuba have been immense. It's not just the millions of barrels of oil that have propped up our economy. Venezuela also pays generously for our doctors, sports trainers and the various "advisers" we send them. The commission fees that our companies charge Caracas for brokering food and other imports generate huge profits. Our diplomatic influence has been boosted by our control over Venezuela's foreign service and embassies. Thanks to deliveries of subsidized Venezuelan oil, our influence over many countries in the Caribbean and Central America has been enormous. We have evicted the USA from there.

That's how high the stakes are.

As you know, the situation here, which had long been difficult, is becoming unsustainable. Eighty-eight percent of the hospitals report that they do not have medicines for their patients, 90% can no longer offer emergency services, 79% say that they are often without water and in 96% there is not enough food. Infant mortality is one of the highest in the world. Absenteeism in schools and high schools is enormous since students and teachers spend most of their day looking for food. In 2017, three-quarters of Venezuelans lost, on average, 11 kilograms of weight. Eighty-nine percent of the population now lives in poverty. The homicide rate is one of the highest in the world. Inflation too.

The oil industry, which generates 90% of the country's export revenue, has collapsed. Today, its crude production is half of what it was when Commander Chávez came to power in 1999. It is estimated that close to three million Venezuelans have left the country.

We are on the verge of killing the goose that lays the golden eggs. Fortunately, the upcoming elections offer us a way out. Maduro is clearly unable to handle the crisis and is losing support rapidly. In the May presidential elections we need a fresh face.

I recommend the following:

1. Make Maduro lose the elections and force him to hand over power to the legitimate winner. This will legitimize Venezuela's democracy before the world. To persuade Maduro to leave power we will offer him an honorary position and a mansion in Havana. But, above all, we will let him know that if he does not cooperate, we are

ready to make sure he loses the enormous fortune he has accumulated. He knows we can do it. When his allies see that he no longer enjoys our support, they will abandon him. We must, of course, also give them "incentives" to align their behavior to our goals.

2. Reach an agreement with the opposition candidate that is most "flexible." We can guarantee that he will win the elections (we still control the National Electoral Council, the body that counts the votes and decides who wins) and we will give him the freedom to act as he wishes on some fronts, especially the economy. But our support will depend on retaining access to Venezuelan oil and staying in control of key posts in the military, intelligence services and, of course, the president's personal security detail. We will also continue to appoint the executives of the national oil company and the top judges.

An additional benefit of this scheme is that it will allow us to continue using Venezuela as a laboratory to learn how to manage Cuba in the future. A partially open political system, where some appearance of democracy is kept and where there are certain freedoms.

But where we remain in power.

April 3, 2018

Four American Tragedies

The election of Donald Trump gives us just one peek into forces that keep the American society divided, tense and confused. America's major political problems are well known: inequality, racism, terrorism, political gridlock and declining international influence, among many others.

With the exception of racism and inequality, these issues don't touch Americans' daily lives directly. Others do, however, in ways that are cruel, tangible and frequent.

One of these is the irresponsibly loose regulation of firearms. The figures are terrifying. The United States accounts for about 5% of the world's population and 48% of its guns. America also has the greatest number of mass murders, especially in schools. Since 2013, there have been more than 300 school shootings in America — an average of about one a week. So far in 2018, there have already been 14 attacks. But in the U.S., the most dangerous place for children and young people is not school, it is the home. Many more are killed by guns in their own houses than in the classroom. The killers are usually family members or acquaintances.

President Trump and the National Rifle Association (NRA) argue that the problem is not guns but rather mental health. But no other country faces this type of attack as regularly as the U.S., and, statistically, mental illness is no more frequent here than elsewhere. All independent studies conclude that the ease with which a weapon can be purchased — even machine guns — is the explanation for these massacres.

Seventy-five percent of Americans want tighter controls on the sale and possession of guns, as well as more restrictions on access to assault rifles. But the wishes of that overwhelming majority are systematically crushed by the NRA, which, though it masquerades as an NGO, in practice serves as a very effective lobby for gunmakers. It claims five million members who vote as a block against politicians who do not blindly support their extreme positions. The NRA also spends money freely to influence elections. It donated $30 million to Donald Trump's campaign and another $3 million to Marco Rubio's. These are minuscule amounts compared to the returns the manufacturers generate through gun sales and whose lucrative interests are well protected by the NRA. This is how a minority imposes its values on the majority.

Another toxic reality for millions of Americans centers on opioids. They can be obtained legally, by prescription, or by illegal means. Illegal consumption of heroin and synthetic opiates such as fentanyl has skyrocketed. In 2015, two million Americans suffered health problems due to abuse of these drugs. About a third of patients who start using opioids to relieve pain end up abusing them. Eighty percent of heroin addicts had previously abused prescription opiates. Every day 115 Americans die from an overdose of these drugs. Nowhere else on Earth are opiates prescribed and consumed as freely as in the United States.

Toward the end of the 1990s, pharmaceutical companies launched a vast campaign aimed at persuading doctors and hospitals that these drugs were suitable for pain relief and, above all, that they were not addictive. The result was a huge increase in prescriptions, overdoses,and cases of addiction. It also, of course, increased the profits of these pharmaceutical companies. The government's attempts to put limits on opioid prescriptions were shot down by the powerful pharmaceutical lobby. Again, the economic interests of a powerful and well-connected few outweighed the welfare of society as a whole.

Even as the United States is brimming with opiates that kill, it faces a serious shortage of medicines that save. This shortage is not because the drugs are not available, but because they are out of reach for millions of Americans who cannot afford them. The price of prescription drugs in the United States is the highest in the world. The average American spends $858 per year on drugs, whereas in the other

19 industrialized countries the average is $400. Twenty percent of Americans say that these high prices force them to ration the doses that doctors have prescribed or prevent them from renewing the prescription when they run out of medicine.

The behavior of some pharmaceutical companies is outrageous. In recent years, companies have increased, without explanation, the cost of insulin for diabetes patients by 325%. The price of Lomustine, a medicine for the treatment of cancer, has increased by 1,400% since 1993, even though its production costs have not increased. The price of EpiPen — an anti-allergy drug — jumped from $7 in 2007 to $500, while the price of 30 capsules of cycloserine, used to treat tuberculosis, rose from $500 to $10,800. In 2015 alone, the price of a basket of the most commonly used drugs increased 130 times faster than the rate of inflation.

Eighty-two percent of Americans want laws that lower drug prices. But... the lobby for the pharmaceutical companies seems to be battling it out with the NRA in the race to spend the most money blocking government initiatives that protect consumers.

Another phenomenon that is killing Americans is climate change. The year 2017 saw the most costly climate events in U.S. history: hurricanes, forest fires, tornadoes, floods and droughts. Extreme weather events are becoming measurably more frequent. California suffered more wildfires than ever, several cities recorded their highest temperatures, and there were prolonged droughts. Hurricane Harvey broke records for rainfall and devastated Puerto Rico, where, coming on its heels, Hurricane Maria wrought even more destruction and left a thousand people dead. In February, it was warmer in the North Pole than in some parts of Europe. How do you explain the timidity with which the United States confronts this problem that, if it continues along its current path, will do enormous damage to its people, especially the poor?

Reducing the emissions that contribute to global warming can be costly for some business sectors, which, naturally, would prefer to avoid those costs or postpone them as long as possible to safeguard their profits. That is why they have contributed so effectively to fostering skepticism, which mitigates the sense of urgency and allows complicit politicians to postpone the necessary initiatives. This tactic is not new. For decades, tobacco companies funded campaigns to make the public believe that there was a "scientific debate" about whether smoking caused cancer.

This debate was fueled by "skeptical scientists" who argued that there was not enough evidence of a causal link between tobacco and cancer. Years later — and hundreds of thousands of deaths later — it was revealed that these "skeptical scientists" were sponsored by cigarette sellers, whose sole purpose was to sow confusion and prevent the government from acting to protect the public health. Something similar is happening with the "scientific debate" about climate change. Reuters has reported that 25 major U.S. companies (Google, PepsiCo, DuPont, Verizon, etc.) fund more than 130 members of Congress, almost all from the Republican Party, who are declared skeptics of climate change and systematically block the initiatives to reduce emissions. ExxonMobil has admitted that for decades it funded organizations whose mission was to cast doubt on the scientific consensus on climate change.

What do these four tragedies have in common? Money. Or, rather, the propensity of some in business who, driven by unbridled greed, abuse their customers and society. They can do it because they have managed to capture the institutions of the State in charge of regulating them and limiting their abusive practices. And also because the government and politicians do nothing to prevent this capture. Faced with a market failure (business behaviors that harm society) they add government failure (inaction due to regulatory capture by private interests). This kind of regulatory capture is lasting only if elections fail to penalize politicians who favor special interests over the interests of voters at large. It is a symptom and a driver of democracy's failure.

The solution is as obvious as it is difficult to achieve: to repair democracy where it is broken.

Nothing could be more urgent.

March 14, 2018

What Zapatero Knows

How would the Spanish feel if they had a government with authoritarian propensities that called for a rush election in which the opposition parties were disqualified, its main leaders were either in jail or in exile, and the organization in charge of guaranteeing that the elections are free and fair was controlled by the same president who was seeking re-election? To be more precise, how would they feel if the country was about to go to the polls and the main opposition Socialist Party (PSOE) was banned and its candidate, Pedro Sánchez, was in jail while Albert Rivera, the leader of Ciudadanos, the party leading in the polls, had to seek refuge abroad to avoid incarceration — or worse?

That would be unacceptable. And, surely, that's something that Spain's former Prime Minister José Luis Rodríguez Zapatero knows full well. Nevertheless, that is the proposal that Zapatero wants the Venezuelan opposition to accept.

When the Venezuelan opposition parties decided to negotiate with Nicolás Maduro's regime about the upcoming elections, they had some very specific objectives: ensuring a transparent, free and competitive presidential election; that all political prisoners be freed; that the political rights of the arbitrarily disqualified opposition candidates be restored; that the National Assembly, which was fairly elected by the people, be recognized; and, most importantly, that the crisis that is decimating the Venezuelan people be addressed. None of this was acceptable to the Maduro government.

And Zapatero knows that.

All the opinion polls show most Venezuelans do not want Nicolás Maduro to continue as president. And the vast majority of them want the transition to be democratic and without violence. They want to vote! But not in rigged elections that make sure that the current government stays in power. Venezuela's National Electoral Council should, in theory, be independent. After all, it is the "electoral referee" and in charge of guaranteeing clean elections. In practice, however, it has been — for almost two decades now — a shameless and unapologetic appendage of the government.

Zapatero knows that.

In Venezuela the vast majority of the media outlets are controlled directly or indirectly by the regime, which uses them as a powerful propaganda tool. They are also the source of constant and merciless attacks on the opposition — which, in turn, is legally prohibited from responding or correcting any of the slanders spread daily by the media.

Of course, Zapatero knows that.

The government has not allowed the presence of experienced and neutral international observers in any of the previous elections. It has already stated that observers from the Organization of American States, which has the most experienced, independent and respected electoral monitor group in the Western Hemisphere, will not be allowed into the country. In contrast, the Maduro government has expressed its enthusiastic welcome to an electoral observation group organized under the aegis of the United Nations. Who does the Venezuelan government want as the leader of this group?

José Luis Rodríguez Zapatero.

In Maduro's Venezuela, the most popular, competent and electorally competitive opposition leaders are in prison, have been disqualified by judges loyal to the government, or have been forced into exile. And yes, Zapatero knows that.

At the age of 27, David Smolansky was elected as mayor of El Hatillo, an area adjacent to Caracas. The youngest mayor in Venezuela's history led a very successful administration and was able to overcome the most Machiavellian maneuvers of a government bent on sabotaging him. The popularity and success of Smolansky proved intolerable for Maduro and his minions. Not surprisingly, the young mayor was accused by the Supreme Court — another appendage of the government — of refusing to use force to stamp out the peaceful protests that occurred in his jurisdiction. He was immediately removed from his position, and an order was issued for his arrest and imprisonment in a jail where political prisoners are known to be routinely tortured. Smolansky refused to surrender and was on the run for 35 days. Finally, he embarked on a risky journey through southern Venezuela that allowed him to enter Brazil via a jungle route. In an honorable gesture, the Brazilian authorities allowed him to enter the country. Today the young politician lives in exile and dreams of returning to work in Venezuela. Smolansky's is not an isolated case. Twelve other mayors have been arbitrarily dismissed, and half of them have been imprisoned and mistreated.

And, of course, Zapatero knows all this.

Recently, Zapatero participated with Pablo Iglesias (the leader of Spain's left-wing party, Podemos) in an act of support for Evo Morales, the president of Bolivia. Morales has been in power for 12 years and now wants to run for a fourth term. The Bolivian Constitution does not allow this: a president can only remain in office for two consecutive periods. In 2016, Morales called a national referendum to eliminate term limits. He lost it. Undaunted, the president appealed to the Constitutional Court, whose magistrates had no problem in deciding that Morales could run once again for the presidency of Bolivia. This was, they ruled, his human right...

The conduct of Evo Morales does not deserve the endorsement and applause of a democrat.

And Zapatero knows it.

March 6, 2018

Education: The World's Biggest Scam?

Every day, 1.5 billion children and adolescents around the world go to buildings called schools. Once there they spend long hours in classrooms where some adults try to teach them how to read and write, math, science and more. Annually, this costs 5% of the world's GDP.

A large part of this money is wasted. An even greater waste is the time lost by those 1.5 billion students who learn little or nothing that will be useful to succeed today's world. The effort that humanity makes to educate children and young people is as titanic as its results are pathetic.

In Kenya, Tanzania and Uganda, 75% of third-grade students do not know how to read a phrase as simple as "the name of the dog is Puppy." In rural India, 50% of fifth-graders cannot subtract two-digit numbers, such as 46-17. Brazil has managed to improve the skills of 15-year-old students, but at the current rate of progress it will still take them 75 years to reach the average mathematics score of students from rich countries; in reading, it will take more than 260 years. These and many other equally disheartening facts are in the new World Development Report, published annually by the World Bank. The central message of the report is that schooling is not the same as learning. In other words, going to school or high school, and getting a diploma, does not mean that the student has learned much.

The good news is that the progress in schooling has been enormous. Between 1950 and 2010, the number of years of schooling completed by an average adult in lower income countries tripled. In

2008, these countries were incorporating their children into primary education at the same rate as higher-income nations. Clearly, the problem is no longer the lack of schooling but rather that once they get there, they do not learn. More than an education crisis, there is a learning crisis. The World Bank report emphasizes that schooling without learning is not only a missed opportunity, but also a great injustice. The poorest people suffer most from the consequences of the low efficiency of the education system. In Uruguay, for example, sixth-grade children with lower income levels fail in mathematics five times more than those from wealthier households.

The same happens with rich and poor nations. The average student in one of the poorest nations performs worse in mathematics and language than 95% of students in rich countries. All of this evolves into a kind of diabolical machinery that perpetuates and increases inequality, which, in turn, creates a fertile breeding ground for toxic politics and all kinds of conflicts.

The reasons for this "educational bankruptcy" are multiple, complex, and not yet fully understood. They range from the fact that many of the teachers are as ignorant as their students and their absenteeism is inexcusably high, to the fact that their students are malnourished or too hungry to pay attention, or that they simply do not have books and notebooks. In many countries, such as Mexico or Egypt, for example, the teachers unions are formidable obstacles to change, and corruption in the sector is often high. What's more, important, sizable portions of the national budgets for education never reach the intended beneficiaries, the students, but rather the bureaucrats who control the system. National leaders usually let this negative trend continue for years, building entrenched and difficult-to-change organizations within governments and unions.

What to do? Start with measuring. For political reasons, many countries are reluctant to be transparent about the result (often dismal) of their students' and teachers' evaluations.

And if a nation's leaders, and the public, do not know which educational strategies are working and which are failing, progress remains elusive.

A second goal should be to start giving more weight to the quality of education. While it is politically attractive to announce that a high percentage of young people in a country go to school, that is of no use if the vast majority of them learn little. Third: start earlier and include school breakfast and lunch. The better the education system is at the early ages, the more capable the children will be as they move through primary and secondary school. Fourth: use technology selectively and not as a magic bullet. It is not. Finally, raise the social and professional status of teachers through pay, training with modern pedagogical techniques and professional credentials.

Perhaps the most important message is that lower-income countries are not condemned to have children who don't learn. In 1950, South Korea was a country devastated by war and had very high illiteracy rate. But in just 25 years it has managed to create an education system that produces some of the best students in the world. Between 1955 and 1975, Vietnam also suffered a terrible conflict. Today, their 15-year-old students have the same academic performance as those in Germany. It can be done. Where there's a will, there's a way.

February 28, 2018

2017

How Christmas Shopping Explains the World

These days, some of the world's largest corporations are out shopping. They are not, however, motivated by the Christmas spirit, but by the goal of taking advantage of trends that are changing the world. What's more, they are willing to pay the highest prices in history for other companies.

But what are they bidding on? Some are betting that our appetite for being connected is growing and insatiable. Others, that the way we consume entertainment and information is changing dramatically and irreversibly.

Have you heard of Broadcom? No; neither had I. Among the hundreds of products it sells is the much-celebrated 16nm Nx56G PAM-4 PHY, which, as you know, is used for internet networking infrastructure (or something like that...). The company defines its business as selling "the technologies that connect the world." If you use a cell phone or the internet, it is very likely that your devices contain Broadcom products. Broadcom wants to buy Qualcomm, another giant manufacturer of semiconductors and products for cell phones, telecommunications and the internet. It has offered to pay more than $103 billion in what would be the highest price paid for a technology company in history. Qualcomm is fiercely resisting but, if the acquisition goes through, nearly every smartphone in the world would have a product or technology from the resulting company, whose sales would exceed $200 billion a year. (To put it in perspective: that amount is equivalent to Saudi Arabia's annual exports.)

This voracious appetite for companies whose revenues depend on technologies that facilitate people's connectivity and mobility reflects demand for their products that is growing at breakneck speed, and all signs suggest it will continue to grow rapidly. Not only because the world's population is growing, but also because the number of users of the internet and of the products it makes possible are also growing fast. An explosion is also expected in the "Internet of Things" (I of C), i.e., the connection between different devices that coordinate with each other. For example, your cell phone wakes you up in the morning, turns on the coffee maker, checks your agenda for that day's appointments and tells your car's navigator where you are going to go so that it has the most convenient routes ready for you. The industrial applications of the I of C are even greater.

We don't know if Broadcom will succeed in buying Qualcomm. But, certainly, its intention unveils interesting features of the future.

These technological changes have also altered the way we entertain and inform ourselves. Television "by appointment" is now a thing of the past. The need to "date" your TV on a day and time set by the broadcasting station to watch your favorite program began to disappear with the rise of VCRs. And now, thanks to streaming technology via the internet, there is a proliferation of companies, such as Netflix, that base their business on the user deciding when and where to watch the program he/she is interested in.

In the communication industries, there has been a strong debate about what is more important (and more lucrative): controlling the production of content or controlling the channels through which this content reaches the consumer? The world's largest media companies have decided that this debate is not for them: they are going to control both content and distribution. And they have the money to do it.

AT&T, the largest of the telecommunications (and therefore content distribution) companies, is trying to buy the iconic Time Warner, the third largest entertainment (and content production) company. In turn, the second largest, The Walt Disney Company, is interested in buying a significant part of 21st Century Fox, owned by tycoon Rupert Murdoch and his family. Murdoch would essentially take Fox

News, the super-profitable and controversial news network. This transaction has sparked much speculation.

One is that Rupert Murdoch's son, James, who is the current head of 21st Century Fox, would replace Bob Iger as Disney's chief executive. The other is that Iger is seriously considering the possibility of being the U.S. presidential candidate in the 2020 election. None of the above is definite and there are bound to be surprises. Although negotiations with Disney are well underway, both Comcast and Verizon have expressed interest in buying 21st Century Fox and could enter the competition by offering prices even higher than the $60 billion that Disney would pay. And even if Disney is the buyer, it is also uncertain whether its board will appoint James Murdoch as an executive (or whether Iger's flirtation with politics will come to fruition).

Perhaps the biggest uncertainty is whether the antitrust authorities will authorize the enormous corporate concentration that these giant acquisitions entail, driven, at their core, by the profound technological change that has in turn radically transformed consumer habits.

What is certain is that, regardless of the outcome of these negotiations, television as our parents knew it, will soon cease to exist.

December 9, 2017

Diasporas: Some Save, Others Kill

The bloody civil war in Sri Lanka between the Liberation Tigers of Tamil Eelam (LTTE) and the Sri Lankan government lasted more than a quarter of a century (1983-2009). Much of the money that financed the LTTE came from Tamils based in Canada, the United Kingdom and other countries. Financial support from the Tamil diaspora prolonged this armed conflict. The same happened in Northern Ireland. Irish groups based in the United States financed the Irish Republican Army (IRA), the armed wing of the secessionist struggle that raged for four decades in Ireland and the United Kingdom.

The list of civil wars that have been exacerbated and lengthened thanks to the financial support that the diaspora of that country gives to one of the parties to the conflict is long, painful and worldwide. From the Balkans to the Horn of Africa and from Central America to Southeast Asia, conflicts have been prolonged by the intervention of what Ethiopia calls "the toxic diaspora." Obviously, the bloodthirsty regimes facing the diasporas are often even more toxic.

Diaspora, Greek for "dispersion," was the word originally used to refer to the exile of Jews from Israel. Over time, it was also applied to other groups that left their countries, spreading throughout the world. Today it is used, somewhat confusingly, to refer both to those places of destination and to a human group.

Life in exile fosters relationships between people who find themselves in the same situation, with whom one shares nostalgia for the old country, ethnic affinities, cultural commonalities and, of course, language. This often generates feelings of empathy and solidarity, which in turn gives these groups a cohesion that allows them to act collectively. Some organize to support social initiatives in their home country and others get involved in their politics. The latter intensifies when there are revolutions, civil wars or political conflicts that deeply divide society.

Often the only real opposition to dictatorships is in the diaspora, which has money and international contacts. Sometimes it succeeds in overthrowing autocratic regimes.

This was the case of Ayatollah Khomeini, who, from Paris, promoted a movement that overthrew the Shah of Iran in 1979.

The possibility of doing politics from a distance and "without getting their hands dirty" also means that the diasporas can afford luxuries that those who confront an autocratic government on the ground often do not have. It is easier to thunder against a repressive regime from thousands of miles away than on the streets of the country or in jail for doing so. Now, YouTube, Twitter or Facebook facilitate remote-controlled politics.

Studies of diaspora interventions in the politics of their home countries have found that they exacerbate polarization and increase the intransigence of the parties, all of which exacerbate and prolong conflicts. Of course, intransigence is not a monopoly of diasporas and is, rather, the basic characteristic of tyrants.

Diasporas not only intervene in the politics of their country of origin but, in some cases, also manage to influence the foreign policy of the country where they reside. In the United States, Cuban exiles and the pro-Israel lobby are good examples. Both have had enormous success in influencing Washington's decisions concerning Cuba and Israel. The U.S. government's six-decade-old failed economic embargo on Cuba, for example, would not have lasted as long without the effective and radical activism of Cuban exiles. Ironically, they are also the exiles whose remittances to their relatives on the island sustain the country's economy.

Like the Cuban diaspora, other diasporas are an invaluable source of poverty relief. Today, more than 250 million people live in a country other than the one in which they were born, and a huge proportion send money regularly to their families and relatives. Last year they sent $440 billion, three times more than the amount that the governments of rich countries devote to helping the poorest nations.

For a large number of countries, remittances are one of the main sources of foreign exchange (in 25 of them they represent more than 10% of the size of their economy). And for millions of families — from India to Colombia and from China to Mexico — remittances from abroad are their main — if not only — source of income.

There are toxic diasporas. But some are also saviors.

December 2, 2017

Corruption: Heroes or Laws?

The good news is that the world is fed up with corruption. The bad news is that the way we are dealing with it is ineffective. We look for leaders who are honest heroes instead of promoting laws and institutions that protect us from the dishonest.

Everywhere, popular disapproval of thieving politicians and businessmen is on the rise. Protests against corruption are massive, global and frequent: India, Mexico, Russia and Thailand are just a few of the many countries where people have taken to the streets. They no longer believe either that corruption is inevitable or that it is futile to try to fight it.

The impact of some of these popular protests has been astonishing: the presidents of Guatemala and South Korea, for example, were deposed and imprisoned. In Brazil, huge marches set the stage for the impeachment of President Dilma Rousseff.

Around the world, there is an enormous desire to remove corrupt leaders and replace them with others whose honesty is beyond question. But is the search for and subsequent appointment of people we believe to have integrity the best antidote to corruption? No.

Choosing honest governors is a lottery. They may indeed turn out to be so, or they may not. In any case, it is not enough to vote for those we presume to be honest; we also need laws and practices that prevent and punish dishonesty. Societies that only bet on an honest leader almost always lose out. Silvio Berlusconi, Vladimir Putin and Hugo Chávez came to power promising to crack down on corruption. And we already know the results.

Moreover, in these times, we need institutions that prevent the fight against corruption from serving as a mechanism for political repression. We are seeing, for example, how this new popular intolerance toward venal politicians is being exploited by the world's autocrats to move against their rivals. Vladimir Putin often accuses those who become too influential of being corrupt and imprisons them. In China, since Xi Jinping took office in 2012, more than 201,000 officials have been put on trial. Some have been sentenced to death. In an anti-corruption raid, Saudi Prince Mohammed al Salman arrested more than 200 potentates, including one of the world's richest men, Prince Alwaleed bin Talal. The governments of Cuba, Iran and Venezuela regularly use corruption allegations to imprison their opponents. Perhaps some fo those imprisoned by the dictators are corrupt. But the real reasons for their detention surely have more to do with their political activism than their alleged dishonesty.

The fight against corruption does not have to be corrupt and, fortunately, genuine efforts to diminish this plague are proliferating. In Argentina, Chile, Colombia, Peru and Uruguay, for example, the Inter-American Development Bank (IDB) is supporting "public innovation laboratories" that are experimenting with new methods of monitoring and controlling government management. In Brazil, a group of data scientists decided to use artificial intelligence techniques for oversight. They chose a concrete case to test their theories: how to limit fraud in the reimbursements requested by deputies to cover their transportation and food expenses when traveling for work. They called their project Operation Love Serenade and collected small donations online. With these funds they created Rosie, a computer script that analyzes MPs' reimbursement requests and calculates the probability that they are unjustified. To no one's surprise, Rosie detected that MPs were often cheating. The team gave Rosie her own Twitter account, where followers instantly learn of their MPs' attempts to charge the state for expenses that have nothing to do with their job.

Rosie is a small example that illustrates big, positive trends in the fight against corruption: the power of organized civil society combined with the opportunities offered by the internet and new advances in technology, as well as the priority that must be given to transparency of information in public management.

To be sure, it is easy to dismiss Rosie as a sideshow that cannot make a dent in large scale corruption. While some congressmen were charging their personal expenses to the State, the Brazilian company Odebrecht was paying $3.3 billion in bribes throughout the Americas. However, skepticism should be tempered. Marcelo Odebrecht, the head of the company, has been sentenced to 19 years in prison. And the deputies are now careful not to abuse with the reimbursement of their expenses.

Things are changing.

November 18, 2017

America's Second Civil War

The Second Civil War that will erupt in the United States will be more devastating than the one that began in 1861. In that first conflict more Americans died than in all the wars that country has fought since then.

But the Second Civil War that will occur at the end of this century will be much worse. The nation will be roughly divided between the "red" states of the south and the "blue" states of the north. Climate change will have drastically altered borders and daily life. The state of Florida, for example, will no longer exist; instead, boats will navigate in what will then be called the Florida Sea. A terrorist attack will have spread a new biological agent that triggers a pandemic that lasts a decade and kills more than 110 million people.

These are not the forecasts of a futurist, but of a novelist. Thirty-five-year-old Omar El Akkad was born in Egypt, grew up in Qatar, and worked as a journalist in Canada. He has covered the war in Afghanistan, Guantanamo prison, the Arab Spring, and racial strife in Ferguson, Missouri. These and other events serve as inspiration for his disquieting first novel, *American War*.

Lately, dystopian novels — stories that depict a frightening future — have proliferated, and this one, certainly, can be included in this category.

The American War of this book occurs between 2074 and 2095 and, although the war's immediate trigger is the assassination of the president of the United States at the hands of a suicide bomber, the context that nurtures it is a society deeply divided in its values, life-styles and political preferences. This extreme polarization boils over after Congress passes a bill banning the use of fossil fuels. Mississippi, Alabama, Georgia, South Carolina and Texas reject the law and declare their independence, starting the Second Civil War.

El Akkad develops the plot from the perspective of the Chestnuts, a "typical" family in this future. Part of being "typical" is that, unlike most Americans today, the war reaches them and they end up living for long years in a refugee camp that is named, with cruel irony, Camp Patience. The author obviously knows well the refugee camps of the Middle East and uses what he has seen to vividly convey the terrible conditions of these precarious temporary cities that almost always end up being permanent.

The circumstances of the Chestnut family are constantly shaken by political conflicts that are nourished by ancestral hatreds, and that are powered by climate change and new technologies. The central character is one of the daughters, Sara T. Chestnut, whom everyone calls Sarat. Dana, her twin sister, dies when her bus is attacked with missiles shot by an unmanned drone. In this story, drones are a constant presence. As is terrorism. At Camp Patience, the young Sarat is recruited and radicalized by an older man who happens to be an agent of the Bouazizi Empire. This unexpected empire has emerged after multiple revolutions in the Middle East and regions of Central Asia have allowed a host of countries to unify into a single nation, head-quartered in Cairo. China and the Bouazizi Empire have the most prosperous economies on the planet, and, after the collapse of the European Union, millions of Europeans emigrate to North Africa in search for jobs that they can no longer find in their own countries. The name of this new empire is loaded with meaning: Mohamed Bouazizi was the young Tunisian man whose immolation in 2010 provoked the popular revolts that ended up overthrowing the dictator of that country and fueling protests in other countries, the Arab Spring. In the novel, the Bouazizi Empire does what it can to foment conflicts and divisions in the United States and prevent this potential rival from recovering. One of its victories occurs when Sarat, working as its agent, manages to infiltrate the ceremony that marks the reunification of the United States and releases a biological agent that triggers the devastating pandemic that will cripple the country for long years to come.

The implicit purpose of many dystopian novels is to illustrate today's world through the description of the future. And El Akkad accomplishes this very well. He has said that when he began writing the book, three years ago, his purpose was to bring his readers closer to the horrors of sectarian violence and show them how the desire for revenge is universal. He also acknowledges that he had not anticipated that his very speculative premise (that a foreign power intervenes in U.S. politics to widen the existing fissures) would, in fact, become the reality that now dominates the national conversation.

But perhaps the single greatest achievement of this novel is that it makes us feel that ominous extreme situations that now seem implausible to us may not be as improbable and remote as we think. And that everything depends on us — and on what we do now.

November 8, 2017

Shifting Borders

If shifting sands are dangerous, shifting borders are even more so. While shifting sands swallow people, shifting borders swallow up whole societies. Seventy years ago, Hitler wanted to change the borders of Europe, while the Japanese Empire wanted to change the borders of Asia. Those attempts cost the lives of 3% of humanity. At the end of those wars, millions of survivors found themselves within new dividing lines, some of which were asphyxiating and impassable. The wall that split Berlin was the most famous of the post-war borders built to imprison a nation.

After World War II, many colonies became independent, changing the boundaries of the surviving empires. In the second half of the 20th century, the movement of large-scale boundary lines diminished, but attempts to redefine them did not end.

In 2014, for example, Vladimir Putin swallowed up Crimea, moving the Russian border. On the other side of the world, the Chinese have been creating new borders. What until a few years ago were small, uninhabited reefs in the middle of the South China Sea are now micro-islands capable of housing Beijing government military bases. By draining sediments and sand from the seabed and compacting them around the reefs and coral atolls, they made them grow to the point where it was possible for them to build ports and airports on the new islets. In this way, China has created a new geographical reality and with it new borders that allow it to claim sovereignty over the adjacent maritime area.

The Chinese are neither the only nor the first to alter the boundaries in the area by creating islands: Vietnam, Malaysia, the Philippines and Taiwan have also done so, albeit more modestly. All want to either protect the territory over which they already exercise sovereignty or expand it. Others want their region to have borders that make it a sovereign country. In Europe alone, there are 21 regions with independence movements that, if successful, would alter the map of the continent and transform its politics and economy.

But these days, a global trend even stronger than independence is the strengthening of borders to make them more impregnable — not to citizens who want to leave, but to foreigners who want to enter. According to a Reuters analysis, since the fall of the Berlin Wall, European countries have built 1,200 kilometers of anti-immigrant fences and fences, the vast majority since 2015. That distance is equivalent to 40% of the length of the U.S.-Mexico border. One of the most enthusiastic fence builders is Viktor Orbán, the prime minister of Hungary, who, moreover, has just sent a bill for €400 million to the European Union for reimbursement of the expenses he has incurred to build his fences.

As we know, Donald Trump also wants Mexico to pay the $21 billion that the wall he wants to build on the common border will cost. Both the European Union and the Mexican government have declined the invitation to pay for Orbán's trellis and Trump's wall.

One of the ironies of these confusing times is that while nationalism, protectionism and isolationism are on the rise, the forces undermining them are increasingly powerful. Cyber viruses and pandemics do not respect borders. Nor do increasingly frequent and destructive hurricanes, cyclones and typhoons. Extreme weather events unite countries in their shared catastrophes.

Protecting national economies from the effects of financial crises in other countries is impossible. Preventing the arrival of new technologies or toxic ideas that alter a nation's economic and political course is increasingly difficult. What border in the world has successfully repelled smugglers of people, drugs, counterfeit goods, weapons and more? None.

Does all this mean that the nation state is in the process of extinction and that nationalisms are not viable in practice? Of course not. States, patriotism and nationalisms are here to stay. And so are borders.

But shifting borders are also here to stay. And those that, regardless of the promises of politicians, in practice fail to give citizens the security they crave.

October 28, 2017

Worse Than Bad Leaders Are the Bad Followers

The world has a leadership problem. There are too many who are thieves, inept or irresponsible. Some are insane. A few combine all of these flaws. But we also have a follower problem. Everywhere, democracies are being shaken by the votes of citizens who are indolent, uninformed or of a naivety only surpassed by their irresponsibility.

We are talking about the British people who, the day after voting to break with Europe, massively googled what Brexit means. Or the Americans who voted for Donald Trump and are now about to lose their health insurance. Or those who believed him when he promised that he would not govern with the usual corrupt elites and now see how lobbyists representing voracious special interests occupy important positions in the White House. They are the citizens who do not waste their time voting because "all politicians are the same" or those who are sure that their vote will not change anything. Surely you know people like that.

Of course we must strive for better leaders. But spare a thought for the quality of our followers. There have always been ill-informed or politically apathetic citizens. As well as those who do not know who they are voting for — or against. But now things have changed and the votes of the indolent, the uninformed and the confused have become a threat to us all.

The internet makes it easier for the worst demagogues, dark interests and even dictatorships in other countries to manipulate disinterested or distracted voters.

The internet is a wonderful source of information, but it has also become a toxic channel for the distribution of lies transformed into political weapons. We are all vulnerable online, but more so are those who, because they are too busy or simply apathetic, do not make the effort to check whether the seductive political messages that reach them are true.

And it is not just the apathetic. At the opposite pole are the activists, whose intransigent positions make politics more rigid. Those who are too sure of what they believe find digital safe havens online where they only interact with those who share their prejudices and where only information that reinforces their beliefs circulates. Social media such as Twitter, Instagram and others force the use of very short messages — the famous 140 characters of Twitter, for example.

This brevity favors extremism, since the shorter the message, the more radical it must be for it to circulate widely. On social media there is no space, time or patience for shades of gray, ambivalence, nuance or the possibility that opposing views have points in common. Everything is either very white or very black.

Naturally, this favors sectarian extremists and makes it more difficult to reach agreements.

What to do?

To begin with, four things.

First, a public education campaign to make us all less vulnerable to the manipulation that reaches us via the internet. It is impossible to achieve complete immunity against cyber attacks that, through lies and misrepresentations, try to influence our vote or our ideas. But that does not mean total defenselessness. There is much that can be done, and disseminating best practices for defending against digital manipulation is an indispensable first step.

Second, it is useless to offer up best practices to those who are not interested in them. A sustained campaign explaining the dire consequences of electoral indolence is equally indispensable.

Third, we must make life more difficult for the manipulators. Those who orchestrate disinformation campaigns must be identified, denounced and, in the most flagrant cases of abuse, sued and prosecuted. These manipulators flourish in opacity and benefit from ano-nymity. It is therefore necessary to make the origins, sources and inter-ests behind the information we consume more transparent. It is necessary to reduce the impunity with which those who are under-mining our democracies operate.

Fourth, stop information technology and social media companies from continuing to act as enablers of the manipulators. Foreign inter-ference in elections in the U.S. or in other countries would not have been possible without Google, Facebook and Twitter. Today we know that at least these three companies profited by selling election ads messages paid for by customers associated with Russian operators. These companies must be forced to use their enormous technological and marketing power to protect their customers. And it must be made more costly for them to continue to serve as platforms for launching anti-democratic aggressions.

October 21, 2017

The Political Hurricane that Is Changing the World: the Middle Class

What do a farmer from Iowa, a graphic designer from Chile, a retiree from the United Kingdom and an assembly line worker from China have in common? Two things: they are members of their country's middle class and they are angry with their leaders. Their disillusionment is transforming politics and triggering surprising events, such as the election of Donald Trump, Brexit, the defenestration of presidents and a global wave of street protests.

In many countries around the developed world, the middle class is rebelling against stagnant or even worsening living standards. Globalization, immigration, automation, inequalities, nationalism and racism open up opportunities for political adventurers selling bad ideas as if they were good.

Of course there were also rich and poor who voted for Trump in the U.S. and Brexit in the UK, and many middle-class people voted against in both cases. However, there is no doubt that, in rich countries, and especially in the U.S., those with middle incomes form the segment that is suffering the most economic damage.

But these upheavals are not only happening in rich countries. The middle classes in Brazil, Turkey, China and Chile share the anxieties that beset their peers in North America and Western Europe. The paradox is that in the last three decades, hundreds of millions of people in Asia, Latin America and Africa have risen out of poverty and are now part of the largest middle class in history. But these people are not satisfied either and are protesting at the ballot box and in the streets.

335

In elections and referendums in Europe and the United States, candidates and programs that were previously unthinkable are proliferating.

Researchers and various institutions such as the World Bank define the middle class as a broad band of incomes, ranging from $11 to $110 per day. And upheavals in this segment of the population are not new. In 2011 I wrote that "the main cause of the coming conflicts will not be the clash of civilizations, but the outrage generated by the frustrated expectations of a middle class that is in decline in rich countries, and on the rise in poor ones." "It is inevitable," I wrote, "that some politicians in developed countries will blame the economic decline of their middle class on the takeoff of other countries." And I warned that prosperity does not always mean greater political stability.

The scale and speed of the expansion of the global middle classes has been truly spectacular. Economist Homi Kharas, an expert on the world's middle class, estimates in a recent study that today 3.2 billion people belong to it, that is, 42% of the total population. Every year, 160 million more people join the middle class. At the current rate of growth, a few years from now, most of humanity will live, for the first time in history, in middle-class or upper middle-class households.

The extent of this expansion varies. While in the U.S., Europe, Japan and other advanced economies the middle class is growing at a mere 0.5% per year, in China and India the middle class is growing at a shocking annual rate of 6%. While it has reached unprecedented proportions in countries such as Nigeria, Senegal, Peru and Chile, the expansion of the middle class is a particularly striking phenomenon in Asia. According to Kharas, the one billion people who will join the middle class in the coming years will overwhelmingly (88%!) live in Asia.

The economic consequences are tremendous. In developing countries, consumption is growing by 6% to 10% per year and already accounts for a third of the world economy.

The political consequences can be just as important. In Europe and the United States, they are already visible in elections and referendums — France, the Netherlands, the United Kingdom, Hungary,

Poland — with the proliferation of candidates and programs that were previously unthinkable. As Bill Emmott, former editor of The Economist, recently wrote: "We live in an era of political turbulence. Two parties barely a year old have seized power in France and in the huge Tokyo metropolitan area. A party less than five years old is leading the polls in Italy. The White House is occupied by a political neophyte, something that causes tremendous unease among Republicans and lifelong Democrats."

Political turbulence is also making itself felt in low- and middle-income countries that are growing very rapidly. As the middle class grows, so do their expectations and demands. Social actors who are more connected, have more purchasing power, are more educated and informed, and are more aware of their rights exert immense pressures on their governments, which often do not have the resources and institutional capacity to respond to these demands.

These countries are beginning to show cracks similar to those in the U.S. and Europe. In Chile — whose economic successes have long made it a model for other nations and has one of the most stable societies in Latin America — there have been violent protests, mass abstention at the polls and even an assault on Congress because citizens want to express their disappointment with a government they feel has failed them.

In China, researchers have observed that between 2002 and 2011 there was a dramatic drop in middle-class confidence in legal institutions, the government and the police, even though it was a period of strong growth and improved social programs. The Chinese government is undoubtedly concerned. In fact, many believe that the country's breakneck growth is a key pillar of Beijing's strategy to placate the middle class: since the government is not going to offer you constitutional democracy, freedom of speech and universal human rights, it would better make sure you at least make a better living, or even get rich. The risk is that a prolonged economic contraction could unleash the political turmoil that the authorities so fear.

The reasons for discontent in the developing world — despite improving living standards — are numerous, but access to information is undoubtedly a crucial factor. Educated and informed people are harder to control. What's more, when billions can see on their cell phones how others live, they are much more likely to be dissatisfied with their situation. They probably think, "I work as hard as they do, so I deserve it too."

That "it" may be higher wages, more affordable health care, better education for their children, more equality, better public services or freedom of expression. However, cheap and widespread connectivity and the information revolution are not the only factors. Urbanization, migration, increasing inequality, and even the new cultural environment and expectations about corruption, authority and hierarchies are also factors.

What is going to happen? The rejection of ""more of the same" and political rearrangements are becoming inevitable: Donald Trump and Brexit are but two manifestations, spurred in part by the revolt of the middle classes in rich countries. The fury of the middle class in poor and middle-income countries is also boiling over. Its consequences are unpredictable.

September 22, 2017

Is a War Between the United States and China Inevitable?

Thucydides, an Athenian who lived about 400 years before Christ, was a bad general but a great historian. His *History of the Peloponnesian War* recounts the conflagration that broke out between Sparta and Athens in the 5th century BC. Many consider this book the first attempt to explain historical events by resorting to analysis and data and not to the designs of the gods.

Based on his study of the causes that led Athens and Sparta to war, Thucydides maintains that it is difficult for a rising power, in this case Athens, to coexist peacefully with the dominant power, which in this case was Sparta. Graham Allison, a professor at Harvard University, has popularized this concept by calling it "the Thucydides Trap." Allison studied 16 situations over the past 500 years in which a nation emerges with the ability to compete successfully with the dominant power. In 12 of these 16 cases the result was war.

All this has profound implications for our times, and that is the subject of Allison's recent book, *Destined for War: Can America and China Escape Thucydides's Trap?* According to him, "if the current course continues, the outbreak of war between the two countries in the next few decades is not only possible, but far more likely than you might think."

Professor Allison's book is not alone in warning of the consequences of the rise of the East and the decline of the West. The subject has stimulated a large number of books, articles and conferences.

339

Gideon Rachman, a journalist for the Financial Times, has written a book entitled *Easternization*, referring to the orientalization of the world. Its central message is that the centuries-long international ascendancy of the Western powers, namely the U.S. and Europe, is coming to an end. According to Rachman, the center of gravity of world power will reside in Asia and, more specifically, in China. Bill Emmot, former editor of The Economist, is also concerned about the fate of the West. According to Emmott, "the West is the most successful political idea" and clarifies that it is not a place but a set of concepts, values, and social and political conditions guided by the preservation of individual freedom, economic openness, and the pursuit of equality and justice for all.

Naturally, the increase in economic inequality that the countries of the West are experiencing and the political problems this has brought about are of concern to Emmott: "Without an open society, the West cannot prosper, but without equality it cannot last." Unlike the other authors, Emmott does not believe that Asia will displace the West. [You can watch the video of my interview with Bill Emmott at www.EfectoNaim.com].

Predictions of a China that succeeds in becoming a global hegemonic power underestimate the weaknesses of the Asian giant. They also assume that the difficulties limiting the international influence of the United States and Europe are insoluble and therefore permanent. But neither the West's problems are insoluble nor China's are insignificant.

The reality is that while China's economic growth is astounding, its social progress indisputable and the modernization of its military intimidating, its problems are equally daunting. Ian Buruma, an expert on Asian affairs, maintains that of all the recent books on the rise of that region, professor Allison's is the worst. According to Buruma, the professor evidences great ignorance about China and minimizes the problems plaguing that country. Despite its rapid expansion, China's economy is fragile and full of misalignments and distortions. Economic inequality has skyrocketed and widespread misery persists in rural areas. The country is an ecological disaster where more than one million people die each year from diseases caused by a polluted environment.

Militarily, China remains far behind the United States, which also has a vast network of allies in Asia that view China with fear and deep historical resentments. Vietnam has had 17 wars with China, for example.

But perhaps the most important objection to the vision of a China becoming the world's leader is that its autocratic model is becoming less seductive and difficult to sustain. Keeping hundreds of millions of people subjugated to the designs of a dictator is a route that in this day and age leads to political instability. And a politically unstable country is not a good candidate to prevail in the conflagrations predicted by Thucydides.

July 9, 2017

Five Ideas That Trump Killed

It is still too early to evaluate the presidency of Donald Trump. However, thanks to his behavior, his policy initiatives and his penchant for shooting himself in the foot, some things are already clear. For example, before Trump's arrival to power there were certain ideas that were widely accepted. But no more.

1. The truth: Trump, his spokespeople, his allies in the media, and other social medias (including Vladimir Putin) have shown that, for them, there are no indisputable facts or data. In fact, there is no such thing as "the truth." Any statement, scientific data or visual evidence such as, for example, photos showing the size of the crowd on the day of the president's inauguration, can be questioned. Confronted in an interview with what appeared to be an irrefutable fact, President Trump's adviser Kellyanne Conway denied it and instead offered what she called "alternative facts." The interviewer, Jake Tapper, replied that, in that case, the alternative facts were simply a falsehood (he did not dare call them a "lie"), to which Conway explained that this was the typical reaction from a hostile media that is out to get the president. The very idea that we can — through reason and the scientific method — come to verifiable truths is under attack. And, as we have seen, politicians who defend their lies with "alternative facts" now have the invaluable resource of social medias. It is ironic that in this age where there is more than enough information, so little truth is in it.

2. That running a big company teaches one how to run the government: This is a zombie idea — we keep thinking it's dead, yet

342

somehow it keeps coming back to life. It is the belief that to be a good ruler it helps to have been a successful entrepreneur. "I am very rich." "I am a great negotiator." "I have created many jobs." These are some of the phrases that Trump repeats incessantly and that, according to him, guarantee that he will be a successful president.

But, as other cases demonstrate (see Berlusconi, Silvio), the skills and the temperament that lead to success in the private sector do not ensure good governance. The chaos and ineptitude that have characterized the government of Donald Trump are only surpassed by the setbacks in his political negotiations both inside and outside the United States.

The next time an entrepreneur aspires to lead the country, he will have to deal with the lesson that Donald Trump will almost certainly leave us: Business talent does not translate well to the public sector.

3. That the president of the United States is the most powerful person in the world: Trump will prove that this is not so. Of course, this president has at his disposal enormous resources and thousands of officials — including the best-armed military mankind has ever known. But the forces that limit the president's performances are equally enormous — and perhaps even more powerful. These limitations to presidential power are domestic and foreign, legal and bureaucratic, political and economic. Despite being one of the presidents with the most imperial temperament, few of his orders are becoming realities. This is not to say that Trump cannot make decisions that will have enormous consequences — such as getting the U.S. out of the Paris Climate Agreement, for example. But these high-impact decisions will be far fewer than he presumes. And it is also telling that there are many initiatives that he wants to block — but can't — such as the investigation into his ties to Russia, to mention one. He is also discovering that gaining power was easier than exercising it.

With Trump the idea that the president of the United States is all-powerful will die.

4. That the longevity of a democracy protects it from corruption and nepotism: In democracies that fail, the Congress, the courts or other state institutions fail to prevent a venal president from using the

prerogatives of his office for the benefit of his private business. Or from naming his relatives to important public positions for which they are not qualified. To a greater or lesser extent this happens everywhere. In African and Latin American countries these abuses become frequent and extreme, while in the United States or the United Kingdom they are comparatively less serious. Until now.

As we know, Donald Trump has appointed his daughter Ivanka and his son-in-law Jared Kushner to high positions. And 200 members of Congress have sued the president accusing him of violating the Constitution for profiting from doing business with foreign governments.

It remains to be seen whether American institutions are strong enough to parry the assault on the healthy checks on executive power that have prevailed until now. In any case, Trump has also done away with the idea that corruption and nepotism only flourish in banana republics.

5. Political apathy: The Trump Government will make it painfully clear to millions of Americans that the elections have very substantial consequences for their lives. Indifference, disinformation, lack of curiosity, a lack of participation in politics, and protest voting without thinking it through have very high costs for citizens. Thanks to Donald Trump, today millions of people have learned this lesson and have become politically active.

June 28, 2017

Exit the United States and Enter... Who?

In last week's column I analyzed one of the biggest surprises in modern international politics: the United States' decision to unilaterally surrender its power and influence in areas in which it had — until now — enjoyed clear leadership. I concluded that column by asking: who will fill these power gaps? I anticipated that it would not be China. I do not think it's Russia either. Then who will it be?

When I wrote that column I did not know that a few days later President Donald Trump would announce his decision to withdraw the U.S. from the Paris climate accord, joining Nicaragua and Syria, the only two countries that did not sign it.

Trump's decision is an excellent example of the rare phenomenon of a superpower giving up power without having it taken away by a rival. Former Secretary of State John Kerry called it "an unprecedented forfeiture of American leadership." Fareed Zakaria, a respected analyst, said that the United States had "resigned as the leader of the free world."

Reactions to the exit of the United States from the Paris Agreement also reveal incipient but interesting trends. Miguel Arias Cañete, European Commissioner for Climate Action and Energy, said that Trump's decision "galvanized" Europeans, and he promised that the vacuum created by the U.S. would be filled by "new broad committed leadership."

In the United States, three governors, 30 mayors, 80 university presidents, and managers of more than 100 large companies announced that they would present the United Nations with a joint plan for the U.S. to meet the emission reduction targets indicated in the Paris Agreement, even if the White House doesn't support it. Jeff Immelt, CEO of General Electric, wrote on Twitter: "Disappointed with today's decision on the Paris Agreement. Climate change is real. Industry must now lead and not depend on government." And in China, Shi Zhiqin, a researcher at the Carnegie-Tsinghua Center, predicted that "while Beijing can only express regret at Trump's action, China will forge ahead with its commitments and cooperate with Europe."

Leadership in this field is shifting from the White House to regional and local authorities, businesses and civil society. And from the U.S. to Europe and China.

But the fight against global warming is not the only area where the United States is retreating. Another — and very important — area is Europe. This was made very explicit by Angela Merkel after her recent meeting with Trump: "The times when we could fully rely on others have passed us by a little bit, that's what I've experienced in recent days. And that is why I can only say that we Europeans must really take our fate into our own hands — of course in friendship with the United States of America, in friendship with Great Britain and as good neighbors wherever that is possible also with other countries, even with Russia. But we have to know that we must fight for our future."

It is an interesting irony that, unintentionally, Trump may be contributing to the geopolitical resurgence of a Europe that he despises and which has been burdened by its economic and institutional problems, the immigration crisis, as well as by Islamist terrorism and Russian expansionism. But even more important is the space these developments open for China to take advantage of the vacuum left by the withdrawal of the United States.

This decline in U.S. international influence precedes the arrival of Trump, although his initial decisions, such as getting the country out of the Paris Agreement or the Trans-Pacific Partnership trade agreement (TPP), will accelerate the process.

Is China then the new leader that will dominate the world?

This prediction, however, ignores important realities that limit the hegemonic capacity of the Asian giant. While China is an economic and military power, it is also a very poor country facing severe social, financial and environmental problems. Nor does its political model seem very attractive to citizens of other countries. This is not to say that China will not have clear leadership in some global issues — such as climate change, for example — or a huge ascendancy in parts of Asia. Or that it will not be part of the decisions that affect the whole world.

But it is one thing to take part in decisions and another, very different thing, to be the one who makes them. Everything indicates that we have entered a post-hegemonic era in which no nation will dominate the world, as it used to happen before. From this perspective, the withdrawal of the United States does not imply its irrelevance. It will not be the superpower it used to be, but it will not cease to have power either. The Pentagon, Wall Street, Silicon Valley, Hollywood and America's universities will continue to be immense sources of international influence.

And the White House? Much less than before.

June 4, 2017

How to Dismantle a Superpower

One of the great surprises that historians will be studying for many years to come is the decision of the United States to give up its world leadership. Moreover, they will have to explain why it did it unilaterally and without anyone taking away the immense power it had accumulated during the last century.

This abdication was not due to a specific decision, but rather the result of a long and complex process. And while the arrival of Donald Trump to the White House accelerated things, the surrendering of power had already been occurring for some time.

The internal political fragmentation of the United States and its difficulty in making fundamental decisions have much to do with the decline of its influence. In 2015, Larry Summers, former Secretary of the Treasury, warned that ideological rigidity and the resulting inability to forge consensus was weakening the country's role in the world. According to Summers: "As long as one of our major parties is opposed to essentially all trade agreements and the other is resistant to funding international organizations, the United States will not be in a position to shape the global economic system." When Summers said this, the example of the damage the United States was inflicting on itself was Congress's reluctance to pass reforms aimed at strengthening institutions such as the International Monetary Fund (IMF). Organizations like the IMF and the World Bank are an important part of a world order that benefits the U.S. Therefore, its strength and relevance should be a priority for Washington. Surprisingly, it is not so.

In the case of the IMF, 188 of its 189 member nations approved the reforms. The U.S. did not, and, without its vote, the needed reforms could not be implemented. After waiting five years for the U.S. Congress to act, the Chinese government decided to create a new international financial agency in which Washington would have no influence. And so there is now the Asian Infrastructure Investment Bank (AIIB), of which 57 countries are members and another 25 nations, including Canada and Ireland, are about to join. From the beginning, the U.S. was invited to join the AIIB, but has yet to do so.

Another recent example of the unilateral transfer of power was Donald Trump's decision to remove the U.S. from the Trans-Pacific Partnership trade agreement, the so-called TPP. The TPP does not include China, and Barack Obama's purpose in proposing it was to create a permanent body to promote U.S. integration with its allies in Asia. Of course, such an agreement also aimed at counterbalancing China's growing influence in the region.

One of Trump's first decisions as president was to withdraw the U.S. from the TPP. China reacted immediately and decisively to take advantage of this unusual gift. Beijing initiated high-level negotiations with the 11 other TPP member countries, offering them attractive trade agreements. The United States was not invited.

But for Xi Jinping, the Chinese president, these new trade agreements were not enough and he decided to push forward an initiative he had proposed in 2013: the New Silk Road.

Invoking the legendary network of roads that in ancient times connected China with the rest of Asia and reached the Mediterranean, President Xi summoned 64 countries to join a huge road, railway, port and airport construction project that would unite China with Asia, the Middle East, Africa, Europe and even Latin American countries such as Argentina and Chile. Sixty percent of humanity lives in these 64 countries and China, and together they represent a third of the global economy. Recently, 44 heads of state attended a meeting in Beijing and signed a communique stating that they "oppose all forms of protectionism [...] and endeavor to promote a universal, rules-based, open, non-discriminatory and equitable multilateral trading system."

This of course contrasts with the protectionist attitude of the current U.S. Government.

International trade is not the only area where Washington is losing power and influence. The fight against global warming and nuclear proliferation, international aid and control of global pandemics, intervention to contain financial crises, regulation of the internet, management of human activity in the oceans, air, space, the Arctic and Antarctica are just some of the areas in which U.S. importance has waned.

Who will fill these power gaps? The answer to this question will define the new world order. In next week's column I will offer some answers. I will give you a hint: it will not be China.

May 27, 2017

Why Do Dictators Like to Appear Democratic?

An interesting paradox of contemporary world politics is the extraordinary contortions that some autocrats take in order appear democratic. Why do so many dictators construct elaborate democratic theatrics even though they know that sooner or later the authoritarian nature of their regime will be revealed?

Some of the reasons are very obvious while others are not. The most obvious is that, increasingly, political power is obtained — at least initially — by votes and not by bullets. Therefore, aspirants must show great devotion to democracy, even if that is not their preference.

The other reason behind the current popularity of fictitious democracies is less evident: today's dictators feel more vulnerable. They know to be afraid of the powerful combination of street protests and social media. This flammable mixture of "hot streets" and incendiary social medias does not sit well with dictatorships. Maybe that's why keeping up a democratic front bolsters their power.

Democracy contributes the most precious ingredient for tyrants: legitimacy. A government that originates from the will of the people is a more legitimate government and, therefore, less vulnerable than a regime whose power depends on repression. Although they are fraudulent, the perception of democracy generates some legitimacy, even if it is transitory.

Vladimir Putin's Russia is a good example of all this. The tricks to which he has resorted to make his government seem democratic are extraordinary. Russia today has all the institutions and rituals of a

351

democracy. But it is a dictatorship.

Of course there are elections in Russia periodically. And these are accompanied by expensive media campaigns, marches, rallies and debates. On Election Day, tens of millions of people make long lines to vote. The small detail is that since 2000 Putin always wins... or the person he designates to keep the position for him until his next turn as president arrives.

That happened in 2008 when Dmitri Medvedev, Putin's prime minister, won the presidential election and immediately gave his former boss the post of prime minister. During Medvedev's tenure there was never any doubt as to who was really in command. After his presidential term, there were elections and, of course, the "new" president-elect was...Vladimir Putin. The power of the presidency and the real power were aligned once more. Obviously, maintaining the appearance that power changes hands in the Kremlin is very important to Putin.

But why? Instead of going through all this trouble, why doesn't Putin just take the mask off and come clean? That would save him from having to abuse the resources of the state to achieve insurmountable advantages over his rivals in the elections and use all sorts of tricks.

Removing the mask would not be difficult. No one would be surprised, for example, if Putin called a referendum to indefinitely extend his term and he won (by an overwhelmingly majority, as always). Nor would it surprise anyone if the Parliament and the Supreme Court endorsed the president's maneuver to keep himself in power. After all, both institutions are fundamental elements of the artificial democratic facade behind which the Russian autocracy is hidden. In 17 years they have not once prevented Putin from doing what he wants.

Russia is not the only dictatorship that wants to appear like a democracy. Recently the Chinese authorities indicated their clear preference for the fate of Syria: "We believe that the future of Syria should be left in the hands of the Syrian people themselves. We respect the Syrian people's choice of their own leaders and development path." It is curious to see a dictatorship advising another dictatorship to let the people decide their fate. In fact, as Isaac Stone Fish, a journalist who spent seven years in China, points out: "One of China's Communist Party Secretary Xi Jinping's favorite slogans refers to the 12 'core socialist values' — of which democracy is second only to national prosperity." Stone Fish also says that at a conference he attended, several leaders of the Chinese Communist Party insisted that, just as with the United States, "China can accurately and credibly be called a democracy."

The Syrian Government asserts the same, while North Korea defines itself as the Democratic People's Republic. Nicolás Maduro, Daniel Ortega and Raúl Castro also argue that their repressive regimes are democracies.

Obviously, democracy is a brand that has become fashionable. This was not always so. In the 1970s, for example, dictators from Latin America, Asia and Africa did not seem to care much about appearing to be democrats. Perhaps because they felt safer than the dictators of today.

April 22, 2017

What Can Trump Learn from Al Capone
and Richard Nixon?

"I could stand in the middle of 5th Avenue and shoot somebody and wouldn't lose any voters," said the current president of the United States when he was still a candidate. He was probably right then, and even today he can still count on a large number of loyal supporters. However, this does not mean that Donald Trump is invulnerable. His stay in the White House could easily be truncated by a massive political revolt or by a judicial process that leads to his removal.

The latter is more likely than the former. It is surprising how often in the United States governors, mayors, members of Congress and the executive branch, as well as other senior officials, lose their office for breaking the law. Not even presidents are immune to catastrophic legal blunders.

These entanglements often occur when a politician or government official tries to cover up a "minor" offense or misconduct that could damage his reputation. For this he lies under oath or obstructs justice, committing a more serious crime than the one he's trying to hide. "What brings you down is not the crime, it's the cover-up," is a phrase that is regularly heard in the circles of power in the United States (and ignored with equal regularity).

This happened to Richard Nixon, who resigned just before being impeached for obstructing justice when he tried to hide his involvement in the Watergate case. And it also happened to Bill Clinton, who was accused of lying under oath in his deposition about his relation-

354

ship with Monica Lewinski. The House of Representatives voted in favor of his dismissal as president, but the Senate acquitted him, allowing him to finish his term. And this just happened to the Alabama governor, Robert Bentley, who has had to resign after being accused of lying and using public funds to hide an extramarital affair he had with his political adviser. Again, the efforts to hide his conduct, and not the conduct itself, were the cause of his departure from office. And it has also happened to General Michael Flynn, the national security adviser appointed by President Trump. Flynn set a record by serving only 20 days in office. He had to resign when it was discovered that — despite his initial denial — the talks he had with the Russian ambassador to the U.S. did include the possibility of easing the economic sanctions against Russia for invading Crimea. His talks with the diplomat were not the cause of Flynn's departure, but rather the lie about their content.

The cases of Governor Bentley and General Flynn are just examples from this week and last month, but the list of the powerful who stop being so when trying to cover up scandalous sexual relations, influence peddling, acts of corruption, misuse of public funds or their role in bad decisions is incredibly long. Donald Trump would do well to learn the lesson.

The other lesson that he should keep in mind is that money leaves fingerprints. That is why "follow the money trail" has become another popular slogan in Washington. Tracing the origins and intermediaries, the kickbacks and all the movements of funds is the best way to find the vulnerabilities of the powerful. In the United States, sex scandals and misappropriation of funds are the two most frequent reasons why political leaders fall. "Following the money" was the slogan that finally put Al Capone in jail, for example. The most famous gangster of the 20th century was accused of all sorts of crimes, including 33 murders, but no one could ever prove it. Only when the authorities succeeded in proving that he had evaded tax payments was Capone sentenced to a long prison term.

Last week, the Associated Press revealed that Paul Manafort, the head of Donald Trump's campaign between March and August of last year, received $1.2 million from a pro-Russian political group based in Ukraine. Manafort, who initially said the report was false, now admits the he received the money, but claims that it was payment for services rendered. We know that the FBI is investigating Manafort for possible contacts with Russian agents who may have been supporting the presidential campaign. It is also known that Donald Trump has refused to make his taxes public. It is difficult for these documents not to come to light. When that happens, "following the money" may offer some very interesting revelations.

Trump would do well to keep in mind how Al Capone and Richard Nixon went down.

April 15, 2017

Donald Trump's Three Wars...
and Those That Are Yet to Come

It is normal for presidents to clash with their political opponents and to have friction with other countries. It is also usual, and indeed healthy, for governments and the news media to not get along; and for presidents to face a bureaucracy that, according to them, does not enthusiastically execute the policies they have promised.

All this is normal. What is not normal is the variety, intensity, vindictiveness and, sometimes, the banality of the conflicts that originate from the new president of the United States. But Donald Trump is not a normal leader.

Presidents often enjoy a period of high popularity at the beginning of their term. Trump, on the other hand, has the lowest approval rating ever recorded in opinion polls. Attempts to realize his main electoral promises are sinking, he faces threatening criminal investigations against members of his team — some of whom have already been forced to resign — and he fails to fill the vacancies that would allow him to govern better. The leaks of information coming out of the White House are incessant. China is rapidly occupying the global leadership positions that the United States is abandoning, and Putin's Russia is on the rise and trying to influence the European elections as much as it did the American presidential elections.

In view of the above, one might think that Trump would try to stabilize the situation and build alliances. But the president is doing the opposite. Instead of reconciling, he seeks confrontation; instead of closing the battle fronts, he opens new ones, and instead of uniting, he divides. These are Donald Trump's three main internal wars.

1. The war against his own party: All political organizations have factions and the Republican Party is no exception. Their internal divisions prevented passage of the bill that would have dismantled the health care reform spearheaded by Barack Obama. Trump's reaction? "We must fight them," referring to the members of his party who were not in favor of his proposal. He has also said that he would support alternative Republican candidates in the midterm elections of 2018 to replace those congressmen and congresswomen who do not support him. The reactions from the dissident Republicans were immediate. "Most people don't take well to being bullied," said Representative Justin Amash of Michigan. "It's constructive in fifth grade, it may allow a child to get his way, but that's not how our government works." Although both parties will make efforts to show that they have overcome their differences, reality will prove that these divisions have lasting effects. Trump will continue waging war against those who do not support his initiatives, even if it means fighting openly against the leaders of his own party.

2. The war against the intelligence community: U.S. intelligence services employ more than 100,000 people working in 17 different organizations. While there have been frictions in the past between this community and the White House, the conflict has never been as strong as it is now. President Trump has said that these agencies are as dishonest as the mass media that disseminate false news. He has also called them "Nazis." For their part, the intelligence agencies issued a report whose conclusion is that the Kremlin influenced the U.S. elections and that Vladimir Putin has a clear preference for Donald Trump. James Comey, the director of the FBI, has confirmed that his organization is investigating a possible collusion of Trump team members with Russian intelligence agents during the election campaign. The president has said that he now has more confidence in the intelligence agencies "because now we have our people in." No doubt. But there are about 100,000 people there who are not yet "Trump people."

3. The war against the Federal Reserve: This war against the U.S.

Central Bank has not yet begun, but it is coming. Presidents like interest rates to be low, which often stimulates consumption, economic activity and employment. But if the fiscal deficit increases, so does the amount of money in circulation and prices start to rise, which means it will be the central bank's duty to raise interest rates to mitigate the risks of high inflation and other economic ills. Again, this tension between the presidency and the central bank, which is common everywhere, could escalate in Trump's case into a conflict with serious economic consequences. While still a candidate, the current president had already expressed his views about the Chair of the Federal Reserve, Janet Yellen. "She should be ashamed of herself," Trump said. Why? Because Yellen said that interest rates may have to be raised.

These three wars are internal, but Trump's pugnacity also manifests itself in international relations. And the biggest danger is that his domestic defeats may motivate him to pick fights abroad. He would not be the first leader of a country that uses an external conflict to distract from his internal problems. Putin can give him lessons on that.

April 1, 2017

Dying White Americans

In the United States, middle-aged white men with less education are dying at an unusual rate. In fact, their mortality rate is higher than that of Hispanics or blacks of the same age and of the same educational level. The mortality of the less-educated whites is also much higher now than it was at the beginning of this century. This is an exclusively American phenomenon. In other developed countries it just doesn't happen.

This is one of the conclusions of an important new study that was just presented in Washington by Angus Deaton and his wife, Anne Case. Deaton is the winner of the Nobel Prize in Economics (2015), and Case is a prominent economics professor at Princeton University.

In 2015, these two economists had already caused a stir with a study that, for the first time, documented the tragic rise in deaths among white Americans with no college education. While in 1999 the group's mortality rate was 30% lower than that of blacks with the same characteristics, by the year 2015 the mortality rate of these whites was 30% higher than African Americans. These changes have erased decades of progress. Over the last century, and continuing today, worldwide mortality has been falling by 2% every year in every country and in every demographic category. But white Americans without much academic preparation are the exception.

What happened? In this group, suicides and deaths from drug overdose and alcoholism increased dramatically. Cancer and heart disease also became more acute, as did obesity. Since 2000, deaths from these causes among non-Hispanic whites ages 50-54 have doubled.

And by 2015 they were dying at twice the rate of white women with the same characteristics (and four times more than white men who managed to go to college).

A common explanation for this tragedy is the unemployment that struck this group of workers, both because of the financial crisis and globalization as well as the automation of production, circumstances that are making low-skilled jobs disappear.

Deaton and Case do not doubt that unemployment and the consequent fall in income are important factors. But according to them, these explanations are insufficient and they maintain that the higher mortality of whites has "deeper causes." How do you explain, for example, that Hispanics and blacks, who also lost their jobs and income, are experiencing increasing longevity? And why is it that among European workers, who were also victims of the 2008 global recession and the ensuing austerity policies, we don't see the same lethal trends that affect white workers in the United States? Moreover, in Europe the longevity of those with fewer years of education (and less income) has continued to rise — and rise faster — than those of Europeans with higher educational levels.

According to the two economists, the deeper causes of this phenomenon have to do with what they call "cumulative disadvantages." These are debilitating conditions and dysfunctional habits that this group has accumulated throughout their life as a reaction to deep economic and social transformations. It typically began with dropping out of high school and an early entry into the labor market in times of plentiful employment and attractive salaries. But this initial "work bonanza" gradually vanished, and other changes in society — the role of women, increased divorce rates and family fragmentation, and geographic mobility — made life more difficult for white men and made them more vulnerable to what Deaton and Case describe as "deaths of despair." They are men who do not see a better future for themselves or for their families.

This hopelessness causes great suffering. In the U.S., half of unemployed men take pain medication and two-thirds consume opioids. The abuse of these drugs has become a very serious epidemic. In 2015, more Americans died of drug overdose than by firearms and traffic accidents. The overwhelming majority of victims? White men.

Two final questions. First: Why do white men of Hispanic origin, with little formal education and bad economic situations, die less? Because they have more hope in what the future holds. They are not longing for the better economic situation they had in the past. They never had it. For them the future can only be better. And even more so for their children.

Second: What is the political reaction of white Americans with high mortality rates? To vote for Donald Trump. More than 60% of them did so.

March 26, 2017

Asphyxiated Arabs

The 22 countries that make up the so-called Arab world represent only 5% of the global population, yet they account for 68.5% of the world's deaths from armed conflict, 57.5% of refugees and 45% of terrorist attacks (2014 figures).

These are some of the appalling realities documented by the United Nations Development Programme's (UNDP) report *Human Development in the Arab World*.

Surprisingly, the focus of this report is not war. It is young people. And it is very appropriate that it be so. Two-thirds of the Arab population is under 30 and half of them are between 15 and 29 years old. It is the group with the highest unemployment rate in the world, and among them, those with the poorest job prospects are women. The global unemployment rate for young women is 16%. In the Arab countries it is 47%. According to the World Bank, over the next three years the Arab countries would need to generate 60 million new jobs to absorb all the men and women who will be seeking employment for the first time. The UNDP report explains that the problem is not only that the Arab economies do not generate enough jobs, but also that their education systems, which are among the worst in the world, do not give young people the knowledge to navigate successfully in today's world or the skills they need to find work.

But while the economies and education systems are not doing well, armed conflicts are booming. Currently 11 of the 22 Arab countries are at war. Moreover, the vast majority of the Arab population has recently suffered an armed conflict, still suffers from one, or has a high risk of being involved in one. Of the 350 million people living in that region, 70 million are in Sudan, Yemen and Somalia. Another 67 million live in Syria and Iraq. Between 1988 and 2014, military expenditures in the region increased by two-and-a-half times, and per capita expenditure on arms became 65% higher than the world average. Since 2009 it has increased 21%.

In short, the UNDP report not only highlights the devastating impact of armed conflict on young people, but it also documents the few economic opportunities they have, the defective health and education services they receive, the widespread discrimination against women, and the limitations that young people have to participate in politics and channel their desires for social and political change. This final point is a critical factor that feeds the frustrations and hopelessness that, according to the report, prevail among young Arabs. For most of them a real future only exists outside their country.

It is important to note that the first of these UNDP reports on the situation of the Arab countries was published in 2002 and broke two traditions: The first was that previous studies on the region had predominantly been carried out by foreign experts. The second was that the automatic response of politicians and opinion makers from the region was to blame the rest of the world. In contrast, since that first report in 2002, the custom has been for a group of respected Arab experts to offer a new perspective every year on the problems and their possible solutions. The authors do not doubt that many of the tragedies of the Arab world are caused by the aftermath of colonialism, imperialism, the Cold War, and the armed interventions of the United States and Europe that overthrew dictatorships in Iraq and Libya, for example. And they also know that the foreign powers subjected — and continue subjecting — the region to their own interests and conflicts. But the novelty of these reports is that they recognize that many of the problems of the region are not imported, but homemade. And that, therefore, they can be alleviated by changing some of the conditions that are not the result of foreign influence, but that originated locally. One of the great merits of these analyses is their pragmatism.

But pragmatism can be a double-edged sword. As is the case with all the work of international agencies, there are issues that this UNDP report prefers, pragmatically, to ignore. Perhaps the most important is the impact on millions of young Arabs of predatory dictatorships and corrupt monarchies that suffocate them and rob them of their future.

March 19, 2017

What Middle Class Do You Belong To?

Six years ago, I wrote that "the main source of the coming conflicts will not be clashes between civilizations, but the frustrated expectations of the declining middle classes in rich countries and growing middle classes in poor countries."

My argument back then — which the passage of time has smiled upon — was that the middle classes in the United States, Europe and other higher-income countries would see their standard of living worsen, while in China, Turkey, Colombia and other emerging countries the economic situation of the poorest would improve. In that same article I pointed out that both rising and falling incomes generate expectations that fuel social and political instability. The surprise, of course, is that rising incomes of people in poor countries are a source of instability. I return to this paradox below. In that 2011 article I also warned that "inevitably, some politicians in advanced countries will exploit this discontent to blame economic decline on the rise of other nations." And I ended by predicting that the international consequences of this class clash, which were not obvious then, would eventually become so.

Well... unfortunately, those obvious consequences are here.

In these times of Brexit, Donald Trump, Marine Le Pen, Geert Wilders, Podemos and other political surprises, there is a proliferation of analyses that try to decipher the forces that nurture "the great rage", that deep discontent that leads voters to choose whoever they want as long as they do not resemble "those of the past." Globalization, immigration, automation, inequality, nationalism and racism are just some of the causes most commonly cited to explain "The Great Rage." But it has struck me that the analyses do not include in their explanation what is happening in Asia, Latin America or Africa. Once again, the dominant narrative treats as global a regional phenomenon occurring mainly in North America and the Old Continent.

The analyses ignore the fact that the middle class, which in Europe and the U.S. is struggling not to lose its economic, social and political preeminence, is in full bloom in the rest of the world. For a family in India that, for the first time, has an income that allows them to have medicine, house, car, television, smartphones and some savings, the defense of white supremacy that motivated many in the U.S. to vote for Donald Trump is unintelligible.

The rise of the middle class in poor countries is the main revelation of a major study just released by Homi Kharas, one of the most respected scholars on the issue. His calculations indicate that today, 3.2 billion people are part of the middle class in the world, i.e. 42% of the total population. For these calculations, researchers and institutions such as the World Bank define the middle class as people with daily incomes between $11 and $110 a day. This segment has been growing rapidly, but at different rates. While in the United States, Europe and Japan it grows annually at 0.5%, in China and India it adds 6% each year.

Globally, the middle class is increasing by 160 million people a year, and if it continues at this rate, in a few years, the majority of humanity will live in middle-class households for the first time in history. Although the middle classes are now more numerous than ever in countries such as Nigeria, Senegal, Peru and Chile, their expansion is primarily an Asian phenomenon. According to Kharas, the overwhelming majority (88%!) of the one billion people who will be part of this stratum in the coming years will live in Asia.

The economic impact of all this is enormous. Consumption by the middle class in lower-income countries is growing at 4% a year and already accounts for a third of the total global economy.

Naturally, the changes that the middle class is undergoing have important political consequences. In Europe and the U.S., we are already seeing these consequences in election results, referendums and the proliferation of unlikely candidates promoting unprecedented agendas. In lower-income countries, where the middle class is growing rapidly, expectations and demands are also growing rapidly. These new, more technologically connected social actors, with more purchasing power, more education, more information and more awareness of their rights, are a source of immense pressure on governments that do not have the capacity to meet these expectations.

The middle class in rich countries feels threatened and will demand actions and results from their governments that maintain their historical standards of living. At the same time, the middle class in emerging countries is more hopeful than ever and will fight for their progress to continue.

As we are already seeing, these divergent political agendas are the source of significant international friction. And they will continue to be.

March 12, 2017

2016

Venezuela: The World's Progressives Can No Longer Remain Silent

Until recently, the government established by Hugo Chávez captivated progressives worldwide. Visiting Venezuela to witness the accomplishments of the Bolivarian revolution became a key item on the agenda for many alter-globalization activists. Venezuela under Chávez garnered widespread acclaim.

That is over. Calamity is no longer celebrated. And blaming the Venezuelan catastrophe on the United States, the opposition or the fall of oil prices only convinces a dwindling group of naïve — or fanatics. The Chavista regime has lost its mask: its militarism, authoritarianism, corruption and contempt for the poor are on full display.

Why did it take so long for the world to catch on? Because Chávez coined a new way of acting in politics in the 21st century by combining a simulacrum of democracy with unlimited power and an oil boom.

The first ingredient was the manipulation of the election system. Chávez quickly understood the importance of not appearing before the world as just another military man who governs autocratically. As long as there were elections, he was a democrat. Very few outside Venezuela seemed to be interested in the boring details about stealthily falsified voter lists, the blatant advantage-taking, the massive use of state money to buy votes or discriminate against the opposition, or the fact that the electoral referees were government party activists.

This is how Chávez became a master in the paradoxical art of destroying democracy through elections. By stealth.

Venezuelans have voted 19 times since 1999, and Chavismo has won 17 times. And after each election, the Constitution was further encroached on, the courts and control bodies further co-opted, institutional counterweights further weakened and liberties further curtailed. The world said nothing.

The torrent of petrodollars that flooded into the country during the long oil bonanza of 2003-2014 was amplified by a massive new debt that today reaches 185 billion unpayable dollars. The money was used for two purposes: to subsidize the consumption of the working-class people who supported Chávez and to bankroll the corruption of the Chavista oligarchy. Meanwhile, the real economy was falling apart. With the economic slowdown and the collapse of public services (security, health, education, etc.), the government's popularity waned, which forced it to switch tacks: it would now tolerate electoral defeats, but not the loss of power. Shortly after losing control of a public institution by electoral means, Chávez proceeded arbitrarily and illegally to take away resources and powers.

When Caracas elected an opposition mayor, Chávez first withdrew the bulk of the office's powers and later Maduro ended up imprisoning him. When voters gave control of the National Assembly to the opposition, the Supreme Court, packed with Chavistas, blocked its every act. Now, the Government speaks openly about shutting down the Assembly altogether.

Hugo Chavez's commitment with democracy lasted exactly as long as his electoral majority did.

Something similar happened with the media. Chávez understood that shutting down independent media would damage his international reputation. But for the Bolivarian Revolution, freedom of expression is an unacceptable threat. The solution was to buy the independent media through private entrepreneurs. The new owners wasted no time transforming them into vehicles for official propaganda. Dozens of journalists were silenced and freedom of the press in Venezuela became a farce: dissidence disappeared from the media that reach the majority of the population. Chavista rhetoric of solidarity with the underprivileged also turned out to be a fraud. Talk of love for the poor covered up the plundering of the country by Cuba and the immense corruption of the military and the Bolivarian bourgeoisie, nicknamed the Bolibourgeoisie. A revealing example of this corruption is the $100 billion in oil revenues that disappeared from the National Development Fund, where they were deposited. The government never accounted for it.

The regime's actions reveal a callous disregard for the poor. While protests by people facing outright hunger are repressed with unusual violence, Chavista leaders appear drunk in social media videos running their luxury yachts aground. While newborn children die due to lack of medicines, the Supreme Court, loyal to the Government, censures the Assembly for having requested international humanitarian assistance. The authorities have no answers to the crisis and their indifference to the suffering of the people is outrageous.

You might think that plundering the public purse of the country with the largest oil reserves in the world should be enough even for the most voracious kleptocratic elite, but no. The regime is also deeply involved in drug trafficking. Anti-drug agencies have dozens of high-ranking Venezuelan government and military officials on their lists of drug kingpins.

Late last year, two nephews of the first lady were taped in Haiti offering hundreds of kilos of cocaine to buyers who turned out to be DEA agents. The nephews are behind bars in New York awaiting trial. Their aunt, the president's wife, has accused the U.S. of kidnapping them. You would think that the world should have lost patience with these aberrations by now. And that has begun to happen, but only timidly. The international community solemnly reiterates its concern for Venezuela, but these statements have had no consequences.

The least we can do to honor the memory of the thousands of murdered Venezuelans and the starving millions is to speak out: the democratic facade of Chavismo has collapsed; the cruel and thieving dictatorship that used to hide behind it is plain for all to see. The world's progressive left cannot remain silent in the face of Venezuela's tragedy. Ideology can no longer justify complicit silence.

July 12, 2016

Brexit and Trump: Politics As Witchcraft

The winner takes it all. This is one of the trends in countries where economic inequality has worsened: a few winners (the 1%) take it all. Or, to be more precise, the winners capture a huge proportion of the income and accumulate most of the country's wealth.

This pronounced economic inequality is one of the factors contributing to another trend in today's world: distrust. Survey-based trust indices in different countries are in free fall. People have very little trust in government, private enterprise, non-governmental organizations or the media. Worse still, institutions that used to be above suspicion are now unable to evade the wave. In recent years, for example, economic and political crises have undermined public confidence in "the experts," while multiple sex and financial scandals have eroded the credibility of the Catholic Church. According to these polls, everywhere and increasingly, people tend to trust mainly family and friends.

There are some exceptions. Sometimes, a normally skeptical population decides to place all its hope in certain leaders or political movements. It is a bipolar reaction: all or nothing. With trust, something similar to what has happened with the economy is happening: the winner takes it all. Suddenly, individuals appear who manage to awaken a faith that breaks all suspicions. We have seen how people's trust in certain leaders is maintained in spite of their proven propensity to distort reality, adulterate statistics, make unfulfillable promises, launch unfounded accusations or simply lie. Never mind that their mendacity becomes obvious.

Donald Trump is a good example of this. The media gives a daily tally of claims Trump makes that, when checked, turn out to be false. This, however, does not dent the enthusiasm of his supporters. Many simply believe that it is the journalists who claim to reveal the falsity of the candidate's claims who are lying. For others, the facts don't matter. Trump offers them hopes, protections and claims that make for an irresistible package, and from which they will not be disenchanted by inconvenient facts and data.

Something similar has just happened with Brexit. One of the most unusual spectacles of the day after the referendum in which the British voted to leave the European Union was to see and hear Brexit leaders deny the promises and facts on which they based their campaign.

No, the amount of money the UK sends Europe is less than they said. No, that amount is not going to be saved or invested in improving the National Health System. No, leaving the European Union is not going to result in fewer immigrants. No, they have no idea how they will fill the institutional and regulatory gaps created by this decision. All of these denials were babbled in front of microphones by Brexit leaders on the day of their victory. The same leaders who just hours before, and for months, maintained the opposite. Again, neither facts nor data matter. Data and facts are for the experts and "the people of this country are fed up with the experts." The latter was said by Michael Gove, one of the leaders of the pro-Brexit campaign (and now a candidate for prime minister), when, before the referendum, a journalist confronted him with the devastating conclusions of a group of renowned experts that included several Nobel laureates.

And these are just two examples of many others we have seen in Spain, Italy and other European countries, as well as in Latin America.

It has become fashionable to speak of a post-truth world. A world where despite the information revolution, Big Data, the internet and other advances, facts and data do not matter. Emotions, passions and intuitions are the forces that guide the political decisions of millions of people. This is not new. Politics without emotions is not politics. But government decisions where data don't matter are not government decisions, they are witchcraft.

As the British will soon discover, being guided by emotions and intuitions alone and ignoring reality always ends up in tears.

July 4, 2016

Brexit and the Italian Stalingrad

To better understand the potency of the forces driving the Brexit hurricane it is useful to recall what happened in 1994 in Sesto San Giovanni, a suburb north of Milan. In its heyday the area was filled with factories, workers and militant communist unions to such an extent that it became famous as the "Stalingrad of Italy." Since the end of World War II, whenever there was a local, regional, national or European election, more than 80% of the voters of Sesto/Stalingrad cast their votes for the Communist Party candidate. This changed in 1994, when a political earthquake as unexpected as Brexit shook the Stalingrad of Italy. It was another year of the crisis that hit the Italian industrial sector hard. That was also the year in which Silvio Berlusconi, allied with the right-wing parties, launched himself as a candidate, directly confronting the left and — specifically — the successors to the communist party.

More than 80% of the people of Sesto San Giovanni voted for Silvio Berlusconi.

The economic crisis, the corruption of politicians and sheer despair led communist voters to kick the table and elect the antithesis of their traditional choices. But apart from indulging in protesting against everything and everyone of the "usual" politicians through their vote, there was very little that the inhabitants of the Italian Stalingrad achieved by helping Berlusconi come to power. Having become prime minister, the businessman neither produced the "new Italian Miracle" with which he had excited his voters, nor did he improve the conditions of the workers, nor did he do much against corruption, another of his promises that led so many to believe in him. In many ways, electing Silvio Berlusconi as Prime Minister was an own goal that the Italians scored (four times!).

The British have just done the same.

Perhaps the earliest and most illustrative example of the British own-goal was provided by the local government of Cornwall, where 56.5% of those who voted in that county in the southeast of England did so in favor of Brexit, which means that there the enthusiasm for the break with Europe is greater than the UK average. But the celebration of that victory was short-lived. The same morning that the result in favor of leaving the European Union was known, the Cornwall council issued an urgent appeal demanding that they be guaranteed the £60 million a year that for 10 years they have received from Europe. And Cornwall's will not be the only own-goal. A startling statistic reveals that the regions of the UK that export the most to Europe were the most likely to vote in favor of Brexit.

Presumably, these areas will be where the most jobs will be lost as exports decline. Another sad example is provided by Dr. Anita Sharma: "I have devoted my career to cancer research, which has been made possible by EU funding. I hope that those who voted for Brexit understand the devastation this will cause to medicine." The United Kingdom and Germany are the countries that receive the most European grants for science.

The most common response to this type of observation is that the vote in favor of Brexit is motivated more by fear of the "excess" of immigrants and their social and cultural impact than by economic calculations. However, another paradox revealed by the statistics is that this concern is more anticipatory than real. The areas where the experience with immigrants is most concrete and real voted to remain in the European Union.

"Let's take back control" is the slogan skillfully used by the pro-Brexit campaign. This is the illusion — taking back allegedly lost control — that was sold well in the UK and is going to be sold well in other countries in Europe by the cohort of "terrible simplifiers," demagogues and opportunists now proliferating on the continent. The devastating results of this quest for "control" took only hours to appear. The most dramatic is that the currency devaluation, which knocked sterling down to 1985 levels, has already caused the economy to contract dramatically.

"Regaining control" is proving prohibitively expensive for Britain. All the more so because it is a delusion. In today's world the control that demagogues promise does not exist. Perhaps this is one of the many lessons to be learned from Brexit. Another lesson — which remains to be seen — is whether societies learn from the mistakes others make.

June 27, 2016

European Own-Goals

"Europeanist: 1. adj. Sympathetic to Europe. 2. adj. Supporter of European union or hegemony."

Based on this dictionary definition, I am a Europeanist.

Yes, I know. This is not an easy cause to champion these days. The list of shortcomings, frustrations and hypocrisies of the "European project" is lengthy. We know it.

However, despite its serious and obvious shortcomings, I still believe that a stronger Europe is indispensable not only for the citizens of the Old Continent, but for all the inhabitants of the planet. And for Europe to be strong, it needs to be more integrated and increasingly able to act in concert.

My Europeanism is based on the conviction that the world would be a better place if European values prevailed over those that today define Vladimir Putin's Russia, Xi Jinping's China or so many other parts of the world where democracy and freedom are not fundamental pillars.

But the winds blowing these days point more to the disintegration of the continent than to its integration, to a future with less Europe, not more. The looming exit of the United Kingdom from the European Union, should Brexit win this week's referendum, would be just one extreme example of the own-goals that Europeans are scoring on themselves. The proliferation of ultranationalist politicians and anti-immigrant proposals is another unfortunate, but very real, example of these own-goals.

Recent public opinion surveys in Europe conducted by the Pew Research Center shed interesting light on all this. In seven of the 10 nations polled, more than half of the respondents are of the opinion that their country should concentrate on dealing with its own problems and let other countries deal with theirs as best they can. Greece is where this view is most popular (83% of respondents), followed by Italy (67%) and France (60%). The country where this opinion is comparatively less popular is Spain (40%).

In general, Europeans think that their country is less important today than it was a decade ago: 52% of Italians, 50% of Spaniards, 46% of the French and 40% of the British think that their country has lost influence in the world. The exception is, of course, Germany, where 62% of respondents think their country is more important today.

The perception that their country's weight in the world is declining is consistent with the perception of great vulnerability and serious threats to national security felt by many Europeans. ISIS tops the list of risks in nine of the 10 countries surveyed. For almost all Spaniards (93%) and the vast majority of French (91%) and Italians (87%), ISIS is the main danger.

The other two most frequently mentioned threats are climate change (66% on average and a fear shared by more than half of respondents in all countries surveyed) and global economic instability (60%). It is worth noting that the perception of climate change as one of the most serious threats has been increasing. That was thought so in 2013 by 64% of Spaniards, while 89% now think so. In France, that perception rose from 64% then to 73% today, and in Italy from 56% to 72%.

Surprisingly, the crisis caused by the massive influx of refugees does not arouse great fears. In the Netherlands, 64% do not rate the crisis as a major threat, as do 76% of Swedes and 58% of Spaniards. In contrast, 73% of Poles, 69% of Hungarians and 65% of Italians do consider the recent wave of migrants a serious threat. But overall, in the ten countries surveyed, more than half of the respondents do not believe it poses a major risk.

Perhaps one of the most unexpected findings of these polls is the support that the European Union still enjoys. Seventy-four percent of those surveyed would like to see the European Union play a greater international role. The three countries where this hope is highest are Spain (90%), France (80%) and Italy (77%). Even more than half of the British (55%) also want this.

What a surprise!

It is good to know that there are more pro-Europeans than how it seems.

June 18, 2016

Latin America's Upheavals: Three Myths

The world is not correctly interpreting the changes taking place in Latin America. In particular, three ideas have become popular that, although they have some basis in reality, do not adequately reflect what is happening in the region.

1. Latin America has repudiated the left and turned to the right. This is not the case. Latin American voters have not experienced some profound ideological mutation, but a profound economic disillusionment. The leftist governments that have ruled Latin America since the beginning of the 21st century have stimulated massive consumption booms with the income generated by the high world prices of the raw materials they export. This obviously made them very popular. As the price of exports fell and, therefore, the capacity of the State to continue financing consumption, popular support for these leaders collapsed. The Kirchner family left power in Argentina and their candidate lost the elections. In Brazil, Dilma Rousseff is out of office and Lula da Silva is discredited. In Venezuela, Hugo Chávez's successor, Nicolás Maduro, presides over an unprecedented economic and political catastrophe. In Peru, Pedro Pablo Kuczynski, a businessman, will be the next president. In Bolivia, Evo Morales was defeated in his attempt to change the Constitution in order to run for a new term.

But these "leftist" political elites, now displaced, will not be out of the game forever. The economic policy corrections that the new Latin American governments will be forced to undertake will be unpopular and will create opportunities for politicians who know how to capitalize on the nostalgia for the good old days of Chávez, Kirchner and Lula.

2. Populism is over. Not so fast. The propensity of politicians to say what voters want to hear never ends. This is a practice of left and right, of secular and religious, of greens and industrialists. No politician can afford to disdain it and that is why populism exists everywhere, from the United States to South Africa. Populism becomes a problem when politicians lose all compunction in proposing what they know they cannot deliver, in promoting seductive policies that in practice are toxic, or in launching initiatives that divide society. And of course, an even bigger problem than the dishonesty of a few populist politicians is the naivety of the millions of followers who believe their enticing lies.

The economic abundance that Latin America experienced at the beginning of this century allowed the "usual" populism to transform into "super populism", thus reaching the unprecedented levels we saw in Chávez's Venezuela and Kirchner's Argentina. That unbridled populism is what is over. Not because people no longer believe in the bad but attractive ideas promoted by populists, but because there is no more money to finance them. In time, "normal" populism will come back.

3. Latin America is finally fighting corruption. In part, yes. But... there is no doubt that the political defenestration of Brazil's president has a lot to do with the gigantic corruption scandal that has occurred during her mandate and that of her predecessor, Lula da Silva. The president of Guatemala was also removed from office and is in jail on corruption charges. In Mexico, the government of Enrique Peña Nieto has been rocked by scandals involving several of its top leaders. Michelle Bachelet in Chile has also been affected by a scandal involving her son and daughter-in-law. In Argentina, former president Cristina Fernández and people close to her are facing serious accusations.

Mass marches protesting corruption have become common in many Latin American countries. The popular repudiation of corruption has also supported new protagonists who are making a difference in this fight: courageous judges, prosecutors and magistrates who are successfully confronting the corrupt, even those whose political or economic power made them seem untouchable.

This new intolerance of corruption is as welcome as the successes of the "corruption-hunting" judges. But beware. The fight against corruption should not depend on the goodwill or courage of individuals, but on institutions and rules that discourage corruption, eliminate impunity and increase transparency in government actions.

Putting public budgets on the internet and allowing everyone to know how public money is spent, reducing the number of discretionary decisions that public officials can make, or developing an efficient and reliable legal framework are examples of more serious ways to fight corruption than betting on the appearance of an honest president or a courageous judge.

June 13, 2016

Giving Money Away: an Inevitable Idea?

Today the Swiss will decide in a referendum whether the state will give its citizens around €2,500 every month. In exchange for what? For nothing. This consultation is key. Not because the proposal will win (according to the polls, it is unlikely to get the necessary votes), but because it may be a forerunner of a worldwide trend. In fact, the idea of guaranteeing a minimum income without conditions to citizens is already being tested in several countries. In Finland, the government randomly selected 10,000 adults to whom it will pay €550 per month for two years. The aim is to measure the impact this income will have on the propensity to work and other life choices made by the beneficiaries.

If this trial is successful, the intention of the Finnish government (which is right-wing!) is to extend this scheme nationwide. Similar experiments are being carried out in Canada, the Netherlands, Kenya and other countries.

The flaws and problems with this idea are obvious. Having a guaranteed income can discourage work. Giving a person material compensation without having produced something of value in return is a questionable proposition from an economic, social and ethical point of view. The risks of corruption and political clientelism in initiatives of this type are high. Finally, this is not a cheap idea. This type of subsidies can become a heavy burden for the State and create huge and chronic deficits in the public budget.

And yet... the trend may prove inevitable.

Globalization and new technologies have created immense opportunities for humanity. From global poverty alleviation to advances in medicine to the empowerment of historically marginalized social groups, the progress is obvious. But it is just as obvious that globalization and technologies that replace workers with machines can also have harmful effects. Job destruction, wage compression and rising inequality have many causes. But we know that both globalization and automation can nurture populism and the toxic political extremism we are seeing in so many countries.

For many, the answer is that while new technologies destroy industries, they also create others that produce as many or more jobs than those that disappear. And that has been happening. However, as technological change accelerates and robots, that at low cost can do many of the tasks a worker performs today, become popular, there is growing concern that new industries and new jobs will not appear in the numbers or at the pace needed to compensate for the job losses and wage reductions. Faced with this situation, the world has three answers.

1. More education and job training for the displaced. This is a priority. But the reality is that, while there are occasional successes in this area, the outcome of training efforts has been disappointing. In most countries — even the most advanced — the budgets devoted to helping displaced workers have been ungenerous, the educational techniques used are seldom effective, and the bureaucracies in charge of these programs are often inefficient. Changing this is urgent.

2. More protectionism. Donald Trump, for example, is just one of the politicians proliferating in the world today who promise to protect jobs by reducing both the number of immigrants competing with local workers and the volume of imported products, which, because they are cheaper, displace domestic production. It is not hard to imagine one of these demagogues promising that, if he wins the election, he will ban the use of robots and other "job-killing" technologies. These proposals are no solution and, in many cases, they cannot even be implemented. Still, millions of people get excited about such promises. I fear that some countries will end up adopting these bad ideas.

3. More guaranteed minimum income. That's right, give away

money for nothing. It may be a crazy idea. But a world where nine low-cost robots can do the work of 140 workers (in China!) is a world where you have to be open to examining all options. Even those that may seem — or be — far-fetched. Permanently high levels of unemployment are unacceptable and unsustainable. Therefore, everything must be tested, always understanding that governing rarely implies choosing between a wonderful policy and a dreadful one.

More often than not, those who govern are forced to choose between the bad and the terrible.

June 5, 2016

A Test and Several Robots

Let's start with a quiz. Was the text below published:
  a) in 1961?
  b) in 1987?
  c) last week?

"The number of jobs lost to more efficient machines is only part of the problem. What worries experts more is that automation may prevent the economy from producing enough new jobs [...] In the past, new industries hired many more people than those who lost their jobs in companies that closed because they could not compete with new technologies. Today, this is no longer true. New industries offer comparatively fewer jobs for unskilled or under-skilled workers, i.e. the class of workers whose jobs are being eliminated by automation."

The correct answer? a) 1961.

The quote is from a Time magazine article from February of that year. But it could have been published last week. And in 1970, or 1987, 1993 or any time in the last half century. Concern about job-destroying technologies is chronic. And, so far, unfounded. Thanks to new technologies, new industries appeared that created more jobs than were lost for technological reasons and increased both productivity and workers' incomes. This had already been predicted in 1942 by the economist Joseph Schumpeter, who called this phenomenon "the gale of creative destruction." According to him, "in the economy there is a process of industrial mutation that incessantly revolutionizes the economic structure from within, destroy-ing it and then creating a new one."

And so it has been. Until now.

It turns out that there will always be some who are sure that "this time it's different" and that the destruction of jobs brought about by revolutionary technological change is of unprecedented magnitude and speed. They believe that the new industries and occupations that are sure to emerge will neither arrive in time nor be sufficient to provide employment and a living wage for the millions of workers displaced by the new technologies. In recent weeks I have had the opportunity to visit different innovation centers and talk with some of the world lead-ers in the field of information technology and robotics. As always, there is a contagious optimism in this atmosphere. But I also found a lot of concern about the impact of new technologies and many doubts about the ability of society, the economy and politics to adapt to them.

The head of a well-known technology company, who asked me not to disclose his name, told me: "We will soon be launching a robot on the market that will be able to perform many of the tasks now given to those with a high school education or less. The robot is only going to cost $20,000. And we are not alone; our competitors in dif-ferent parts of the world are at the same thing. When these cheap, reliable, efficient robots become popular, I have no idea what jobs could be offered to people who don't have skills and abilities beyond what you learn in high school. But I also think this technological rev-olution is unstoppable. I don't know what the solution is."

In another example, these days Uber has announced that it began testing driverless cars. And it's not just Uber. Google, Mercedes-Benz, General Motors, Toyota and Tesla are just a few of the dozens of companies that are investing in this technology. Driverless vehicles are as inevitable as the $20,000 robot.

On this, Andy Stern, the former president of the U.S. labor union SEIU, has said that the popularization of driverless vehicles would destroy millions of jobs. "There are three and a half million truck drivers in the U.S., and so I see the possibility of the greatest disloca-tion of the labor market in human history," Stern says.

But Marc Andreessen, one of Silicon Valley's most respected investors and founder of Netscape, among other companies, takes a drastically different and much more optimistic view. According to him, "robots are not going to produce unemployment, they are going to unleash our creativity. To defend the idea that a huge group of people will be unemployed because we will have nothing to offer them is to bet against human creativity. And I have always done well when I have bet against human creativity."

Andreessen is right. But we urgently need to apply maximum creativity to make this transition less traumatic. How to guarantee a certain level of income for those who suffer the negative consequences of this revolution has to be part of any conversation about the wonderful potential of the new technologies.

May 29, 2016

Obama, the Disappointed

There is no doubt that Barack Obama ends his presidency having disappointed many of those who, with their votes, brought him to the White House in 2008.

The list of these disappointments is long and varies with each group. For some, the disappointment is that Obama has not closed the prison in Guantanamo Bay, for others it is his reliance on drones, or the fact that he has not intervened militarily in Syria, or that he has not intervened in Libya or made a pact with Iran. Also for not having sent more bankers to jail, or for having let inequality in the United States remain so high and wages so low. And the list, of course, goes on.

The president responds by emphasizing his accomplishments, comparing today's better situation to the crises he inherited, and pointing to the financial, political and international constraints that limited his ability to do more. There is no doubt that Obama experienced firsthand the limitations of power in these times. And that has led to his own list of disappointments. Not only has the president disappointed many, but many have disappointed him as well.

Lately, Barack Obama has been publicly reflecting on his presidential experience. Through lengthy sessions with reporters and meditative speeches, the president has hinted at some of his disappointments.

Perhaps the most obvious of his disappointments is with some leaders of allied countries. David Cameron and Benjamin Netanyahu are two examples. In a major interview with Geoffrey Goldberg in

The Atlantic magazine, Obama was candid in blaming Cameron in particular, and other European leaders such as Nicolas Sarkozy, for letting Libya become the disaster it is today. According to Obama, the stabilization and reconstruction of Libya after the overthrow of Muammar Qaddafi was a task for Europe, which, once again, the continent irresponsibly ignored, waiting for Washington to come to the rescue. Europe's inability to play an international role commensurate with its weight in the world is one of Obama's clearest disappointments during his time in the White House. He already knew this, but he confirmed it by experiencing firsthand Europe's failure to act as the global power it is in negotiations that are critical to its own future.

The Israeli prime minister has also been a constant source of irritation to his American counterpart. Obama is convinced that he has been a loyal, generous and reliable ally of Israel and that, in contrast, Netanyahu has been a disloyal, ungrateful and disdainful partner. Netanyahu's determination to survive in power by any means necessary in the hurricane-tossed domestic politics of his country has led him to engage in behavior unacceptable for one who claims to be an ally. His famous speech before the U.S. Congress on the eve of the disputed Israeli elections (orchestrated behind the back of the White House, in coordination with the leaders of the Republican Party), which Netanyahu used to denounce Obama's policies, is only one of the many examples that have surely reduced the President's sympathy for Bibi.

The leaders of major Arab countries and especially Saudi Arabia are also on the list of the American president's disenchantment. Obama has been very explicit about the urgency with which the Arab world should address the dysfunctions and failures that prevent hundreds of millions of its young people from taking advantage of the opportunities of today's world without abandoning their faith and traditions. Or the need to overcome the age-old confrontation between Sunnis and Shiites that causes untold violence and suffering. Obama knows that his exhortations in this regard have fallen on deaf ears. And that this deafness feeds one of the main sources of instability in the contemporary world.

But perhaps the greatest frustration of the U.S. president is with the elites of his country. Elites that are increasingly fragmented and whose need to defend their privileges makes them incapable of acting with a vision of the country and of the long term. In this they are not unique and reflect a global trend that is observable in more and more countries.

In the case of the United States, Obama has been explicit in pointing out that the political circles that today do not know what to do to stop Donald Trump are the same ones that for years legitimized the myopic narrative that today embodies the virtual presidential candidate of the Republican Party. They are the groups that promised that derailing Obama's presidency was their priority, that sowed doubts about the president's true nationality or the possibility that he was a radical Muslim infiltrating the White House, that his health care reform would lead to the creation of "death panels" that would decide which seniors would be entitled to which medical treatments or that, as Marco Rubio repeated, Obama's real purpose is to weaken the U.S.

In the face of all this, anyone would be disappointed.

May 11, 2016

A Miracle in Barcelona

Last week I witnessed an event that was at once rare, extraordinary and marvelous. I attended for the first time the Sant Jordi festival in Barcelona.

It turns out that, every year on April 23, the Ramblas in the capital of Catalonia are filled with roses, books and people.

The celebration of St. George's Day, patron saint of that region, is, of course, very old. Linked to the legend of the saint, the custom became popular in the 15th century, according to which on that day men give their beloved a red rose. From the thirties of the last century, the holiday coincided with the celebration of Book Day. And thus began the practice that, in exchange for the rose, women give a book to their men.

To say that these customs have caught on does not do justice to what happens in Barcelona on that day. In the Catalan capital, 1.6 million books and almost six million roses were sold on Saturday, April 23. Almost a thousand bookstores set up stalls on the Ramblas, where it is estimated that more than a million people strolled. Hundreds of authors, many from other countries, settled down to sign copies for their readers. That Saturday the bookstores turned over about €21 million, equivalent to 10% of their sales for the whole year.

The crowds of people, young and old couples, whole families, mothers with their babies and a wide variety of people of all ages interested in books, in talking to their favorite authors — or new authors they had never heard of before — or simply strolling through streets full of roses and books created a wonderful atmosphere. In other parts of the world, outdoor events that attract millions of people are usually accompanied by quite a lot of alcohol and a certain feeling of insecurity. Not at Sant Jordi. I didn't see anyone drunk or in threatening or aggressive attitudes. And although, like the rest of Europe, Spain is on high alert for the threat of new terrorist attacks, that danger seemed to be the furthest thing from the minds of those who took to the streets. On that day, street crime, violence or terrorism did not exist. This was a celebration of conviviality and culture rarely found elsewhere.

So much so that Markus Dohle, one of the foreign participants, told me that his dream would be to have an event like Sant Jordi in Manhattan, where he lives. "Can you imagine Broadway full of stores selling books?" he told me. It's not a disinterested wish. Dohle is the top boss of Penguin Random House, one of the world's largest publishing empires, and its headquarters are on Broadway. Dohle was not the only foreign visitor to look on Sant Jordi with a certain envy. Many of us from other countries imagined promoting something just as ambitious in our own cities. There are many book fairs and festivals. Some are even bigger. But none of them has the air of joy and civilization that Sant Jordi has. That is why it is surprising how relatively little known this event is outside Spain. The opportunity to turn it into an international destination should be seized.

Another reason why I felt that Barcelona was living a miracle is that, in theory, the passion for books, and specifically for old-fashioned paper books, should no longer exist - or at least not with the strength that I perceived at Sant Jordi. Today we are told that paper books are on their way to extinction. That they cannot compete in cost and convenience with e-books, and that in the future they will only be decorative pieces or museum relics. Experts also tell us that social medias and other revolutions in information technology make our attention increasingly fragmented and we have constant distractions, all of which are not conducive to reading. In this day and age, the 140 characters of a Twitter tweet dominate, not the 500 pages of a good book. Who has time to read books these days?

But it seems that the passionate readers who attended Sant Jordi's Day didn't get the memo. They are still reading. And on paper. And so, every year they create a "rare, extraordinary and wonderful thing." This week, don't follow me on Twitter. Read a book.

May 5, 2016

A Panamanian Story (and Not the One You Think)

Panama's party has been spoiled. Instead of celebrating the expansion of its iconic canal, the small Central American country has consolidated its image as the place used by the world's powerful to hide money. Someone turned over to the media the secret information of thousands of Panama-based companies that served to maintain the anonymity of their owners. Its publication will surely have an impact equal to or greater than the Wikileaks or Edward Snowden's leaks.

But there is another interesting Panamanian story that has nothing to do with the so-called Panama Papers. Instead, it has to do with international trade, dictatorships, the internet, global warming and... China.

It begins with Panama's decision, in 2006, to double the capacity of the canal that saves a 12,700-kilometer detour for ships transiting between Asia and Europe. In view of the increase in world trade, which has tripled in volume since the 1950s, Panamanian authorities thought it was a good idea to expand the canal to allow more ships and more goods to pass through it and to increase the country's revenues. This assumption seemed safe when international trade was growing every year at twice the rate at which the world economy was expanding. But now it has slowed: 2015 was the fifth year in a row in which international trade growth fell below its historical average, a trend not seen since the 1970s and one that will continue this year. In 2007, international flows of funds, goods and services reached 53% of the global economy. In 2014 they fell to 39%.

Is this slowdown in exports and imports between countries simply a transitory bad patch? In part yes. But, according to the International Monetary Fund, the slowing trade between countries is also due to more structural and permanent causes, specifically: China and the internet.

The Asian giant — in addition to growing more slowly — is trying to move from an economy based on exports and manufacturing to one where domestic consumption and services have more weight. In addition, Chinese factories are now producing more intermediate products that they used to import. Both of these things reduce China's international trade. But there is more. While trade in goods is slowing, the international flow of digital information is booming: it doubled between 2013 and 2015 alone.

The consulting firm McKinsey estimates that, in 2016, individuals and organizations will send 20 times more data to another country than in 2008. One of the innovations that has huge implications for global trade is 3-D printing technology. Today, instructions can be emailed to a printer anywhere in the world to manufacture, for example, an airplane part. General Electric estimates that, by 2020, it will be shipping 100,000 parts around the world via the internet rather than ships.

But the Panama Canal not only faces less potential demand for its services, but also more competition. Wang Jing, a Chinese businessman, announced in 2013 that he would build an alternative canal through Nicaragua. This work would require the largest earth movement in the history of the planet and involves enormous risks to the environment. Its financing was and remains mysterious and its feasibility doubtful. But Nicaragua's limited democracy allows President Daniel Ortega to go ahead and give his enthusiastic support to Wang, a businessman as opaque as the project he is promoting.

Obviously, if built, the Nicaraguan canal would take away market and profitability from the Panamanian one. But few believe it will become a reality.

What is a new and unstoppable reality is the global warming that is melting the Arctic and allowing cargo ships to sail through what used to be an impassable ice barrier. Use of this northern route is still infrequent, but if the current rate of melting continues, in the future a cargo ship could save two weeks of sailing from Shanghai to Hamburg by this route. Or the cost of paying Panama to use its canal.

This is how the small Central American isthmus has become a laboratory where the effects of the major global trends shaping the world today — from corruption in China to climate change or the internet — is in plain view.

April 17, 2016

'Continuismo' Is More Dangerous Than Populism

Populism will never go away, not in Latin America and not all over the world. Populism is found on the right and on the left, among environmental politicians and among those who deny climate change, among protectionists and among those who promote economic openness. It is found among the most religious politicians and among secular leaders.

As long as there are people who want to hear feel-good promises, there will be politicians who will tell them what they want to hear. In a world of rapid change, of new threats that are difficult to understand, and full of uncertainties, those who promise security and certainty give assurances and alleviate anxieties, attract followers.

The problem with the populism that existed in Latin America in the first decade and a half of the 21st century is that it was amplified by the economic bonanza that the region experienced. Now the bonanza is over and, with its end, so is the possibility of financing the hyper-populism experienced in Venezuela or Argentina and, with lesser excesses, in the rest of the region.

There is no doubt that the results of the presidential elections in Argentina, the legislative elections in Venezuela, the defeat of the referendum through which Evo Morales sought to continue in the presidency of Bolivia, as well as the fall in popular support for Rafael Correa, are due to voter fatigue with regimes that have governed them for more than a decade.

But there is more. The poor economic situation also diminished

401

the population's tolerance for corruption. The institutional removal of Otto Pérez Molina from the Guatemalan presidency, the massive popular protests calling for Dilma Rousseff's resignation, and the corruption scandals hounding Lula da Silva and the presidents of Mexico and Chile are also signs that impunity for the corrupt is less tolerated in Latin America.

But it is important to understand that a greater threat than populism is presidential re-election. If a government is inept, indecent or insensitive to the cries of the people, in the next election the voters will get rid of it. But a bad president who manages to perpetuate himself in power perpetuates bad government.

This sacred rule of democracy, alternation, is in trouble in Latin America. Presidents who come to power by the ballot box but quickly manage to cheat rules, control the electoral tribunal, buy legislators, judges and magistrates, or use public funds for their re-election, have become a frequent phenomenon in Latin America.

A common trick is to promote changes in the country's constitution. It is often presented as an initiative to fight corruption and social exclusion, modernize the State and other laudable objectives. But the real objective is to concentrate power in the Executive, lengthen the presidential term and allow the president to be reelected.

Latin America has entered a stage in which governments will no longer have so much money for populist programs. Hopefully it will also enter a stage in which no president can be reelected. This may have costs, but they will always be lower than having presidents who govern to prolong their stay in the presidential palace. Latin American presidents: one term and then out of office. Forever.

April 10, 2016

Zika, ISIS and Trump

They couldn't be more different. Zika is a virus, ISIS is a terrorist group and Trump is... Trump. Yet all three have shocked the world. And it turns out they have more in common than meets the eye. They are the 21st century version of ancient phenomena: epidemics, terrorism and demagoguery.

The Zika epidemic began in 2015, ISIS was born in 2014, and Donald Trump announced his candidacy for the United States presidency in 2015.

However, none of the three are new. The Zika virus was first identified in 1947 when it was found in a monkey in a jungle in Uganda. ISIS leaders have a long history in other Islamist terrorist organizations. And as early as 1987, Donald Trump announced to the media that he planned to run for president of the United States. That plan did not prosper, but in 2000 Trump ran for the presidency in the Reform Party primaries.

While there have always been epidemics, terrorists and demagogues, their recent manifestations have taken the world by surprise. And we have no answers.

The Zika virus is suspected to be transmitted mainly by the Aedes aegypti mosquito. In February, the World Health Organization declared that both the sudden increase in Brazil of newborns with cranial defects (microcephaly) and people affected by Guillain-Barré syndrome (a rare condition affecting the nervous system) constituted a worrying international public health emergency. Aedes aegypti is well known to health authorities and scientists, but the new virus it transmits, Zika, is not. Substantial investments are being made to prevent outbreaks and contain the epidemic. Scientific research has also intensified to find vaccines and cures. But the reality is that the international community is not prepared to deal with the epidemic and much is unknown about the threat or how to combat it. It is an old virus that has acquired a new potency.

Exactly the same can be said of Islamist terrorism. It has been around for a long time, but its lethality has been increasing to unprecedented extremes. Compared to the more recent atrocities of Boko Haram or ISIS, the horrendous terrorist acts of Hezbollah seem almost quaint. Even for Al Qaeda, ISIS violence is unacceptable. The central command of the organization led by Osama bin Laden issued a statement distancing itself from ISIS and clarifying that it has no ties to that organization. "Al Qaeda is not responsible for the acts of ISIS," the statement insists.

ISIS tactics and actions have not only shocked Al Qaeda. Its ruthlessness, efficiency and methods of recruitment and financing and its novel use of social media, as well as its military tactics, also took governments with long experience in dealing with Islamist terrorism by surprise. "ISIS is different" is the resigned and repeated acknowledgement heard in the security agencies of threatened countries.

That's the same thing said of Donald J. Trump by Republican Party leaders trying to block his candidacy and by political analysts who never imagined the businessman could get this far: "Trump is different." Just as ISIS has done with respect to terrorism, Trump's actions in American politics are unprecedented. And it's not just about how unusual his threatening messages and aggressive proposals are. Trump has also changed the traditional ways of financing presidential campaigns, the use of the media or the relationship with his party's establishment. His ability to make millions of people believe him in unfulfillable promises, or get them excited about the idea that it is enough for him to be president for everything to be better, are realities that have analysts perplexed.

Another factor that Zika, ISIS and Trump have in common is

that all three are products of globalization. As Science magazine reports, the virus arrived in Brazil from French Polynesia and the ease of travel and increase in tourists for the World Cup caused it to spread rapidly. There are already Zika outbreaks in 30 countries and territories in the Americas.

For its part, ISIS owes to globalization the ease with which it can recruit jihadists in Europe, send trained terrorists back to the West, sell oil or manage its finances internationally or collect donations worldwide.

And what would Donald Trump be without the Mexicans he claims are "invading" the U.S., the 11 million "illegal aliens" he promises to extradite or the Chinese workers who have millions of Americans unemployed?

In many ways, Trump, the Republican mogul, is as anti–globalization as his adversaries on the left.

Zika, ISIS and Trump are the continuation of old phenomena. But in their current version they are more potent — and more dangerous — manifestations of the phenomena they represent. We are prepared for none of it.

9 de abril de 2016

The Numbers of Terrorism

In my article last week — published before the recent attacks in Brussels — I wrote about the myths of jihadist terrorism in the United States. Perhaps the most striking of the data I mentioned there is that, from September 11, 2001 to today, only 45 people were killed by Islamist terrorists in the U.S. By comparison, in Brussels terrorists claimed 31 lives in a single day and last November's attacks in Paris killed 130 innocents. In 2014 there were a total of 37,400 murders perpetrated by terrorists worldwide.

To provide some context on the Brussels tragedy, in this article I expand the focus of the analysis to the rest of the world. The data come primarily from START, the National Consortium for the Study of Terrorism, a research center at the University of Maryland, and from a compilation by Anthony Cordesman, an expert at the Center for Strategic and International Studies (CSIS) in Washington.

Terrorism has always existed, but in the 21st century both the number of attacks and the number of victims has increased rapidly. In the last 15 years, terrorist attacks have grown from fewer than 2,000 to nearly 14,000. And fatalities have increased ninefold.

But this increase has occurred neither in North America nor in Europe. Five countries — Iraq, Pakistan, Afghanistan, Nigeria and Syria — have accounted for 57% of attacks since the turn of the century. Most of the attacks were not against targets in the Western world, but between Shiite and Sunni Muslims.

While lethality has increased, actions resulting in more than 100 deaths are rare. This number has been exceeded most often in a single attack in Iraq (29 times), Nigeria (13), Pakistan (6), and India and Syria (4 each). More than 90% of terrorist attacks achieve their most immediate objectives, the killing of civilians, police, military or civil servants. This high success rate is due to the proliferation of the use of homemade explosives that are often set off by suicide bombers, another practice that has also increased considerably. Fifty-eight percent of all attacks are carried out with explosives and 34% with firearms; the remaining 10% are due to other methods. Only 4% employ both firearms and explosives, but experts expect this combination to increase, as their lethality is almost three times that of attacks using only firearms.

Between 2000 and 2014, 40% of all terrorist attacks were perpetrated by groups that could not be identified. The remaining 60% is accounted for by a small number of organizations: the Islamic State (ISIS), Boko Haram, the Taliban, Al Qaeda in Iraq and Al Shabab are perpetrators of 35% of all attacks that occurred worldwide in the last 15 years. Between 2013 and 2014, ISIS perpetrated more than 750 attacks. One of the preferred targets of terrorists are means of transportation, especially buses and trains (they concentrate 62% of the attacks in this category).

Terrorism is on the rise and is also becoming globalized. Its protagonists, its targets, its tactics and the way it is organized are changing. So are the capacities of Western states to deal with it. In some respects, societies have strengthened their defenses against terrorists. In others, they are still very vulnerable, as the attacks in Brussels have shown.

The consequences of these terrorist actions in Europe (and the U.S.) are devastating, to the extent that they shake important principles such as freedom of movement or privacy of communications. They also have an impact on public spending, travel, coexistence and integration within and between countries. In other latitudes, terrorist groups threaten the viability of certain countries and shape geopolitical struggles.

In Spain, ETA killed nearly 1,000 people in five decades. But the political and social consequences of its terrorist acts are still being felt.

There are no simple solutions for the threat of terrorism. It is a diverse phenomenon that will not have a single solution. But within this complexity there is one statistic worth keeping in mind. The average homicide rate worldwide in 2014 was 6.24 deaths per 100,000 population, while deaths from terrorism were 0.47 per 100,000. This means that, that year, for every 13 homicides there was one person killed by a terrorist.

Terrorism's numbers are relatively low when compared to other causes of death. But its consequences are disproportionately large.

Terrorism is not the most lethal threat of the 21st century. But it is changing the world.

March 27, 2016

Myths of Jihadist Terrorism

Since the September 11, 2001, attacks, terrorists have killed 93 people in the United States. Nearly half, 45, were victims of jihadists. The remaining 48 died at the hands of terrorists who had nothing to do with Islam. They were murders motivated by hatred against doctors and nurses who perform abortions, by paranoid anti-government fanaticism or by neo-Nazi ideology.

Analysis of more than 330 people sentenced in the U.S. since 9/11 for crimes related to jihadist terrorism reveals a profile that contrasts with commonly held beliefs about who these terrorists are. When they committed these crimes, they were, on average, 29 years old. A third of them were married and another third had children. They had attained the same level of education as the average in the U.S. and the incidence of mental problems in this group was lower than the U.S. average. Another important fact is that all of the lethal Islamist-motivated attacks were perpetrated by U.S. citizens or legal residents.

In short: the Islamist terrorists who have acted in the U.S. after 9/11 are surprisingly ordinary people. And they did not come from abroad. They are Americans who have always lived, or lived most of their lives, in that country. It is also worth noting that, in the United States, a person is 3,000 times more likely to be killed by a bullet fired by one of their own countrymen, with no ideological motivation, than by a jihadist.

This data comes from *United States of Jihad*, a recent book by Peter Bergen, an expert on Islamist terrorism who rose to fame in 1997 as the producer of the first televised interview with Osama bin Laden. The book offers a detailed dissection of what Bergen calls "home-grown terrorists." These are Americans who are radicalized, becoming soldiers in a holy war against non-believers, particularly against the West, and which is inspired by an extreme and distorted interpretation of Islam. Of particular concern are the so-called "lone wolves," terrorists who act alone and without having had major contact with international networks or other suspects. Their isolation makes it extremely difficult to detect them before they commit a terrorist act.

The big question is: Why? What makes people who, at first glance, show no major differences with the rest of the population, decide to become jihadists? We don't know.

Experts have no consensus on the answer.

Some things, however, are clear. Radicalization toward jihadist violence has different determinants and contexts in different countries. The young Frenchman who murders innocents and then commits suicide by shouting "Alahu akbar" has had a different life experience than the one who does something similar in the United States. In France, for example, less than 10% of the population is Muslim but 70% of its prison population is. This is not the case in the U.S., although it is the country with the highest percentage of its incarcerated population. The integration of Muslims into economic and social life in the U.S. is more harmonious than in other countries.

Another frequent — but far from universal — characteristic among jihadists is the existence of a triggering episode: some personal frustration, serious economic difficulties, grief over the loss of a loved one or a failed love affair.

But not everyone who goes through something like this becomes a terrorist.

Jihadism can also be reached through more complex and less obvious psychological processes. The American Psychiatric Association has published an interesting article in its monthly newsletter that recapitulates the results of the most recent research on the subject.

The psychiatrists focus their explanation on the need of all young adults to achieve a certain "existential relief." They add: "This involves discovering who you are, where you belong, what you value, what gives meaning to your life, what you can aspire to be and how you can prove yourself to the world... For young people who are marginalized and sometimes in transition between one society and another, the process of identity formation can be a hopeless task."

Psychiatrists conclude that "the reasons why young people join terrorist organizations have little to do with being poor, Muslim or psychopathic and more to do with the vulnerabilities of human nature, which are made worse by certain aspects of Western societies [...] For young Westerners who are in transition and feel marginalized, lonely, lost, lost, bored, spiritually and existentially dispossessed and overwhelmed by too much freedom, ISIS and other shallow but contagious ideologies will remain tempting as instant solutions to the deep difficulties inherent in the human condition."

This psychological insight does not provide many practical ideas about how to prevent jihadist terrorism. But at least it unmasks the prejudices that pass for unquestionable facts and makes us see how dangerous it is to adopt policies based on false assumptions.

March 19, 2016

Mediterranean Surprises

Greece, Turkey, Syria, Lebanon, Israel and Egypt define an area as beautiful as it is historically transcendent and conflict-ridden. This is where written language and mathematics, bureaucracies and democracy, Christianity, Islam and Judaism were born, as well as the Byzantine empire, among many other ideas and institutions that form an indelible part of humanity's heritage. But the nations of the eastern Mediterranean have also formed, and continue to form, a very dangerous neighborhood.

Civil wars, insurrections, invasions, famines, genocides, droughts, pirates and mercenaries have made the region one of the most unstable on the planet.

One of the surprises that the eastern Mediterranean holds for us today is that, in this very modern 21st century, instability in the area has reached levels worthy of the Middle Ages. In the most recent issue of Foreign Affairs magazine, analyst Kenneth Pollack writes: "The modern Middle East has not been a peaceful place, but it has never been as bad as it is now [...] The Middle East has not seen so much chaos since the Mongol invasions of the 13th century."

As we know, in times of globalization, conflicts also tend to globalize and that is how isolated street protests in Syrian cities escalated into a terrible civil war that contributed to the rise, among others, of the Islamic State and generated the largest number of displaced people in Europe since World War II. But while all this is going on, the eastern Mediterranean has given us another surprise that has gone mostly

412

unnoticed: some of the world's largest hydrocarbon deposits, especially gas, have been discovered under its seabed.

At the beginning of this century, oil prices hovered around $100 per barrel, and this encouraged energy companies to explore areas that were not previously economically attractive. Exploration and production costs were high, but so were prices. A series of technological innovations in the search for oil and gas, as well as advances in methods to exploit deposits located tens of kilometers below the seabed, made previously unreachable areas commercially attractive. The new efforts were yielding results. They started slowly: interesting deposits were found, but not particularly large ones. In recent years, however, there has been a boom in discoveries of fields with huge oil and gas reserves. According to the U.S. Geological Survey, the Levant Basin, which stretches from Egypt in the south to Turkey in the north, contains 122 trillion cubic feet of gas and 1.7 billion barrels of oil.

Some estimate that there is twice as much gas and about 3.8 billion barrels of oil.

These are huge numbers. For example, the Tamar and Leviathan fields, discovered off the shore of Israel, are larger than most North Sea gas fields and their reserves could supply all of Europe for two years. And these are just two fields. Last August, off the coast of Egypt, the Zohr field was discovered, a gas field equivalent to 5.5 billion barrels of oil. There have also been discoveries in the waters off Cyprus, and exploration efforts in the rest of the basin have accelerated.

These discoveries change the energy map of the region and of Europe. And they have enormous geopolitical consequences. Egypt, Israel and Lebanon will be able to export energy. Moreover, the proximity of these new hydrocarbon sources to Europe poses a serious threat to Russia. Its economy is critically dependent on the gas it sells to Europe and runs the risk that its Mediterranean competitors will take away its European customers. The impact of these new riches in this conflict-prone region is difficult to gauge.

But nothing is simple in the Levant. In addition to armed conflicts, civil wars and precarious governments, there are protracted disputes between Lebanon and Israel over their borders, and between

Turkey and Greece over Cyprus. These disputes leave the sovereignty of huge marine areas in limbo.

But the most serious threat to the energy potential of the eastern Mediterranean is the fall in oil prices. If the new prices — between $40 and $50 per barrel — become established as the norm, the newly discovered fields in the Levant Basin will be of little consequence. On the other hand, if prices rise and new technologies continue to drive down production costs, energy from the eastern Mediterranean will have a global impact that is now unimaginable.

March 12, 2016

China: The Tangle Is Not Just Economic

In my previous column I described the economic difficulties China is going through. The lowest economic growth in 25 years, massive capital flight, huge uncollectible debts and a sharp fall in the stock market are some of the symptoms that the Asian giant's economy is not doing well. Macroeconomic upheavals always generate turbulence in other areas. Here are some of the rare micro-events, which have macro-implications for China, its government, its people and, inevitably, for all of us.

1. The Communist Party represses the working class. In January 2011, there were eight work stoppages in China. This January, 503. According to the Chinese Labor Bulletin, there were 2,774 strikes in 2015, twice as many as in 2014. The increase in unrest has led the government to crack down hard on labor leaders. International observers have warned that while Chinese labor organizations have always suffered systematic attacks and pressure from the Government (tax audits, mafia violence, police harassment), repression has intensified. As an article in The Washington Post points out, the regime seems determined to stamp out labor activism for good. "It is a cruel irony that the Communist Party represses its workers," it concludes.

2. Guo Guangchang is called the Chinese Warren Buffet. He is a billionaire who controls China's largest private company, Fosun. Last December, Guo disappeared. It was said that he was "collaborating with certain investigations by the authorities." Days later, and without further explanation, he reappeared addressing Fosun's shareholders' meeting.

415

Yang Zezhu, one of the best-known leaders of the Chinese financial sector, fared much worse than Guo. In January, he threw himself out of a window. He left a note explaining that his suicide was because the Communist Party's disciplinary body was investigating him for "personal reasons." These are just two examples of a staggering number of leading businessmen who have "disappeared," suddenly resigned, emigrated or been arrested. The list includes the top echelon of the business sector. One of President Xi Jinping's priorities is the fight against corruption. And the disappearance and detention of businessmen is undoubtedly a manifestation of this crusade. But it also reflects the fact that the anti-corruption fight also serves to eliminate potential rivals and consolidate power.

3. Sometimes books also disappear... and I mean company books. Recently, police had to use two backhoes to dig 1,200 books containing the accounts of one of China's biggest financial frauds out of a deep hole. Ding Ning, 34, is the founder of Ezubao, one of the best-known investment houses. The company promised a 15% annual return to those who deposited their money there, and 900,000 people took them up on it. And they lost a collective $7.6 billion, which, it is now known, Ding used for his own purposes. Ezubao's is the biggest and most visible of the Ponzi schemes plaguing the Chinese financial sector. But it is not the only one.

4. And publishers, booksellers, and writers... Publisher Lee Bo, 65, a British citizen based in Hong Kong, also vanished in December. His wife reported to the police that Lee had been kidnapped and taken to Beijing. A few days later she withdrew the report and explained that her husband had traveled voluntarily to assist Chinese police in an investigation. Four other people associated with Lee's publishing company have been missing since last year. Small detail: the company is known for publishing books that are critical of the Chinese leadership.

Another publisher, Yiu Man, 73, was finalizing the publication of *The Godfather Xi Jinping*, a critical book written by dissident Yu Jie. But he was unable to publish it because he was sentenced to 10 years in prison. His crime? The government accused him of bringing drums

416

of industrial paint from Hong Kong to Shenzhen without paying customs duties. Naturally, the crackdown on publishers causes critical books to disappear and their authors to go into exile, go into hiding or stop writing.

5. And words and numbers. Professor Frank Fukuyama has just identified the words that disappeared from the Chinese edition of his latest book. Among others: "Mao," "the Tiananmen protests," "the great famine," "corruption" and "the rule of law." There is also a long list of words that do not appear in internet search engines or are deleted when typed in social media search boxes. Statistical data indispensable to evaluate the economic situation have also vanished. Others have been clearly faked.

In short: censorship, propaganda, the concealment of information, harassment, imprisonment of dissidents, activists, businessmen and anyone who protests against the regime. These are some of Beijing's responses to the social and political consequences of its economic crisis. Governments often aggravate crises with their reactions. This is a case in point.

27 de febrero de 2016

China Missteps

For 35 years, the Chinese economy grew, on average, by more than 10% every year. This meant that, every seven years, the Asian giant's income doubled. As a result, China today is a different country than it had been for centuries. This transformation is not only obvious in its modern cities, its huge industrial sector, its exports or the fact that it is the world's second largest economy. The most important change is that 500 million Chinese are no longer poor. In 1981, at the beginning of the economic reforms, 85% of the population lived in conditions of misery, while now the poor make up 7% of the population.

China's progress has radiated to the rest of the world: it has become the main buyer of raw materials, a major exporter of manufactured goods, the largest buyer of debt bonds issued by governments and companies in the Western world, and a major investor, especially in less developed countries. Today, what has so often been said about the U.S. can be applied to China: if China sneezes, the world catches a cold. Or more precisely: what happens in China affects you. And these days the Chinese economy is not only sneezing, it is sick.

The symptoms are many. The most obvious is that in 2015 its economy grew at the slowest rate in 25 years. And for the past four years, growth has been slower than the previous year. Then came a stock market crash and a chaotic currency devaluation. This was followed by massive capital flight. In January alone $110 billion flowed out of China, while during the whole of 2015 the net flow of capital abroad was $637 billion, an unprecedented amount and a serious indi-

418

cator of distrust. A population that on average saves 30% of its income sees how the value of its currency falls and prefers to keep its savings outside its country and in other currencies.

But the most worrying symptom is the immense and growing debt that has been accumulating. This debt, which in 2007 was equivalent to one and a half times the size of the entire Chinese economy, has tripled. The main indebtedness is in local governments, which financed the construction of an enormous amount of unjustifiable infrastructure works (buildings, roads, airports) that have remained unused or unfinished. Now the central government will be forced to absorb these losses, which will increase the fiscal deficit.

What happened, and how did China's successful economy get into such a tangle? The answer can be summed up in two words: boom and bust. When an economy grows at high speed for three decades, so do waste and bad investments, corruption and many mistakes that the bonanza allows to be covered up or ignored. On the other hand, the global crisis that broke out in 2008 led the Chinese authorities to launch the biggest economic stimulus ever known. Their goal was to prevent the problems in the U.S. and Europe from spreading to the Chinese economy: high growth had to be maintained at all costs. And so it was: government spending soared, as did credit and the injection of money into the economy. This effort succeeded in preventing the Chinese economy from collapsing, but it fed the distortions that plague it today.

What is going to happen? China needs to move from an economy based on investment (especially in infrastructure) and manufacturing exports to a model driven by domestic consumption and service sector growth. This requires the government to pursue reforms that are unpopular in the short term, but which would put the country on a sustainable path.

Unfortunately, this does not look like it will happen anytime soon. The Premier, Li Keqiang, has just ordered an intense "information campaign" aimed at explaining that the economy is fine and that the problems are mainly about "communication." But censorship and propaganda do not make the difficulties go away; rather they tend to aggravate them.

So, is China caught up in a tangle? It is. And it is going to get even more entangled. The social pact between the Communist Party and the population so far has been that, in exchange for more jobs and better wages, people passively accept their lack of freedom.

This pact will be difficult to maintain. Economic problems will exhaust the political patience of the Chinese people.

February 20, 2016

World In Numbers

The world is changing at such a speed that it is difficult for us to process, interpret and digest the magnitude of these transformations, and even more so, to anticipate their consequences.

A report by Goldman Sachs offers an arbitrary but revealing quantitative sample of the changes that occurred between 2010 and 2015.

In that period, the world oil supply increased by 11% and its price fell by 60%. The price of iron fell even more, 77%, and that of food, 30%. What prices increased? Among others, cocoa (+11%) and lithium (+27%). These increases are driven by demand from a new, larger middle class that eats more chocolate and buys more cell phones with lithium-ion batteries. Users of these phones went from 19% of the world's population to a whopping 75%, and their price fell by 58%. Almost all of humanity will soon have access to mobile telephony, contributing to the already rapid digitalization of everyday life.

In 2010, Facebook had 600 million monthly active users. Today, 1.6 billion people use it monthly. YouTube received 24 hours of videos every minute, while last year it received 400 hours a minute. On eBay, six suits were sold every minute in 2010 and now 90 are sold, while the number of travelers staying in rooms and houses offered through Airbnb jumped from 47,000 to 17 million. The articles available on Wikipedia increased by 20 million (from 17 to 37).

In those five years we also witnessed an energy revolution. The price of oil plummeted and the U.S. overtook Saudi Arabia and Russia as a crude oil producer. The price of an LED light bulb fell by 78%, the price of a Li-Ion battery by 60% and the cost of solar energy by 37%. The fuel efficiency of a Ford truck (F150) increased by 29%. In 2010, the most valuable company in the world was Petrochina. In 2015 it was Apple.

Profound changes also occurred in the world of work. Wages remained stagnant in the most advanced countries, while in China they increased by 54%. Many think that unemployment and low wages are due to automation and robots displacing workers. Indeed, in the U.S., the number of industrial robots sold in the last five years grew by 89%, but the total number in use remains low and the impact on employment is not significant. But it will be.

And this concern about jobs and incomes leads us to point out other important changes that have occurred in the past five years. Economic inequality has always existed, but in the last five years it has acquired enormous visibility. Among other things because, while globally it has declined, in the most advanced countries it has become more acute, becoming a central topic of national debate everywhere, which is a good thing. The danger, of course, is that this problem in the hands of demagogues often leads to policies that, instead of reducing inequalities, increase them. But, undoubtedly, the matter requires urgent and effective attention.

Another recently published work also sheds interesting light on the major transformations underway. It is the Annual Global Risks Report, which has been published by the World Economic Forum for the past decade. This report is based on the perceptions of 750 renowned experts from different fields and countries on the main risks facing the world. For several years, the financial crisis was at the top of the list of concerns. No longer. In the 2016 edition, climate change (which for the past three years was among the top five risks) emerges as the most serious and high-impact danger. It is followed by the proliferation of weapons of mass destruction, conflicts over water scarcity and involuntary migratory movements. The report notes that there are already 60 million displaced persons (if they were to form a country, refugees would be the 24th most populous on the planet). The report also attaches great importance to cybercrime, which already causes $445 billion in annual losses and is growing rapidly.

But perhaps, along with global warming, the most important change in recent years is the increase in our ability to alter biology. In 2010, specifying a genome sequence cost $47,000. Five years later, it's done for $1,300. And the price keeps dropping.

Is this a risk or an opportunity?

February 13, 2016

Printed in the United States
by Baker & Taylor Publisher Services

Printed in the United States
by Baker & Taylor Publisher Services